ENGLISH

Curriculum B

KEY STAGE TWO
SCOTTISH LEVELS C-E

READING

Published by Scholastic Ltd,
Villiers House,
Clarendon Avenue,
Leamington Spa,
Warwickshire CV32 5PR
Text © 1995 George Hunt
© 1995 Scholastic Ltd

AUTHOR
GEORGE HUNT

EDITOR
NOEL PRITCHARD

ASSISTANT EDITOR
JOEL LANE

SERIES DESIGNER
LYNNE JOESBURY

DESIGNER
SUE STOCKBRIDGE

ILLUSTRATIONS
LIZ McINTOSH

COVER ILLUSTRATION
JONATHAN BENTLEY

INFORMATION TECHNOLOGY CONSULTANT
MARTIN BLOWS

SCOTTISH 5–14 LINKS
GILL FRIEL

Designed using Aldus Pagemaker
Printed in Great Britain by Ebenezer Baylis,
Worcester

British Library Cataloguing-in-Publication Data
A catalogue record for this book is available from the
British Library.

ISBN 0-590-53368-1

Contents

Introduction

Scholastic Curriculum Bank is a series for all primary teachers, providing an essential planning tool for devising comprehensive schemes of work as well as an easily accessible and varied bank of practical, classroom-tested activities with photocopiable resources.

Designed to help planning for and implementation of progression, differentiation and assessment, *Scholastic Curriculum Bank* offers a structured range of stimulating activities with clearly-stated learning objectives that reflect the programmes of study, and detailed lesson plans that allow busy teachers to put ideas into practice with the minimum amount of preparation time. The photocopiable sheets that accompany many of the activities provide ways of integrating purposeful application of knowledge and skills, differentiation, assessment and record-keeping.

Opportunities for formative assessment are highlighted within the activities where appropriate, while separate summative assessment activities give guidelines for analysis and subsequent action. Ways of using information technology for different purposes and in different contexts, as a tool for communicating and handling information and as a means of investigating, are integrated into the activities where appropriate, and more explicit guidance is provided at the end of the book.

The series covers all the primary curriculum subjects, with separate books for Key Stages 1 and 2 or Scottish Levels A–B and C–E. It can be used as a flexible resource with any scheme, to fulfil National Curriculum and Scottish 5–14 requirements and to provide children with a variety of different learning experiences that will lead to effective acquisition of skills and knowledge.

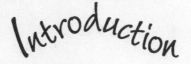

SCHOLASTIC CURRICULUM BANK ENGLISH

The *Scholastic Curriculum Bank English* books enable teachers to plan comprehensive and structured coverage of the primary English curriculum, and enable pupils to develop the required skills, knowledge and understanding through activities.

Each book covers one key stage. There are four books for Key Stage 1/Scottish levels A–B and four for Key Stage 2/Scottish levels C–E. These books reflect the English programme of study, so that there are titles on Reading, Writing, Speaking and listening and Spelling and phonics.

Bank of activities

This book provides a bank of activities that can be used in many different ways – to form a framework for a scheme of work; to add breadth and variety to an existing scheme; or to supplement a particular topic. The activities are designed to encourage children to develop as enthusiastic, responsive and knowledgeable readers.

Lesson plans

Detailed lesson plans, under clear headings, are given for each activity and provide material for immediate implementation in the classroom. The structure for each activity is as follows:

Activity title box

The information contained in the box at the beginning of each activity outlines the following key aspects:

▲ *Activity title and learning objective.* For each activity a clearly stated learning objective is given in bold italics. These learning objectives break down aspects of the programmes of study into manageable, hierarchical teaching and learning chunks, and their purpose is to aid planning for progression. These objectives can easily be referenced to the National Curriculum and Scottish 5–14 requirements by using the overview grids at the end of this chapter (pages 9 to 12).

▲ *Class organisation/Likely duration.* Icons ✝✝ and ⏱ signpost the suggested group sizes for each activity and the approximate amount of time required to complete it.

Previous skills/knowledge needed

Information is given here when it is necessary for the children to have acquired specific knowledge or skills prior to carrying out the activity.

Key background information

The information in this section outlines the areas of study covered by each activity and gives a general background to the particular topic or theme, outlining the basic skills that will be developed and the ways in which the activity will address children's learning.

Preparation

Advice is given for those occasions where it is necessary for the teacher to prime the pupils for the activity or to prepare materials, or to set up a display or activity ahead of time.

Resources needed

All of the materials needed to carry out the activity are listed, so that the pupils or the teacher can gather them together easily before the beginning of the teaching session.

What to do

Easy-to-follow, step-by-step instructions are given for carrying out the activity, including (where appropriate) suggested questions for the teacher to ask the pupils to help instigate discussion and stimulate investigation.

Suggestion(s) for extension/support

Ideas are given for ways of providing easy differentiation where activities lend themselves to this purpose. In all cases, suggestions are provided as to ways in which each activity can be modified for less able or extended for more able children.

Assessment opportunities

Where appropriate, opportunities for ongoing teacher assessment of the children's work during or after a specific activity are highlighted.

Introduction

Opportunities for IT

Where opportunities for IT present themselves, these are briefly outlined with reference to particularly suitable types of program. The chart on page 158 presents specific areas of IT covered in the activities, together with more detailed support on how to apply particular types of program. Selected lesson plans serve as models for other activities by providing more comprehensive guidance on the application of IT, and these are indicated by the bold page numbers on the grid and the 🖥 icon at the start of an activity.

Display ideas

Where they are relevant and innovative, display ideas are incorporated into activity plans and illustrated with examples.

Other aspects of the English PoS covered

Inevitably, as all areas of English are interrelated, activities will cover aspects of the programmes of study in other areas of the English curriculum. These links are highlighted under this heading.

Reference to photocopiable sheets

Where activities include photocopiable activity sheets, small reproductions of these are included in the lesson plans together with guidance notes for their use and, where appropriate, suggested answers.

Assessment

The system of level descriptions in the National Curriculum presents the teacher with the task of matching the typical performance of individual children with a set of descriptive statements. In this book, each activity presents advice on what the teacher should look out for during the course of

the activity. The notes made while observing the children can contribute to a descriptive profile of the child's performance, compiled and refined throughout the school year, which might also be supported by annotated samples of the work that the child produces. The important point is that assessment is integrated into everyday performance.

At the end of each chapter there are activities which are designed to provide a summative measure of a range of key competencies linked to the type of reading dealt with in that chapter. These activities do not differ in their organisation from the preceding ones, and focus on a number of learning objectives covered in the chapter. Assessment activities are indicated by the ✍ icon.

Photocopiable activity sheets

Many of the activities are accompanied by photocopiable activity sheets. For some activities, there may be more than one version; or an activity sheet may be 'generic', with a facility for the teacher to fill in the appropriate task in order to provide differentiation by task. Other sheets may be more open-ended to provide differentiation by outcome. The photocopiable activity sheets provide purposeful activities that are ideal for assessment and can be kept as records in pupils' portfolios of work.

Cross-curricular links

This book emphasises that reading and writing skills should not be taught in isolation, but integrated into the work children do in other areas of the curriculum. Information retrieval strategies are not confined to study skills lessons, but can be developed through the perusal of texts on topics of contemporary concern. Where photocopiable pages have been supplied for particular activities, these are intended as

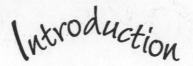

demonstration materials, providing opportunities to rehearse procedures which can then be applied to more relevant texts. In many cases, the activities open routes for links between different subject areas – techniques for mathematical representation are applied to media texts; the musical dimensions of spoken and printed language are explored; historical change and geographical variation in language usage are examined; and throughout, children are encouraged to respond to all forms of printed material via a range of types of graphic representation.

Cross-curricular links are identified on a simple grid which cross-references the particular areas of study in English to the programmes of study for other subjects in the curriculum, and where appropriate provides suggestions for activities. (See page 160.)

READING

The aim of this book is to help teachers to fulfil the National Curriculum requirement that at Key Stage 2, children 'should be encouraged to develop as enthusiastic, independent and reflective readers.'

There is, perhaps, the hint of an assumption in this quotation that the job is largely one of continuing the good work that has been done at Key Stage 1: that the early years have laid a foundation of basic skills upon which the primary teacher builds and consolidates a more complex superstructure.

Although the job of maintaining continuity is crucial, most Key Stage 2 teachers will recognise the view that one simply has to extend and elaborate an existing set of skills as an oversimplification. Many children will enter Key Stage 2 without such skills. Others, drifting away from books towards the attractions of more strident or mysterious media, will be in the process of divesting themselves of established competencies which have not been presented in a sufficiently stimulating way.

Accordingly, the activities set out here attempt to meet the needs of a broad range of abilities and interests. The main emphases are extending the range of children's reading, encouraging personal responses to literature, stimulating curiosity about the many forms of print, and heightening critical awareness of its many functions. However, these goals are not seen as higher-level objectives, to be aimed for only after 'basic skills' have been mastered; rather, they are regarded as fundamental requirements which teachers should try to develop as a key aspect of all reading experiences. Thus activities which seek to develop phonological awareness are embedded in creative investigations rather than in a decontextualised drill, while activities aimed at developing responses to whole texts are presented in ways which are adaptable to children who are at the earliest stages of learning to read.

An underlying concern is that the activities should reflect a view of reading as a communicative, recreational and problem-solving process, rather than the practice of a set of discrete skills. Accordingly, the chapters have been organised by genre, so that there is an emphasis on providing children with a range of experiences of authentic texts.

The main aspects promoted by this general approach are:
▲ an emphasis on the use of a wide range of natural language texts;
▲ a complementary role for word games and other forms of linguistic play;
▲ a central role for teacher demonstration;
▲ shared reading and shared writing;
▲ discussion of texts by partnerships and small groups, reporting back to the whole class.
▲ integration of reading with writing, speaking and listening;
▲ encouragement of teachers and children to develop their own texts;
▲ a positive approach to language diversity;
▲ critical consideration of texts within the social contexts of production and consumption.

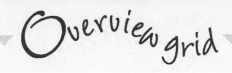

Learning objective	PoS/AO	Content	Type of activity	Page
Fiction				
Oral storytelling.	1a; 2b. A	Involving the children in storytime – telling and retelling favourite stories.	Whole-class speaking and listening; audio and visual recording; reading and writing.	14
Encouraging children to reflect on the content and scope of their own reading.	1a, b, c, d; 2b; 3. C, D, E	Keeping a record to show reflective commentaries on reading experience.	Individual reading and writing accompanied by occasional group discussion and 'tutorial time' with the teacher.	15
Awareness of word order and sentence structure.	1a; 2a, b; 3. B, C	Shared writing; segmenting and reconstructing sentences.	Group composition (shared writing) followed by reading and discussion in pairs.	16
To develop sight vocabulary.	1a; 3. A	Identifying selected words in a familiar text and matching them with isolated words.	Small-group reading and discussion.	18
To use semantic, syntactic and graphophonic information to reconstruct a familiar text.	1a; 2a, b; 3. B, C	Restoring deletions to a text that the children have helped to compose themselves.	Shared creative writing in a small group, followed by reading and discussion; opportunities for using IT.	19
Use of semantic, syntactic and graphophonic information; story writing.	1a, c; 2a, b; 3. C, D, E	Reconstructing a 'damaged' account of an event based on an historical incident.	Paired reading and discussion of photocopiable sheet; paired or individual writing.	21
Reflection and prediction.	1a, c; 2b; 3. B, C, D, E	Discussing sequenced chunks of a story; completing a story orally or in writing.	Group discussion of a photocopied story or story starter; group or individual writing or oral storytelling.	23
Awareness of discourse structure of narrative texts.	1a; 2b, c, d; 3. B, C, D, E	Reconstructing a story in which the paragraphs have been scrambled.	Group reading and discussion; use of photocopiable sheet; opportunities for writing and IT.	24
Developing the ability to use inference and deduction.	1a, c, d; 2a; 3. C, D, E	Reading a traditional story; selecting words for a missing piece of dialogue.	Individual reading of photocopiable sheet followed by group discussion.	26
Responding to narrative; prediction; awareness of genre characteristics.	1a, c, d; 2b; 3. D, E	Reading story starters from a range of genres, and writing suitable continuations.	Individual reading, then group discussion and reading aloud.	27
Responding imaginatively to plot and characters.	1a, c, d, 2b, 3. D, E	Transforming favourite stories into scripted drama.	Group reading and discussion; collaborative writing and performance.	28
Awareness of moral issues in fiction.	1a, c, d; 2b; 3. C, D, E	Discussing the relative culpability of characters in a story based on a fairy tale.	Individual reading of the story followed by group discussion.	30
Awareness of didactic fiction and traditional moral tales.	1a, b, c; 2b; 3. C, D, E	Discussing fables and other moral tales to identify the intended message.	Group or individual reading followed by group discussion and opportunities for shared or individual writing.	31
Helping readers to visualise the settings of stories.	1a; 2c, d; 3. C, D, E	Representing the geographical setting of a story as a map.	Whole-class listening to a story, then discussion of a visual representation of its setting, using a photocopied map.	32
Inference and imaginative response to fictional characters.	1a, c, d; 2b; 3. B, C, D, E	Exploring, in words and pictures, reflections on characters in stories.	Paired discussion about favourite characters; individual drawing and writing.	33
Developing awareness of changing relationships between fictional characters.	1a, c, d; 2b; 3. C, D, E	Developing a chart showing relationships between characters in a story.	Whole-class listening, followed by visual representation of the story content.	35
To reflect on similarities between stories from different times and cultures.	1a, c, d; 2b; 3. D, E	Storytime discussion of motifs in fiction read-aloud.	Whole-class listening and discussion; opportunities for shared writing.	36
Extending children's knowledge of different fictional genres.	1a, c, d; 2b; 3. D, E	Exploring genre characteristics working from story starters.	Small-group reading, discussion and oral storytelling. Opportunities for 'publishing' own work.	38
Sharing literary preferences and building a bibliographical database.	1a, c, d; 2b, d; 3. C, D, E	Writing and sharing book reviews; compiling a simple bibliographical database.	Whole-class discussion, then individual work on reviewing and compiling information.	39
Awareness of story structure; developing the range and quality of reading resources.	1a, c, d; 2b; 3. D, E	Analysing key points in stories; developing a recommended read-aloud programme.	Two small groups working collaboratively on reading and annotating stories.	42

READING

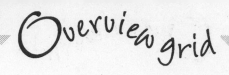

Learning objective	PoS/AO	Content	Type of activity	Page
Developing critical awareness of the range and quality of reading resources.	1a, c, d; 2b; 3. D, E	Assessing contemporary and historical reading resources.	Whole-class discussion of equal opportunities; small groups working on aspects of the survey and reporting back to the whole class.	43
Critical reflection on favourite stories; formulating and communicating opinions about literature.	1a, c, d; 2b; 3. C, D, E	Writing to an author about questions raised by a book.	Whole-class discussion followed by individual reading and writing.	45
Developing oral reading skills; summative assessment.	1a, c, d; 2b; 3. B, C, D, E	Selecting a favourite snippet of a story to read aloud.	Individual reading aloud, supported by the teacher.	46
Enabling children to articulate their experiences of, and attitudes towards, literature.	1a, c, d; 2b; 3. A, B, C, D, E	Discussing recent reading and texts for future reading with the teacher.	One-to-one discussion between child and teacher.	48

Information books

Learning objective	PoS/AO	Content	Type of activity	Page
Fostering appreciation of information books and knowledge of the distinctive language patterns of these books.	1a, b, c; 2b, c; 3. A, B, C, D, E	Promoting information books with teacher demonstration of how to use them.	Whole-class listening and discussion.	50
Familiarising children with library layout, classification and procedures for locating information.	1a, b; 2c, d; 3. A, B, C, D, E	Developing awareness of library organisation.	Small groups working under supervision in library.	51
Identifying information needs in relation to a specific topic.	1a. C, D, E	Drawing a 'knowledge map' of a given topic, and generating questions to be answered.	Whole-class and small-group discussion with shared writing in small groups.	52
Developing the ability to skim information texts for relevant information.	1a, b, c; 2b, c; 3. C, D, E	Formulating purposes for reading particular texts and classifying information in the text as relevant or irrelevant.	Children working in pairs or small groups.	54
Developing note-taking skills; skimming for the gist of a text.	1a, b, c; 2b, c; 3. C, D, E	Formulating questions, then underlining relevant words in the text.	Working in pairs for the underlining, then comparison of results within small groups.	55
Development of note-taking skills; identifying different types of information in a text.	1a, b, c; 2b, c; 3. C, D, E	Identifying different types of information in selected texts by underlining key phrases.	Group or whole-class discussion, followed by reading and underlining in pairs and reporting back to group or whole class.	57
Developing comprehension by creating visual representations of the ideas in a text.	1a, b, c; 2b, c; 3. C, D, E	Comparing written and graphic representations of a set of ideas in a text.	Whole-class comparison of text and graphic representation, then individuals reading and creating their own drawings.	58
Developing note-taking skills; co-ordinating information retrieved from various sources.	1a, b, c; 2b, c; 3. C, D, E	Representing relationships between the ideas in selected texts in note form.	Teacher demonstration and whole-class discussion of the procedure, then individual reading and note taking.	59
Developing comprehension and scanning skills.	1a, b, c; 2b, c; 3. C, D, E	Matching portions of text to parts of a diagram representing information in the text.	Small group working collaboratively and reporting to the whole class.	60
Developing awareness of chronological organisation of information.	1a, b, c; 2b, c; 3. C, D, E	Matching main events from a chronologically organised text to points on a timeline.	A small group working as individuals, then comparing results.	61
Developing comprehension and scanning skills; co-ordinating information from various sources.	1a, b, c; 2b, c; 3. C, D, E	Constructing a tabular representation of items of related information from a variety of texts.	Small group or whole class, working in pairs and then comparing results.	63
Developing strategies for summarising in writing information retrieved from texts.	1a, b, c; 2b, c; 3. C, D, E	Using information gained from reading to finish a sequence of open-ended sentences.	Whole class or smaller group, working in pairs and then comparing results.	64
Awareness of different ways in which ideas might be organised in an information text.	1a, b, c; 2b, c; 3. C, D, E	Discussing alternative ways to reconstruct a 'shuffled' text.	Whole class working in small groups and comparing results.	65
Developing personal responses to information texts.	1a, b, c; 2b, c; 3. C, D, E	Writing and sharing questions inspired by a selected text.	Whole-class discussion followed by groups reading chosen texts, then individuals writing/exchanging questions.	67
Developing personal responses to information texts and awareness of social and political issues.	1a, b, c; 2b, c; 3. D, E	Assuming the role of protagonists in various discussion activities.	Role plays prepared by small groups with opportunities for whole-class question and answer sessions.	68
Developing topic-specific vocabulary; focusing on selected emphases in an information text.	1a, b, c; 2b, c; 3. C, D, E	Discussing possibilities for words deleted from a passage according to selected criteria.	Whole-class discussion followed by paired work to restore words to the passage.	70

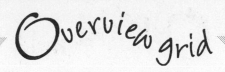

Learning objective	PoS/AO	Content	Type of activity	Page
Raising awareness of the social values found in information texts.	1a, b; 2b, c; 3. D, E	Examining contemporary and historical texts to identify bias, inaccuracy and omission.	Whole-class introduction, then surveys conducted by small groups reporting back to the whole class.	71
Familiarising children with the structure and language of information texts.	1a, b, c; 2b, c; 3. C, D, E	Creating an information book on a selected topic.	Whole-class discussion followed by open-ended work by individual children.	72
Familiarising children with the use of information books.	1a, b, c; 2a, b; 3. C, D, E	Responding to set information tasks, using the library.	Small groups of children working individually, observed by the teacher.	74

Poetry

Learning objective	PoS/AO	Content	Type of activity	Page
Stimulating interest in poetry and developing read-aloud skills.	1a, c, d; 2b; 3. C, D, E	Displaying and performing favourite poems.	Whole-class listening; groups and individual contributions to performance and display.	76
Raising awareness of rhythm and rhyme and of poetic aspects of everyday speech events.	1a, c, d; 2b; 3. C, D, E	Collecting contemporary and historical playground rhymes.	Flexible group size for research; whole-class sharing.	77
Raising awareness of rhythm and rhyme and of poetic aspects of everyday speech events.	1a, c, d; 2b; 3. B, C, D, E	Making an anthology of contemporary and historical nursery rhymes.	Flexible group size for research; whole-class sharing.	78
Raising awareness of rhythm and rhyme and of poetic aspects of everyday speech events.	1a, c, d; 2b; 3. D, E	Reading, solving, composing and collecting contemporary and historical riddles.	Flexible group size for research; whole-class sharing.	80
Extending knowledge of initial letter-sounds; appreciation of alliteration.	1a, c, d; 2a, b; 3. C, D, E	Brainstorming words beginning with the same letter or blend and using these words to compose tongue-twisters.	Whole class initially, then children working individually.	82
Extending knowledge of initial letter-sounds; appreciation of alliteration.	1a, c, d; 2a, b; 3. C, D, E	Restoring alliterative elements to poems from which these have been deleted.	Small-group reading and discussion; shared or individual writing.	83
Extending knowledge of rhyming patterns; developing scanning skills and media awareness.	1a, c, d; 2a, b; 3. C, D, E	Examining environmental print and a range of media for instances of rhyme.	Individuals and flexible groups working on scanning; whole-class sharing of display and publication.	84
Developing awareness of onomatopoeia and other aspects of phonology.	1a, c, d; 2a, b; 3. C, D, E	Collecting and playing with onomatopoeic words.	Whole class.	85
Appreciation of nonsense poetry; relationships between sounds of words and their meanings.	1a, c, d; 2a, b; 3. C, D, E	Developing appreciation of relationships between word sound and meaning.	Whole class or small groups.	87
Appreciation of the visual layout of written language.	1a, c, d; 2b; 3. C, D, E	Exploring ways of representing memorable spoken language.	Small groups working at the word processor.	88
Developing personal response to poetry.	1a, c, d; 2b; 3. C, D, E	Responding to poems by writing in a variety of ways.	Whole-class introduction followed by individual writing.	90
Developing personal response to poetry.	1a, c, d; 2b; 3. C, D, E	Responding to selected poems through a variety of types of drawing.	Whole-class listening followed or accompanied by individual drawing	91
Enhancing awareness of the structure of ideas in poems.	1a, c, d; 2b; 3. C, D, E	Reconstructing a shuffled poem.	Whole class or groups, working in pairs.	92
To develop children's use of a range of textual cues in reading.	1a, c, d; 2a, b; 3. C, D, E	Restoring words, phrases or longer units of text deleted from a selected poem.	Whole class or flexible group, reading and writing in pairs.	94
Encouraging children to seek out and share enjoyable poetry.	1a, c, d; 2b; 3. C, D, E	Compiling personal collections of favourite poems.	Teacher demonstration followed by individual work.	96

Instructional texts

Learning objective	PoS/AO	Content	Type of activity	Page
Raising awareness of the features and range of uses of procedural text.	1a, b; 2b, c; 3. C, D, E	Collecting, sorting, displaying and using a wide range of procedural texts.	Whole-class introductory session followed by open-ended work by individuals.	98
Developing critical awareness of and knowledge about language.	1a, b; 2b, c; 3. C, D, E	Assessing the readability of a procedural text, then improving it (if necessary) by rewriting.	Pairs or small groups.	99
Exploring different ways of representing written language; developing comprehension.	1a, b; 2b, c; 3. D, E	Presenting procedural texts in graphic form.	Small groups working in pairs.	100
Raising awareness of organisational features in procedural texts.	1a, b; 2b, c; 3. C, D, E	Reconstructing a 'shuffled' procedural text.	Small groups or pairs working with a photocopiable sheet.	102

READING

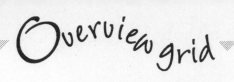

Learning objective	PoS/AO	Content	Type of activity	Page
To raise children's awareness of procedural texts in the classroom and how they are structured.	1a, b; 2b, c; 3. C, D, E	Restoring procedural texts from which words and phrases have been deleted.	Whole-class discussion.	103
Developing the ability to write clear instructions.	1a, b; 2b, c; 3. C, D, E	Inventing games and writing rules and instructions.	Small groups.	104
Developing links between literature and writing, and the ability to write clear instructions.	1a, b; 2b, c; 3. C, D, E	Writing procedural texts inspired by reading fiction.	A group of children working with response partners.	105
To encourage children to use procedural texts.	1a, b; 2b, c; 3. C, D, E	Selecting and using a procedural text.	Children working individually.	106
Media				
Familiarity with the range of text types within a newspaper.	1a, b, c, d; 2b, c; 3. D, E	Evaluating characteristics of a range of newspapers.	Whole-class discussion followed by group activity.	108
Developing awareness of different styles of writing.	1a, b, c, d; 2b, c; 3. D, E	Investigating/writing types of headline and related articles.	Whole-class discussion, then group or paired work.	110
Demonstrating the distinctive syntax and vocabulary of different styles of journalism.	1a, b, c, d; 2b, c; 3. D, E	Generating parodies of newspaper headlines.	Whole-class introduction, then small-group activity.	111
Developing critical awareness of journalistic writing; developing information retrieval strategies.	1a, b, c, d; 2b, c; 3. D, E	Developing critical analysis of a selected article.	Group or paired work. Whole-class feedback.	112
Developing critical language awareness in relation to vocabulary choices in newspapers; scanning skills.	1a, b, c, d; 2b, c; 3. D, E	Identifying vocabulary used in relation to males and females in the media.	Small group reporting back to the whole class.	113
Identification of biased language.	1a, b, c, d; 2b, c; 3. D, E	Discussing examples of biased reporting and the possible sources of bias.	Whole class working in pairs, then plenary discussion.	114
Raising awareness of the range and purposes of written language in the environment.	1a, b, c, d; 2b, c; 3. D, E	Collecting and evaluating a variety of environmental print.	Whole-class introduction, then activities in small groups.	115
Raising critical awareness of different types of persuasive language.	1a, b, c, d; 2b, c; 3. D, E	Collecting, sorting and analysing junk mail.	Whole-class introduction, research in small groups and plenary feedback.	116
Developing writing skills and awareness of the distinctive language features of comics and cartoons.	1a, b, c, d; 2b, c; 3. C, D, E	Using a range of comics and cartoon strips as a basis for language activities.	Whole-class, flexible-group and individual work.	117
Familiarising children with the conventions of drama scripts.	2b; 3. D, E	Written work and role-play based on the investigation of drama scripts.	Whole-class, flexible-group and individual work.	119
Familiarising children with spelling patterns and dictionary conventions.	1a; 2a, c; 3. D, E	Matching words in a crossword matrix to their definitions.	Children working in pairs, individually or in small groups.	120
Extending knowledge of spelling patterns, word structure and dictionary conventions.	2a, c. C, D, G	Composing assemblies of words based on similar roots; using dictionaries.	Whole class or flexible groups.	121
Developing awareness of structure and meaning relationships between words.	1a; 2a, c; 3. D, E	Collecting and discussing words related to a particular stimulus.	Whole class or flexible groups.	122
Extending knowledge of letter-sounds, dictionary conventions and experience of wordplay.	1a; 2a, c; 3. D, E	A game in which words are invented and given meanings.	Small groups.	123
Raising awareness of the distinctive language of news broadcasts; developing reading-aloud skills.	1a; 2b; 3. C, D, E	Writing a parody of a news broadcast.	Children writing co-operatively and reading aloud individually.	124

Fiction

This chapter has two main aims: to develop children's reading fluency and to enable them to reflect on the quality and personal relevance of what they read.

The former aim is approached through activities which explore the structures of a range of narrative texts. At sentence level, the reader's attention is directed towards the syntactic, semantic and graphophonic elements of written language, and children are encouraged to use these elements in their reading. At discourse level, the distinctive styles and structures of stories are examined. Aspects such as characters, settings and themes are introduced, and children are helped to recognise recurrent motifs in stories from a range of traditions. Each activity focuses on a story or story fragment; in the case of the latter, the children are given the opportunity to rebuild the entire edifice.

The development of personal response is approached in a variety of ways. Critical awareness is fostered through discussion of favourite books with other children and the teacher, through more individual procedures such as the keeping of personal reading diaries, and through activities which invite children to represent in other media the ideas that they have encountered in literature.

FROM READING TO TELLING

To provide children with the opportunity to retell their favourite stories to the class, without having to rely on the printed page.
†† *Whole class.*
🕐 *20 minutes.*

Key background information

The tradition of oral storytelling has enjoyed a revival in recent years. By encouraging children to participate in this tradition, we can help them to make stories they find in books their own, develop oral skills and, perhaps, display creativity. The latter possibility arises from the fact that retelling need not always be faithful to the original stimulus.

This type of activity should be established as a regular practice as early in the school year as possible, so that the children have plenty of time to become accustomed to it. This is particularly important for less confident children. Children who speak languages other than English should be given the opportunity to use these languages in storytelling, regardless of the language of the original story. As well as enhancing the confidence and creativity of the teller, the experience of hearing the same story told in different ways, and in different languages, will provide a vivid and entertaining celebration of literary and linguistic diversity for all the children.

Preparation

Practise oral storytelling yourself. Start off with simple, familiar narratives, and build up your confidence by rehearsing with a tape recorder. When you begin to tell stories to the class in this way, draw attention to the fact that you are practising a time-honoured tradition of which they can become a part.

About a week before the lesson outlined below, tell the children that you would like volunteers for a storytelling session to be held in a week's time, and that children who are interested should begin to practise retelling their favourite short stories.

Resources needed

A wide selection of short-story books in the classroom.

What to do

Ask all the children to sit in a circle, or in any other arrangement where the storyteller is in a central position and has the focused attention of the rest of the class. You could provide a storyteller's chair for this purpose, or establish a convention that the storyteller wears a special garment or holds a special object.

The session should then proceed as it would for a routine storytime. Children who are unaccustomed to storytelling may need support if they falter, though this should happen less frequently as the activity becomes an everyday part of normal classroom work.

Suggestion(s) for extension

Children who enjoy oral storytelling may want to share this skill with classes other than their own. A video of school storytellers could be made, perhaps incorporating storytellers from the wider community. Children who are particularly interested can be helped to search for further information about storytelling in different cultures.

Common Bonds edited by Alan Howe and John Johnson (Hodder & Stoughton, 1992) is a good teachers' resource for classroom storytelling.

Suggestion(s) for support

Children who find it difficult to 'perform' in front of a large group should not be coerced into doing so. However, many such children might enjoy storytelling as part of a small circle. Alternatively, as one of your reading time activities, children who have read different stories and wish to share them can be encouraged to pair up with a partner and to exchange stories orally.

Assessment opportunities

Storytelling allows the teacher to make incidental assessments of the oral abilities of those children taking part, as well as providing information about the range of reading done by these individuals. It would be a great pity, however, if this were allowed to overshadow the main aim of the activity, which is simply the enjoyment of story.

Other aspects of the English PoS covered

Speaking and listening – 1a, b, c, d; 2a, b; 3a, b.

INTRODUCING A READER'S NOTEBOOK

To keep a record of thoughts and feelings about particular books during reading in order to encourage a more careful consideration of the story.

†† *Whole class, preferably taken a group at a time according to their reading ability and fluency in writing.*

🕒 *20 minutes per group.*

Key background information

This activity requires children to start keeping a record of their immediate reactions to the stories that they are reading and/or listening to. This will provide a basis enabling them to compare their perceptions of fiction. The record should be maintained throughout the year, or for longer if feasible; so the best time to start this activity would be during the first term. However, in order to conduct the lesson outlined below you will need to have a good idea of the reading and writing abilities of the children in your class, so some time after the first half-term break would probably be the best time to do this.

Preparation

Select three or four stories, one for each of the groups in your class, and make a copy for each child in the group. These passages can be short stories, or the first chapters of novels that you think might appeal to the group and encourage them to read further. If you are working with children at the earliest stages of reading development, a short story for reading aloud should be included.

After you have introduced this lesson you will need to talk to one group at a time, so it is essential that you prepare work for the other groups which they will be able to carry out more or less independently.

Resources needed

Copies of the chosen story, one notebook for each child.

What to do

Introduction

Distribute the notebooks and explain to the children that they are going to use them to keep a record of their thoughts about the stories that they are reading or listening to. Tell them that for this activity they will need to read or listen to a story, and after a certain point they are to stop and write down whatever comes into their mind about the story. Because these notebooks are for the children's own use, and for making spontaneous notes, assure the children that they should not be too anxious about spelling and handwriting.

Development

Work with one group at a time. Distribute the stories, and allow the children to read them silently. (If you are working with readers who cannot yet read independently, read a story or 'story starter' aloud to them.) After a given time, or when the children have all read a certain amount of the story, ask them to open their notebooks and to write down all of the things that they can remember thinking about while they were reading (or listening to) the story. Preferably this should be done without discussion between the children. You might encourage them to include:

▲ pictures that they saw in their heads as the story unfolded;
▲ predictions about what might happen next;
▲ opinions about people or events in the story;
▲ opinions about the quality of the story;
▲ experiences of their own that the story reminded them of.

Encourage the children to include quick sketches and doodles if this is their preferred way of responding to the story. Children who are literate in other languages should be encouraged to respond in this language if they want to. While they are doing this, do the same thing yourself.

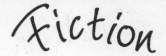
After the children have been given time to write and draw their responses, they should be allowed to share these with other members of the group and to talk about any differences that have emerged. If you think that it will help the discussion, share your own responses to the story with the children.

Conclusion

If you have used only the first part of a story for this activity, make sure the children have the opportunity to finish it for themselves so that their expectations can be revised or confirmed.

Remind the children of the ways in which this activity might be helpful. Encourage them to repeat the activity on an individual basis during their own reading time.

Suggestion(s) for extension

Children who are group-reading novels or other works of fiction can be encouraged to keep a reader's notebook and to share their responses to specific parts of the book.

Suggestion(s) for support

If children find writing difficult, you can scribe their responses for them. Readers' notebooks can be incorporated into individual reading-aloud sessions, allowing the child to add her own voice to the teacher's comments.

Assessment opportunities

Children's readiness to respond in writing or with drawings to the reading that they are doing can be observed by the teacher; but you should expect many responses to be highly idiosyncratic or laconic.

Other aspects of the English PoS covered

Speaking and listening – 1a, b, c; 2a, b.
Writing – 1a, c; 3a, b.

SEQUENCING: FAMILIAR TEXT

To encourage the children to use syntactic, semantic and graphophonic information in order to reconstruct shuffled texts that they have composed themselves.
†† *Shared writing in groups of six to eight children, then children working in pairs within each group.*
⏱ *One hour.*

Key background information

This activity will help to integrate children's reading and writing abilities, and also develop their ability to co-ordinate their attention to different sources of textual information when they are reading. It is best used as a regular activity for children at a relatively early stage of reading development.

Preparation

If you do not already use shared writing as part of your language activities, introduce it to your class. *Through Writing to Reading* by Brigid Smith (Routledge, 1994) provides a valuable account of the theory and practice of this approach to literacy.

Before conducting the lesson outlined below, inform the children involved that they will soon be working co-operatively on the composition of a story. Offer them some optional themes or titles that they might like to start thinking about, perhaps based on a story that you have recently shared with them or related to a topic that is currently being explored by the class.

Resources needed

Shared writing materials (a flip chart, paper and a felt-tipped pen), strips of card, scissors. A word-processing program with at least two terminals, to be shared by a group of six children.

What to do
Introduction

Ask the children to pool ideas for the story, writing them down on the flip chart. Discuss these ideas with the children, and try to negotiate an overall shape for the story orally before you start on the actual writing. When this has been agreed, write the story out according to the children's dictation, helping them to select appropriate vocabulary and sentence structures.

The length of this phase of the lesson will depend on the attention span of the group you are working with. It is not essential to complete the whole story before proceeding with the next phase, but you do need at least one coherent episode consisting of five or six sentences. A portion of text exceeding this length might be rather unwieldy for the purposes of this lesson.

Exploring word order in this way will raise children's syntactic awareness, as well as giving an opportunity to point out the role of capitalisation conventions.

Development Two

Instead of copying the story on to a clean sheet, you can type it up on a word-processing program. Show the group how you can manipulate the order of the sentences using the 'cut' and 'paste' commands, then allow them to reconstruct the original order or explore alternatives using these commands. The shuffling and re-ordering of phrases, and of words, in individual sentences can then be done in the same way.

Whichever procedure is used, after the original order has been restored or an alternative order created, encourage the children to talk about how they managed to complete the task.

Conclusion

Reread the reconstructed story. If it is incomplete, help the children to finish it through shared writing; then plan the arrangements for its illustration and publication, perhaps using the procedure outlined below.

Suggestion(s) for extension

Groups working on sequencing and story writing can exchange photocopies of completed stories which have been word-processed and cut into strips consisting of sentences or paragraphs.

Each group should sequence these strips and then arrange them on to the pages of their own handmade books, indicating where illustrations should be placed when appropriate. The children should be encouraged to examine published picture books, which will provide a model of different possibilities for the positioning of text and pictures. When an order has been agreed on, the 'paste ups' can be retyped, illustrated and published, and the finished product compared with the version produced by the author(s) of the original story.

Once children have become accustomed to sequencing, they can play with word and sentence order at the computer, scrambling and unscrambling texts for each other. The teacher should control the level of difficulty of the original text, enter the text on to the machine, and ensure that such games do not become a substitute for the creation and communication of whole texts.

Suggestion(s) for support

If difficulties occur in the sequencing of sentences or phrases, remind the children of the course of the whole story, and encourage them to scan the problem sentence for significant words whose recognition might crystallise the meaning of the whole sentence. Repeat this procedure for the other sentences and help the children to determine their temporal relationship to each other.

Development One

Help the children to read the story or story beginning through together, then copy it in separately written sentences on to a clean sheet. Cut the sheet up into strips, each containing a separate sentence, and shuffle them. Ask the group to reconstruct the text in its original order, intervening only if frustration sets in. Note that during this activity, the children might light upon an alternative and perhaps preferable order for the sentences.

After the text has been reconstructed, assign each pair a sentence of their own and cut this up into its separate phrases. For example, the sentence *Every day the planet-eating slug slithered nearer to the Earth* could be cut up into: *Every day / the planet-eating slug / slithered nearer to the Earth,* or *Every day / the planet-eating slug / slithered nearer / to the Earth.*

Ask the children to arrange the shuffled phrases back into their original sentences, exploring alternative patterns if these are possible. For example: *the planet-eating slug / slithered nearer to the Earth / Every day.*

When this has been done, cut the reconstructed sentences into separate words. Again, allow the children time to re-order them, discussing different possibilities with their partners. The process of shuffling individual words is quite likely to produce coherent sentences whose meaning differs from the original. For example: *the planet Earth slithered nearer to the slug, eating Every day.*

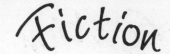

If difficulties occur in the sequencing of words, remind the children of the meaning of the whole sentence. Set out the first word or two for them, reading the word or words as you do so, then ask them to anticipate what word will come next. When this word has been identified orally, ask the children to focus on its initial sound and to scan the available words for one that begins with the corresponding letter or blend of letters. If there is more than one such word available (slither, slug), focus their attention on other structural cues such as the word's length and its ending, until the appropriate word has been found. If none of this works, show the children the target word instead of allowing frustration to develop, before moving on to the next word.

Assessment opportunities

Listen carefully as the children discuss possibilities for sequencing. This will enable you to make judgements about their syntactic awareness, knowledge of word meanings, sight vocabulary and phonic knowledge.

Opportunities for IT

Instead of copying the story on to a clean sheet you can type it up on a word processor. The easiest programs for this activity are those which use a mouse to mark and move text. Show the group how you can manipulate the order of the sentences by marking or highlighting the sentence and then either *cut* it to the clipboard, move the pointer to the new position and then *paste* it back, or *drag* the highlighted section to the new position. Once they can do this, children can be left to reconstruct the original order or explore alternatives using these commands. Children could print out the final versions of the altered text.

Display ideas

Words and phrases for sequencing into sentences, and sentences for sequencing into stories, can be written on card and attached to a sequencing board with either Blu-Tack or Velcro. The children can use this for occasional shuffling games, under the same conditions as the computer sequencing game described above.

Different ways of 'pasting up' the layout of completed stories can be made into a display which could help children to make decisions about the design of their own books.

When the sequencing has been completed, high-frequency or other particularly useful words (for example, particularly vivid words contributed by the children, or words related to the topic which occur in other curriculum areas) can be displayed, used for word games, or added to a child's personal dictionary or thesaurus for use in independent writing.

Other aspects of the English PoS covered

Speaking and listening – 1a, b, c; 2a, b; 3a, b.
Writing – 1a, b, c; 2a, b, c, d; 3a, b, c.

KEY WORDS AND PHRASES IN FAMILIAR TEXT

To develop sight vocabulary by focusing attention on key words and phrases in a text composed by the children themselves.
†† *Shared writing in groups of four to twelve children.*
🕐 *30 minutes.*

Key background information

The immediate recognition of a corps of words is an important foundation for fluent reading. Between 100 and 200 'heavy-duty' words comprise more than 50 per cent of the texts that children are likely to encounter (*Beginning to Read*, Marilyn Jager Adams, MIT Press 1990, pp160–161). This activity does not prescribe the memorising of such words in isolation, but encourages children to focus on a personal vocabulary that is perceived in a variety of written contexts.

This activity should be conducted regularly with children in the early stages of reading development, who can then begin to extend their sight vocabulary from this corps of meaningful words.

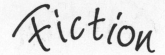

Preparation
See 'Sequencing: familiar text' on page 16.

Resources needed
Shared writing materials, and a set of masking cards with windows sufficiently large to enable the children to focus on selected words and phrases from the completed text (as shown in the illustration).

What to do
Introduction
See 'Sequencing: familiar text' on page 16.

Development
When the shared story or its first chunk has been completed, read it through with the group, then ask them to select from the text four or five words or phrases that are of particular significance to the story. These might be the names of characters, vivid adjectives or verbs, important spoken phrases or repetitive refrains.

Isolate these items one at a time from the text, using the masking cards. Ask the children to read the words or phrases aloud, and to point out any distinctive features (spelling patterns, word length, relationship to other known words) or similarities between the words. Write the selected items out on separate cards, and ask the children to take the cards and match them to the words and phrases in the story.

Conclusion
Read the story again, and finish it off if this has not already been done.

Suggestion(s) for extension
The cards bearing the selected words and phrases can be added to personal word collections. These can be referred to in future stories and used for a variety of word games.

Once children are accustomed to focusing on words in this way, the same procedure can be used to help them recognise words which carry less significance. Children can also be encouraged to focus on words which are phonically similar or related in meaning.

Suggestion(s) for support
Children who are unable to recognise isolated words should be encouraged to refocus on the whole story. Read the story out to the child, using clear intonation; then pause at the selected word or phrase, directing the child's attention to the first sound of a word or the first word of a phrase.

Assessment opportunities
Note the child's ability to recognise words instantly. If the child cannot do this, observe the strategies she uses for working the word out: reliance on memory, attention to context, sounding out.

Display ideas
Completed stories should be illustrated and published both as big books and as smaller personal copies. Selected words and phrases can be added to a class thesaurus.

Other aspects of the English PoS covered
Speaking and listening – 1a, b, c; 2a, b; 3a, b.

RECONSTRUCTING A FAMILIAR TEXT

To encourage the children to use syntactic, semantic and graphophonic information in order to reconstruct shuffled texts that they have composed themselves.

†† *A shared writing group of four to twelve children.*

🕐 *40 minutes.*

Key background information
This activity aims to integrate children's reading and writing abilities, and to help them co-ordinate their attention to different sources of textual information when they are reading. It is best used as a regular activity for children at a relatively early stage of reading development.

Preparation
See 'Sequencing: familiar text' on page 16.

Resources needed

Shared writing materials, a collection of cards of various sizes (large enough to cover a range of words from the text that you will be writing with the children).

What to do

Introduction

See 'Sequencing: familiar text' on page 16.

Development

When the story, or at least a coherent chunk of it, has been completed, read it through with the children, then cover a selection of words with the cards. The criteria used for 'deleting' these words will be determined by your knowledge of the needs of the group you are working with. You should consider:

▲ Random deletions, perhaps every tenth word (more frequent deletions will make the text very hard to read for beginner readers).

▲ Deletion of particular parts of speech (selected adjectives or verbs, for example).

▲ Deletion of words which share a specific phonic element. It can be particularly useful to cover all words beginning with a specific letter or blend of letters, leaving the beginning of the word exposed. An alliterative text emerging from the 'Alliterative word web' activity (page 82) would be useful here.

▲ If the story is based on a topic that you are following with the class, it might be useful to delete examples of specific vocabulary related to that topic.

When the deletions have been made, ask the children to read the story again, to pause at the deletions and to discuss what the hidden words might be. In order to do this, encourage the children to read back and read on, asking themselves what will make sense in the context of the sentence and of the story as a whole. To focus the children's attention on the initial letters of the words, a disclosing card can be used (as shown in the illustration). As each letter is revealed, ask the children to guess the word, bearing in mind the syntactic and semantic constraints as well as the evidence provided by the exposed letters.

Conclusion

When all the restorations have been made, reread the story and ask the children to try to describe what they were thinking while working out the identities of the missing words.

If the story is unfinished, complete it now or make arrangements for its completion, illustration and publication.

Suggestion(s) for extension

See the Document Restoration activity on page 21 for one way of extending this type of activity to unfamiliar texts based on stories and themes from topics you are working on.

Shared stories or adaptations of those familiar from storytime can be word-processed, particular words can be

deleted and children can reconstruct the stories working in pairs. Discussion, and the use of text which has personal significance, is essential or the activity will degenerate into a vapid gap-filling exercise.

The use of the text disclosure program *Developing Tray* (RML) will enable children to collaborate on the production and manipulation of such texts.

Suggestion(s) for support

The process of identifying uncertain words can be supported by oral storytelling in which children are encouraged to anticipate what comes next. Asking children to predict, from time to time, what course a story is likely to take is a simple but valuable practice. Occasionally pausing while reading with natural intonation, and encouraging the children to predict the next word, is a more focused strategy which should help to develop the children's awareness of syntactic and semantic cues in reading.

Assessment opportunities

Observe the cues that the children are using in order to make the word restorations. Note any positive signs that children are *combining* cues, or any symptoms of them over-relying on one system – for example, labouring over initial letters without due attention to context, or guessing from context without due attention to graphic information.

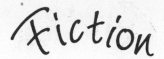
Opportunities for IT

Any of the texts used for this activity could be word processed by the teacher beforehand. It is then a simple matter of deleting the words which are the focus of the activity. Different activities can be produced for different groups from the same text. These can be printed out in suitable font sizes for different groups.

Some groups might complete the activity working at the computer itself. The editing facilities of the word processor give children an opportunity to add and edit the missing words as the discussion develops. The activity will also help to develop children's ability to read from the screen itself.

Other aspects of the English PoS covered

Speaking and listening – 1a, b, c; 2a.
Writing – 1a, b, c; 2a, b, c, d; 3b.

DOCUMENT RESTORATION: THE *MARIE CELESTE*

To develop the following strategies in order to restore the text of a document in which several words have been semi-obliterated:

▲ *attention to initial letters and other graphophonic features;*

▲ *attention to the syntax and semantics of the surrounding context;*

▲ *attention to the cohesive links which bind the sentences of the text together.*

All of these strategies will be used simultaneously.

†† *Pairs.*

🕐 *30 minutes.*

Key background information

This activity attempts to provide a topic-based context for using the strategies outlined above. In the follow-up work, opportunities are offered for creative writing based on the reading task.

Preparation

Prior discussion of contexts in which damaged documents would have to be restored will be helpful.

The text used should be based on a current topic, or on some item in the news in which the children have shown an interest. For example, if the children are working on a topic in local history, the document might be a letter from a damp-ravaged archive, or a diary entry, or a newspaper clipping, giving a contemporary account of a famous event. Photocopiable sheet 126 provides one such example which might be used as part of a topic on The Sea.

The deletions should focus on those phonic elements which you think the children need to concentrate on, and should be positioned in such a way that children will be able

to use their general knowledge as well as their graphophonic awareness. There should not be more than one deletion in a sentence, or more than 20 deletions in the whole document. In order to focus the children's attention, you might prepare an authentically dilapidated document by crumpling, staining and tearing a copy of the text that the children will be working with.

As with the 'Reconstructing a familiar text' activity on page 19, a text disclosure computer program (such as *Developing Tray*) can be used to prepare the text and to give the children further practice in this type of activity.

Resources needed

Documents and rewrite sheets based on the model given on photocopiable sheet 126 (or use the sheet itself if this is appropriate). A more authentic-looking model of such a document, prepared by the teacher. A poster-sized copy of the document (A2 or A1), large enough to be visible to the whole group. Shared writing materials, if the teacher intends to support the creative writing work in this way.

What to do

Introduction

Present the children with your simulation of the damaged document. Invite them to speculate on its origins and how it might have got into its present state. Explain that the objective of this activity is to restore the text to wholeness by working out what the damaged words are, and by writing the missing conclusion of the text.

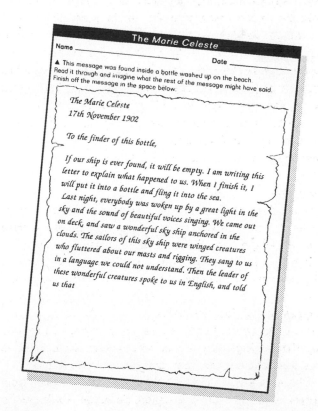

The Marie Celeste

Name _____

Date _____

▲ This message was found inside a bottle washed up on the beach.
Read it through and imagine what the rest of the message might have said.
Finish off the message in the space below.

The Marie Celeste
17th November 1902

To the finder of this bottle,

If our ship is ever found, it will be empty. I am writing this letter to explain what happened to us. When I finish it, I will put it into a bottle and fling it into the sea.
Last night, everybody was woken up by a great light in the sky and the sound of beautiful voices singing. We came out on deck, and saw a wonderful sky ship anchored in the clouds. The sailors of this sky ship were winged creatures who fluttered about our masts and rigging. They sang to us in a language we could not understand. Then the leader of these wonderful creatures spoke to us in English, and told us that

THE MARIE CELESTE
17TH NOVEMBER 1902

To the finder of this bottle,
If our s... is ... found, it will be ...
writing this ... plain what hap...
when I finis... but it into a bo...
fling it into the ...

Last night everybody ...
light in the s... and the s...d of ...
singing. We came out on deck, a...
wonder... ...y sh... anchored in t...
s... of this s... sh... were winged ...
fl...ttered about our masts and ...
us in a language we could not u...
the leader of these wonderful cr...
in English, and told us that ...

Development

Give each pair of children a copy of the document. Read the first two or three sentences to them, using natural intonation at a slightly slower pace than normal. When a damaged word is reached, ask the children to supply a likely restoration, and to explain why they think that the word they have given is suitable.

Using the poster, demonstrate how various sources of information should be considered together when working out a damaged word:

▲ the meaning of the preceding text (read back);
▲ the meaning of the following text (read on);
▲ the length and visible pattern of the surviving part of the word;
▲ the possible sounds represented by any surviving letters.

When this has been done, allow the pairs to work on the document without your assistance.

Conclusion

The group should compare their versions of the restored text, and discuss any differences of opinion. Children can then be helped to write the missing portion of the document, either alone or in pairs, independently or through shared writing with the teacher acting as scribe.

Suggestion(s) for extension

Other types of document could be explored in the same way (for example, wills, treasure maps, recipes for magic potions or miracle cures, 'lost' works by famous poets, novelists and dramatists).

The complexity of the task can be increased by making more deletions, allowing more alternatives for missing words or requiring closer attention to more remote parts of the text.

Suggestion(s) for support

Run through the entire text as an oral cloze procedure if the children are unfamiliar with the activity. That is, read the text aloud using natural intonation and pause at those portions of the text where a restoration is required. Remember that the spelling of the restored words is not as important as their *identification* through the clues given.

If the group lacks confidence in writing, or is at a very basic level of reading ability, the entire activity can be done through oral cloze. In this case, the teacher can sit with the children around the poster text, and write in the restorations after the children have discussed alternatives and agreed on an acceptable version.

Assessment opportunities

Observe the cues that the children are using in order to make the restorations. Note any positive signs that children are combining cues, or any symptoms of them over-relying on one system, for example, labouring over initial consonants without due attention to context, or guessing from context without due attention to graphic information.

Display ideas

Completed documents, with suitably authentic damage, can be put on display, though this will only work if the children have produced completed texts through creative writing beforehand.

Opportunities for IT

The initial text could be prepared on a word processor and the deletions made by the teacher before starting the activity. Children can then either work from the printed versions of the text, or at the computer screen.

Other areas of the English PoS covered

Speaking and listening – 1a, b, c; 2a.
Writing – 1a, b, c; 2a, b, c, d; 3b.

Reference to photocopiable sheet

Photocopiable sheet 126 can be used if relevant to a current class topic.

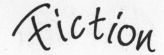
WHAT HAPPENS NEXT?

To reflect on the events of an unfolding narrative and discuss ideas about what will happen next.

†† *Small or large groups, working in pairs or as a whole class.*

🕑 *30 minutes.*

Key background information

Anticipating what will happen next in a text is an important part of reading: the reader combines background knowledge with the information provided by the text in order to construct possibilities for the rest of the story. In this activity, children are encouraged to share their predictions and to justify them by reference to what they have read and how it relates to previous experience (including previous reading experience).

Preparation

Build prediction into your routine sharing of literature with the class. You could do this by regularly reading out the opening passages of short stories or novels and asking the children what sort of narrative is likely to unfold from this beginning. This strategy can often motivate children to read the rest of the story or book for themselves.

Select a story at an appropriate level for the group you are working with. Cut it into chunks, each consisting of a sentence or a paragraph, depending upon the density of information in the story and the reading stamina of your group. Mount each chunk on a piece of card. Make enough sets of cards for each pair of children to have a set of their own. If you prefer to work with the whole group/class, the chunks can be copied on to an OHP transparency.

There is no need to prepare a whole story. If only part of a story is used, the children can be encouraged to finish it off themselves, either orally or in writing, or they can be given the complete version to read independently.

Photocopiable sheet 127 can be used as a starter activity. This is based on 'The Enchanted Pig' from *The Red Fairy Book* by Andrew Lang (Dover, 1966).

Resources needed

Photocopiable page 127 or story cards you have prepared yourself. Alternatively, you could use an OHP and your chosen story segments copied on to transparencies.

What to do

Introduction

Explain to the children that the purpose of this activity is to make thoughtful guesses about how a story might evolve.

Development

Distribute or project the first story chunk on to a screen. Ask the children to read it silently, and to think about what might happen next. The children can discuss their predictions in pairs or among the whole group, and you should encourage them to make explicit the text details and aspects of background experience on which these predictions have been based.

When this has been done, distribute or project the next chunk of the story and repeat the process. If at any point predictions are found to be mistaken, discuss how the author has managed to thwart the reader's expectations, and encourage the children to amend their predictions.

Conclusion

If you have been using part of a story, invite the children to finish it off themselves either orally or in writing. Ask them to try to describe the strategies that they have used in making their predictions, and discuss how effective writing plays on the reader's expectations: sometimes confirming them, and sometimes thwarting them in order to provide a surprise. Encourage the children to share with the class times when they have enjoyed unexpected twists and surprise endings in stories.

Suggestion(s) for extension

Fluent readers can be encouraged to incorporate predictions into their reading notebooks (see 'Introducing a readers' notebook' on page 15). Children who are group-reading the same novel can compare their predictions at set points in their reading. This should not be done too frequently, as unwarranted interruptions will destroy interest in the story.

Children who enjoy writing can prepare a story on the word processor, placing sequential chunks on separate pages. Other children, in pairs or threes, can then read the chunks, using the 'page down' command only after they have discussed what might come after the passage that they have just read.

Suggestion(s) for support

The entire activity can be conducted orally, with the teacher reading all the chunks aloud, or helping less confident children

---

Prediction (1)

There was once a head teacher who ran an enormously posh school, so exclusive and expensive that only her own three daughters could afford to go there. Two of them were sensible girls, but the youngest was very mischievous.

One day, the head teacher announced that she had to go on a long journey to visit another school. She told her daughters that she was leaving them in charge of her own school.

'You may play in the grounds and stroll in the orchard,' she told them, 'and you may enter any room in the school, except for the tiny room at the very top of the bell tower. That room is extremely dangerous.'

When the daughters found themselves alone, they soon became bored with the grounds and the orchard, and they took to exploring the school. Within a week they had searched every room, but none of them dared to approach the tiny room at the very top of the bell tower. Then one day when her sisters were picking apples in the orchard, the youngest daughter decided to climb the staircase to the top of the bell tower. At first she had no intention of going into the forbidden room. She just wanted to enjoy the view from the staircase windows – but when she reached the door of the tiny room at the very top, something made her open it and step inside.

There was nothing in the room except an old school desk, and a curious old exercise book which lay on the desk. She was about to open the book when she saw the writing on its cover. It said 'On no account should this book be opened.'

The youngest daughter was frightened and wanted to leave the room, but something made her stretch out her hand to the book and open it. What she read inside froze her blood.

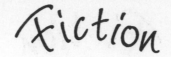

to read from the OHP or from an enlarged text. Subject to the point made above about restricting the number of interruptions, prediction should be encouraged when individual children are reading to the teacher.

Assessment opportunities
Note how well the children are able to support their predictions with detailed reference to the story so far and to their previous reading or other experience.

Opportunities for IT
Children who enjoy writing can prepare a story on a word processor. If they place each sequential 'chunk' on a new page, children can read each chunk and then use the 'page down' command to move on to the next chunk only after they have discussed what might come after the passage they have just read.

A more sophisticated approach would be to use a multimedia authoring package. If each chunk is put on to a separate page, visual arrowed links can be created which move children to the next chunk. It would even be possible to add prompts with questions the children might consider.

Other aspects of the English PoS covered
Speaking and listening – 1a; 2a, b; 3b.
Writing – 1a, b, c; 2b, e.

Reference to photocopiable sheet
Page 127 is an incomplete story which can be finished off by the children either in writing or as an oral game.

SEQUENCING UNFAMILIAR TEXT

To read a story in which the paragraphs have been jumbled together and use textual clues to put them into a coherent order.

†† *Small or large groups, with the children working in pairs or groups of four.*

🕐 *30–45 minutes.*

Key background information
Sequencing activities appeal to most children in the same way that jigsaw puzzles do. They help children to develop reading skills by focusing the reader's attention on the means by which text hangs together: chronological markers, pronouns and sentence connectives, for example.

Preparation
Choose a story which your group will be able to read with some help. (Or use photocopiable page 128 or 129, whichever is most appropriate.) The story should be short and pithy. The first two or three times you try this activity,

use a complete story with which the children are familiar. Cut the story up into six to eight segments. As with prediction activities, the length of the segments will depend on the density of the text and the reading stamina of the children in the group. Mount each segment on a piece of card, and ensure that you have a complete set of pieces for each pair or group of four.

Resources needed
Photocopiable page 128 or 129, or your own story cards.

What to do
Introduction
Explain to the children that they are going to read a story, but first of all they will need to put the pieces of the story into the correct order. Distribute the cards and allow the children time to read them through. Ask the children to identify clues which suggest where in the story particular chunks might go.

Development
Allow the children to work in their groups, intervening only if frustration is evident. Where difficulties are encountered, encourage the children to discuss different possibilities – there is not always a single best sequence. You could provide prompts which draw children's attention to such features as:
▲ phrases which indicate the beginning or ending of the narrative;

Death conquers all

'What are you running away from, old fellow?' said one of the youths.
'From Death,' said the old man. 'I have seen Death hiding in a cave and I must escape from him.'
'We're not frightened of Death,' said another one of the young men. 'Show us where he is hiding, and we'll show Death who is master around here.'

While he was in town, the younger man began to think about how rich he would be if he had all of the money himself. He bought plenty of food and wine, but he also bought poison and poured it into the wine bottle.

They began to count the gold in order to divide it up fairly between them. After a while, they became tired and hungry. They decided to have dinner, so the youngest man was sent to the nearest town to buy food and wine.

The man dropped his sticks and fled from the cave. Further down the beach he ran into three youths who were lounging on the sand.

The old man pointed along the beach and then hurried away. The three young men walked down the beach and soon found the cave. When they saw the chest full of gold inside it, they forgot all about Death and began to rejoice at their good luck.

When the young man returned to the cave, his two companions stabbed him to death. Then they sat down to eat the food he had brought and to drink the poisoned wine. Within minutes, they too were dead. Death had conquered after all.

There was once an old man who found a cave by the sea while he was gathering driftwood after a storm. Looking into the mouth of the cave, he saw a large sea-chest standing open, and in the chest was more gold than any person could count in a day.

While he was away, the older men began to talk about how much more money they would have if there were only two of them to share it. They decided to kill the younger man when he returned.

Later still, a fox padde[...]
'Go to sleep, youn[...]
freeze.'
But the young fro[...]

The next thing he kn[...]
water of the pond. A[...]
they were making fu[...]
'Never mind,' he [...]
sleep than any othe[...]

Winter came. The y[...]
settle into the mud[...]

The young frog ig[...]
to stay awake for [...]
gone to sleep in [...]
on the river bank[...]

Later, a hedgeho[...]
and saw the you[...]
'Go to sleep.[...]
freeze.'
But the youn[...]

Once upon a ti[...]
was like. All of [...]
frogs had to go[...]
awake would [...]

The young frog jumped into [...]
the mud and fell fast asleep.

As he sat there, the geese who were flying south for Winter looked down and saw him.
'Go to sleep, young frog,' they said. 'Winter is coming and you will surely freeze.'
But the young frog stayed awake.

▲ to whom or to what the pronouns, or other referring devices in a particular sentence, are referring;

▲ clues given by sentence connectives such as *later, suddenly,* and *at last.*

When the pairs or groups of four have worked out a coherent order for the story, encourage them to compare this with the one worked out by other partnerships.

Conclusion
Ask the children to describe the clues they have used in working out the order of the chunks, and discuss any instances of viable alternative sequences.

Suggestion(s) for extension
The complexity of these tasks can be increased to the point where even adults have genuine difficulty in agreeing on a sequence. This can be done by selecting texts in which the segments allow different ordering possibilities, by increasing the number of segments, and by shortening the length of each.

Children can also be encouraged to prepare short stories that they have read themselves for other children to sequence, or to write stories for this purpose. A word-processing program which allows the user to move portions of text to different locations would be a useful resource for this purpose.

Suggestion(s) for support
The simplest way of beginning this activity is to take a highly familiar story, divide it into a beginning, middle and end, and ask the group to talk through the order in which it should be reassembled and the reasons for this. This will give children a broad view of the features which structure a text. If children find the more extended activity difficult, sit down with the group, help them to read each chunk, and talk through the possibilities, drawing their attention to the text features referred to above.

Assessment opportunities
Note the children's awareness of the cohesive features of the story, and their ability to identify and evaluate different possibilities for sequencing.

Opportunities for IT
Children can also be encouraged to use a word processor to prepare short stories for other children to sequence. They could use stories that they have read themselves or write their own. The completed story should be saved on disk so that it can be retrieved later. The children can then use the 'cut' and 'paste' commands or the mouse to drag portions of the text into different locations. Other groups of children could use the same software and commands to re-sequence the text which could be checked against the original. Copies of the text could be printed out at each stage and used for

work away from the computer. The children should also be introduced to the 'load' and 'save' commands so that they can return to the work at a later date.

Display ideas
This activity can be incorporated into the everyday work of the class by means of a sequencing board. A bank of segmented story sets can be collected, mounted on Velcro-backed card and placed next to a cloth-covered board. A different set of cards can be put up each day for children to work with in their own time. Encourage them to set up the board themselves, and to contribute their own segmented stories to it.

Other aspects of the English PoS covered
Speaking and listening – 1a, b, c; 2a, b.

Reference to photocopiable sheets
Photocopiable pages 128 and 129 provide examples of stories which have been divided into eight segments; page 128 (based on 'The Pardoner's Tale' from Chaucer's *Canterbury Tales*) is intended for a more advanced level than page 129.

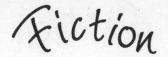

THE MISSING PIECE

To discuss and consider the events of a story in order to formulate a sentence to fill a gap in the story.
†† *Any size group. A good whole-class activity.*
🕐 *20 minutes.*

Key background information
In this activity the children will read a traditional Turkish story, 'Nasr-ed-Din and the End of the World'. A crucial sentence has been omitted, and the purpose of the activity is to encourage the children to reflect on the events of the narrative in order to identify what these words might be.

Although the missing phrase is 'the world ends tonight' or words to that effect, the children might come up with alternative ideas that make equal sense.

Preparation
Prepare a copy of photocopiable sheet 130 for each child or pair of children in the group. If you are unfamiliar with the figure of Nasr-ed-Din, talking to a member of the Turkish, Armenian or Balkan community would be the best way of finding out about him. If this is impractical, *Tales of the Hodja* retold by Charles Downing (OUP, 1964) is a good source of information.

Resources needed
Photocopiable sheet 130.

What to do
Introduction
Tell the children about the Nasr-ed-Din and relate two or three stories about him in order to give the children a flavour of these tales.

Explain to them that this activity resembles a jigsaw puzzle with a piece missing that they have to create themselves, using the clues provided by the rest of the story.

Development
Provide the children with copies of photocopiable sheet 130 and allow them to read the story silently, providing support wherever necessary. When they have done this, encourage them to share ideas about the missing words. They should 'test' each others' suggestions by rereading the story and deciding which of the suggestions fits best. Can they suggest a title for the story?

Conclusion
Read the version of the story to the children with the 'official' completion, and ask for their opinions on how this compares

with their own ideas. Encourage them to look for more Nasr-ed-Din stories themselves.

Suggestion(s) for extension
The procedure for this lesson can be applied to any story whose denouement depends upon a single phrase or sentence. There are many other Nasr-ed-Din stories which could be explored in the same way. Children could also select or compose their own stories for this type of exercise.

Suggestion(s) for support
Children who find it difficult to read the story unassisted can be supported by shared reading. Enlarge photocopiable sheet 130 to poster size and read it with the children.

Assessment opportunities
Observe the children's ability to use the storyline to solve the problem. This involves making and evaluating hypotheses based on what has been read.

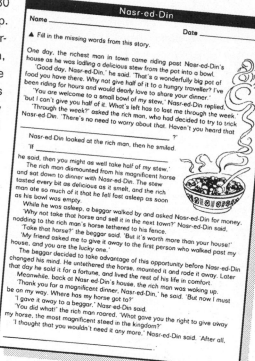

Opportunities for IT
After the children have decided on their replacements for the missing pieces they could use a word processor to insert their missing pieces into a copy of the text. The missing sections could be represented by stars or other symbols. Although the sections would be easily identifiable, children could be shown how to use the 'search' command to move to the missing sections. Once they have typed in their sections, the children could use the bold, italic, underline commands, other font styles or colours to make their insertions stand out from the rest of the text. Their version could then be printed and used as part of a class display. Children should save their work with their own filename in order to preserve the original text for another group to use.

Display ideas
The children can prepare a cartoon strip version of the story, with the 'crucial words' omitted from the appropriate speech balloon. This can then be presented as a puzzle to children who have not participated in the activity.

Other aspects of the English PoS covered
Speaking and listening – 1a; 2a, b.

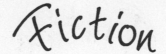

ROTARY STORY

To identify distinctive features of different types of narrative, and reflect these in creative writing.

✝✝ *A small group, or several small groups (4 to 6 children in each).*

🕐 *Approximately one hour.*

Key background information

This activity is most appropriate for children who can write independently, though a similar activity can be conducted orally.

Preparation

Read the 'story starters' on photocopiable pages 131 or 132 and try to write continuations of them yourself. Copy the photocopiable page suitable for the level of the children; then cut out the separate paragraphs and mount each one at the top of a page, so that you have one page for each child in the group.

Resources needed

The 'story starters' on photocopiable pages 131 or 132. If there are more than four children in each group, you will need to make enough copies to ensure that each child has a choice of story to start from.

What to do

Introduction

Explain to the children that the purpose of this activity is to write stories for the enjoyment of the rest of the class, or whatever other audience the group chooses, and that they will be writing co-operatively.

Distribute the story starters, read each one aloud and encourage the children to identify what type of story is most likely to grow from each one. Let each child choose the starter that they would like to work on first.

Development

Allow the children about 10 to 15 minutes to write the next paragraph or two of the story. When they have done this, they should be encouraged to read it carefully and make any necessary amendments before passing it on to the next person in the group. The person receiving this chunk should then read it carefully before writing, so that their continuation is consonant with what has already been written. The stories are rotated around the group, with 10 to 15 minutes of writing being allowed for each turn. Each child should initial any segment that they have written. The amount of time allowed for each contribution can, of course, be shortened or lengthened according to your knowledge of the children's attention span, and how the activity goes on the day.

Conclusion

When the pages return to the person who made the first contribution, the children can take turns reading out the

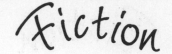

stories so far and discuss their development in terms of consistency and continuity. Where inconsistencies occur, these can be evaluated in terms of whether they make the story more interesting or simply spoil the flow. A group decision can be made about whether the stories should be finished off by individuals working independently, or by further rotations.

Completed stories can be redrafted and published in future writing sessions.

Suggestion(s) for extension
Capable writers can create a bank of story starters, based on their reading of a wide range of fictional genres.

Suggestion(s) for support
Working with a group of children sitting in a circle, the teacher can read aloud one of the starters and encourage each child in turn to add to it orally, telling them to base their contributions as closely as possible on what has gone before. This process can then be repeated with as many of the other starters as the teacher thinks suitable. Each of them should be discussed and compared with others before the oral game begins. The stories thus created can be written up as a shared text, or can be recorded on tape and written out later. They can then be added to the reading resources of the class.

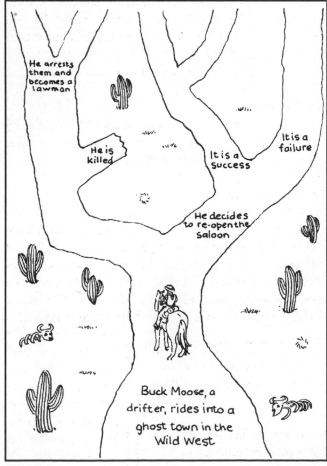

Figure 1

Assessment opportunities
Note how well each child's contribution is based on a careful and appreciative reading of the preceding text. Remember, however, that breaks in the stylistic register of a story are not necessarily due to inattentive reading. Look for creative departures from the preceding pattern as well as careful continuities.

Display ideas
As well as appearing in straightforward book form, the stories can be displayed in formats which allow the children to see how different narratives can grow from the same starter. A story tree can be constructed in order to show this (see Figure 1) with the additional branches used as an invitation to create variants on the stories already completed.

Other aspects of the English PoS covered
Speaking and listening – 1a, b; 2a, b; 3a, b.
Writing – 1a, b, c; 2a, b, c, d; 3a, b, c.

Reference to photocopiable sheets
Pages 131 and 132 provide story starters based on fairly clear-cut genres. The first sheet is intended to be simpler and more open-ended than the second.

READING TO DRAMA

To select a favourite story and transform it into a scripted drama.

Small groups.

An initial session of about 30 minutes, with an open-ended follow-up.

Key background information
Many children enjoy the process of transforming a story into a play that can be performed. It is, however, a complex business, and needs to be tackled carefully in order to avoid a superficial approach which will trivialise the original story, frustrate the participants and bore the audience. If the teacher guides the children through this process, they can be helped to reflect on plot and characterisation, and to consider different ways in which these elements can be interpreted.

Preparation
Provide opportunities for the children to read and perform stories set out as playscripts. (Several reading schemes now incorporate such texts.) Talk to the children about the links between stories and plays – television serials based on well-known children's books should provide an accessible starting-point for this.

Well before you intend to conduct the lesson, ask the children to think about stories that they would like to perform as plays, and encourage them to discuss their preferences with each other so that groups based on particular choices

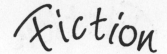

can be formed. You may have to veto choices that are too unwieldy in terms of length or number of characters. Many stories from mythology are amenable to this kind of treatment, having strong simple storylines and a manageable number of characters.

When the children have made their choices, conduct a drama session in which each group enacts an improvised stage version of their chosen story. The aim of this preliminary session is for the children to agree on the overall shape of the story, and to share ideas for setting, action and dialogue. It should also demonstrate the usefulness of a script in the planning of a more 'public' dramatisation of the story.

Resources needed
Shared writing materials.

What to do
Introduction
The children should decide whether they want to present the story as a spoken play only, perhaps involving a narrator, or as a more theatrical production involving the use of scenery and props. They should also consider their intended audience, as this will inform the discussion surrounding the creation of the dialogue. They can then sit in a circle and retell the story orally, taking responsibility for one role each.

All of the characters involved should be identified and their names written out by the teacher or scribe. A scene structure for the play should also be agreed. If the children have opted for a theatrical presentation, details of settings for each scene can be determined at this point.

Development One
Assign the roles of characters in the story to individual children, who then speak in role as the story unfolds, with the teacher or scribe 'taking dictation' from each character in turn. At the end of each scene, the group can comment on the dialogue and make any necessary amendments.

Development Two
The group as a whole can work on the dialogue, with the teacher or scribe writing down the agreed version.

Whether the play is to be staged or only spoken, the children need to be reminded that the bulk of the story has to be conveyed through dialogue – so particular attention has to be paid to the amount of explicit information in each character's speech. There must be enough to make the story comprehensible to the audience, but not so much that the dialogue becomes overloaded and artificial.

| George | I told the two men that if they waited here any longer the traffic warden would come along and give them a parking ticket. |
| Policeman | Could you describe them to me again so that we can issue a description? *(Policeman gets out notebook and pencil.)* |

Conclusion
The children should read aloud (in their roles) through the script so far, and assess how effectively it tells the story and how faithful to their own visions of the characters the dialogue sounds. This is best done by recording the read-through on tape and then listening to it critically. If time permits, immediate amendments can be made; or they can be postponed until the next session.

The children should be encouraged to talk through the stages of the process in which they have just been involved, as a preparation for subsequent sessions leading to publication and performance.

Suggestion(s) for extension
Once the entire script has been finalised, the children can explore the use of other media to support the drama, such as visual backdrops and background music. Decisions about what form these supportive types of representation will take should be justified by reference to the text.

Suggestion(s) for support
The preliminary drama session can be recorded on video or audiotape and used as a support for the shared writing of the script.

Assessment opportunities
The children's comprehension and appreciation of the story will be reflected in the dialogue that they create. This will provide evidence of their ability to assess and adapt their ideas as a result of attentive listening, and their competence in creating and negotiating ideas through oral language.

Display ideas
The different stages in the process of transforming a story into a play can be photographed and displayed with captions and extracts from the evolving playscript.

Opportunities for IT
Once the children have moved on to creating a script, they can use a word processor or DTP package to assist them with the drafting and re-drafting as the script develops. If children use a word processor, they need to be taught how to use the formatting commands to present the script in a standard format which makes it easy to use. This should involve the use of tabs to separate the speaker's name from the dialogue. If possible, children could use hanging indents so that the dialogue is set in from the speaker's name. These could be set up as styles in advance.

An alternative approach would be to use a desktop publishing package and create a master page. If two columns are created, speakers' names can be placed in the first column and the dialogue in the second as shown at the bottom of page 29. This approach avoids the need to use indents and tabs, although if extra dialogue is added children need to make sure that the names stay with the speech.

In both approaches, the stage directions and other scene information can be written in italics. If possible, a style could be set up to make this easier. Copies can be printed for each actor and the final scripts could be used as part of a display or bound to make a book.

Other aspects of the English PoS covered
Speaking and listening – 1a, b, c, d; 2a, b; 3a, b.
Writing – 1a, b, c; 2a, b, c, d; 3a, b, c.

WHO'S TO BLAME?

To prompt the children to discuss the behaviour of the characters in a story, justifying their judgements of who is most and least blameworthy by referring back to the text.

†† *Whole class, working in groups of four.*

🕐 *30 minutes.*

Key background information
This is a reading and oral activity. It can be adapted to explore issues in any topic in which the morality of people's behaviour is under discussion.

Preparation
Prepare one copy of photocopiable page 133 for each child.

Resources needed
Photocopiable page 133.

What to do
Introduction
Invite somebody in the class to tell the traditional story of Red Riding Hood. Discuss the roles of heroes, villains and victims in traditional fairy tales. Ask the children if they know of any stories, including ones from films, comics or television programmes, in which these roles are not so clear-cut. Explain that they are going to read a story in which traditional roles have been altered.

Development
Distribute the copies of photocopiable page 133 to the children. Ask them to read and discuss the story and to try to come to an agreement, within each group of four, over the relative culpability of the characters.

Conclusion
Discuss, with the whole class, the orders of blame arrived at by different groups. Encourage the children to justify their choices by referring to specific parts of the text.

Suggestion(s) for extension
Children can reconstruct the story as a drama activity, then prepare a court case in which they take on the roles of defence counsel and/or prosecutor for the four people in the story.

Some children might want to try adapting other fairy stories in a similar way.

Suggestion(s) for support
If children find it difficult to read the story sheet independently, they can read in partnership with more capable peers or with the teacher or another adult. Alternatively, the activity can be started with a 'read-aloud' by the teacher, using a poster-sized copy of the text as a support. An audiotape could also be used, with the teacher stopping the tape at appropriate points for discussion. Remember that in this activity, accurate reading of the story is much less important than a readiness to discuss the behaviour of the characters in the story.

Blue Riding Hood (2)

The wolf tucked into the cakes, not realising that foxgloves are poisonous. He was on his third cake...

Blue Riding Hood (1)

Once upon a time there was a clever young woman called Blue Riding Hood who enjoyed playing tricks on people.

Every Sunday, Blue Riding Hood walked through the forest to her grandmother's house, where the old lady gave her dinner in exchange for a basket of cakes.

One Sunday morning, Blue Riding Hood strayed from the path to pick some foxgloves to sell at the market. When she had finished, she realised that she was lost. She wandered about for an hour before sitting down on a tree stump, sobbing in frustration.

'Don't cry,' said a gentle voice. 'Are you lost?'

'What does it look like?' Blue Riding Hood snapped, looking up into the beautiful brown eyes of the great big wolf who had stepped out of the trees.

'There's no need to worry,' the wolf said. 'I know the way to your grandmother's house and I will guide you there.'

The wolf took Blue Riding Hood's basket full of cakes between his teeth and led her out of the forest. By the time they arrived at Grandmother's house, it was getting dark.

'Here we are,' the wolf said. 'Now that I have helped you, will you pay me?'

'What do you want?' Blue Riding Hood said suspiciously, taking up the basket that the wolf had set down.

'Nothing much,' the wolf replied. 'Just those lovely cakes in your basket; half for me and half for my poor starving cubs.'

'You can't have any of them; those cakes have got to pay for my dinner.'

'If you won't give me the cakes, I will have to take them. I hope it won't be necessary for me to bite you in order to do so.'

'I was only joking,' Blue Riding Hood said, thinking quickly. 'Take the cakes, but let me spice them up a bit for you first.'

Blue Riding Hood stripped the petals off the foxgloves and sprinkled them over the cakes.

'Eat them up quickly while they're still fresh,' she said, 'and take the rest home to your poor hungry children.'

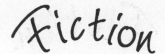

Assessment opportunities

Note how closely the comments made by individuals are based on reference to events in the text.

Opportunities for IT

As part of the extension activity children could use a word processor or DTP package to write a script for the court case. The teacher and children could use the ideas in 'Reading to drama' on page 28 for setting out and writing the script. Alternatively, children could use a word processor to help them adapt other fairy stories in a similar way. It may be possible to use an art package or commercially available clip art, or resources from CD-ROMs to illustrate the new story. The new versions could be printed out and used as a part of a class display.

Display ideas

Adapted fairy stories can be displayed as illustrated 'zigzag' books, surrounded by printed-out statements for the defence or prosecution of the featured characters.

Other aspects of the English PoS covered

Speaking and listening – 1a, b, d; 2a, b; 3b.
Writing – 1a, b, c.

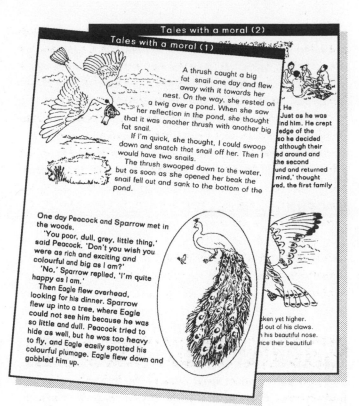

Tales with a moral (2)
Tales with a moral (1)

A thrush caught a big fat snail one day and flew away with it towards her nest. On the way, she rested on a twig over a pond. When she saw her reflection in the pond, she thought that it was another thrush with another big fat snail.

If I'm quick, she thought, I could swoop down and snatch that snail off her. Then I would have two snails.

The thrush swooped down to the water, but as soon as she opened her beak the snail fell out and sank to the bottom of the pond.

One day Peacock and Sparrow met in the woods.

'You poor, dull, grey, little thing,' said Peacock. 'Don't you wish you were as rich and exciting and colourful and big as I am?'

'No,' Sparrow replied, 'I'm quite happy as I am.'

Then Eagle flew overhead, looking for his dinner. Sparrow flew up into a tree, where Eagle could not see him because he was so little and dull. Peacock tried to hide as well, but he was too heavy to fly, and Eagle easily spotted his colourful plumage. Eagle flew down and gobbled him up.

TALES WITH A MORAL

For children to discuss examples of stories that attempt to teach a moral lesson, and then to verbalise the ethical dimension in such stories and compose their own stories to illustrate moral maxims.

†† *Whole class, then pairs or small groups.*

🕐 *30 minutes.*

Key background information

The use of storytelling to convey moral messages or uncomfortable truths is a common element in many traditions. The parables of the New Testament, Aesop's fables and the *Panchatantra* stories (traditional Indian tales) are well-known examples of this custom.

Discussion of such stories can help children to think beyond the immediate events depicted in their reading and enable them to identify the underlying message of such events and its application to the wider world.

Preparation

Start to share tales that have a moral with the children as part of your reading or storytelling programme. Encourage them to think beyond the story and to verbalise the moral.

Resources needed

A copy of *The Puffin Book of Fabulous Fables*, edited by Mark Cohen (Puffin 1991). Other books which contain moral tales (any edition of Aesop's fables would be appropriate). You should preferably provide examples in which the moral is not stated explicitly at the end of the story. (Photocopiable page 135 or 136 can be used as an alternative.)

A selection of maxims, written on cards large enough for all children in the class to read, some relating to the stories to be presented and others not – such as 'Beauty is only skin deep', 'Wisdom is strength' and 'A fool and his money are soon parted'.

What to do
Introduction

Read *What's a Fable?* by Hans Andersen to the children from the Puffin collection, or read the first story on sheet 135 or 136. Ask the children to think about what the story is trying to do, besides entertaining the reader or listener. Can any lesson about human behaviour be learned from a story about an animal? If the children fail to identify the wider implications of the story, you will need to prompt them with examples of human behaviour that illustrate the 'problem' addressed by the fable. You will also have to deal with any responses that identify a valid moral, but focus on peripheral aspects of the story (for example, 'It's wrong to steal' in relation to the fox story). Once the moral has been identified, invite the children to think of as wide a range of similar situations as they can.

Development

Distribute your collection of moral tales, or the relevant photocopiable sheets, to the children. Allow them time to read the stories – individually, with a partner or in a small group – and to discuss them afterwards. Ask the children to try to agree on a moral for the story or stories that they have discussed with their partners; then present a selection of maxim cards to the children, some of them based on your own interpretations of the stories and others derived from fables with which the children are not yet familiar.

Ask them to match their own verbalisations of the morals of the stories with those you have presented, and to set aside the maxims that do not appear to be related to any of the stories. Talk through any disagreements with the children.

Conclusion
Read through those maxims that have not been matched with any of the presented stories, and ask the children to try to devise stories which illustrate such maxims in an entertaining way. This can be done 'on the spot' as a prompt to spontaneous oral storytelling if you have a particularly fluent group; or it can be assigned as something to think about for a future storywriting or storytelling session.

Suggestion(s) for extension
Children can conduct their own research into moral tales from a range of cultures. The acknowledgements in the Puffin collection will provide some leads, as will any good collection of folk-tales from around the world.

Suggestion(s) for support
Fables can be expanded into poster-sized texts and used for shared reading in a small group.

Assessment opportunities
Make a note of individual children's ability to think beyond the immediate events of the story, to identify underlying messages and to consider alternative messages.

Opportunities for IT
Children could use a word processor to write their own moral tales to add to a class display on this topic.

Display ideas
Make a display of fables and other types of moral tales in your reading area. Encourage the children to read these stories and to formulate their own interpretations of what they are trying to teach. Many such stories are very concise, so it would be a good idea to make poster-sized copies of the stories and to display them alongside a question sheet on which children can write their own formulations of the moral. Children's own moral tales can be added to this display.

Other aspects of the English PoS covered
Speaking and listening – 1a, b, c; 2a, b.

Reference to photocopiable sheets
Pages 135 and 136 provide a selection of short fables at different levels of readability.

STORY MAP

To select relevant information from a story and use it to make a map showing the setting of the story.
†† *Small groups or whole class.*
⊕ *One hour.*

Key background information
In this activity, the children are encouraged to create an illustrated map showing an environment featured in a story that they have read or listened to. This requires them to focus on the points in the story that are relevant to the task, and to convert them into visual form.

Figure 1 shows one such map, based on the story *Nothing to Be Afraid of* by Jan Mark (Puffin, 1982). You can, of course, substitute any story more relevant to the interests of your class, provided that it has a sufficiently strong geographical element to it. This work can form part of a topic on Places or on Literature.

Preparation
Make an OHP or an enlarged version of Figure 1. Rehearse a reading of the story *Nothing to Be Afraid of* to your class.

Resources needed
A copy of *Nothing to Be Afraid of*. Another story, or selection of stories, likely to appeal to the children. These should be related to a theme that the children have been exploring (for

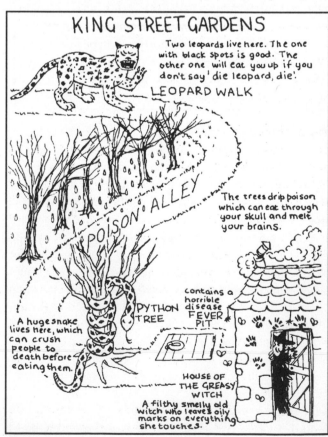

Figure 1

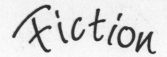
example, stories about exploration or stories written by your 'Author of the Week'). The settings of the stories should be suitable for map-like representation.

What to do
Introduction
Read *Nothing to Be Afraid of* to the class or group. Discuss the story and ask the children to picture the layout of the park in their heads. Encourage them to sketch a map of the park, labelling the sites of the main events in the story, and ask them to discuss it in relation to the story and to compare it with their own sketch maps. Figure 1 provides a model for such a map.

Explain that they are going to make another map, based on a different story that they will be reading.

Development
If you are using a selection of stories, provide an introductory synopsis of each and allow the children to choose which one they want to read. The reading can be done silently or aloud (if the same story is given to each child), individually or in collaboration.

When this has been done, the children can create their own maps based on their interpretations of the stories.

Conclusion
Allow plenty of time for the children to share their work with each other. It is particularly valuable to compare and discuss different interpretations of the same story. Discuss possibilities for displaying the work with the children.

Suggestion(s) for extension
Children can be encouraged to create maps as a stimulus for writing their own stories.

Suggestion(s) for support
The activity can make up part of a follow-up to a read-aloud session. If working with a small group, the map can be drawn by the teacher (or a volunteer from the group) on a larger scale with its details determined by the children. This can then be reproduced on a smaller scale for each child, and used as a support for individual or shared reading.

Assessment opportunities
Note the degree of correlation between the information given in the story and the information shown on the map. Remember that a lack of correlation might be due more to creative reinterpretation of the story than to misunderstanding.

Display ideas
Maps can be displayed in conjunction with chunks of the story. Differing interpretations of the same chunk are particularly interesting to display.

Other aspects of the English PoS covered
Speaking and listening – 1a, b; 2a, b.
Writing – 1a, b, c; 2a, b, c.

VISUALISING CHARACTERS

To deepen children's involvement in stories by helping them to reflect on the characters that they meet in their reading.

†† *Whole-class introduction, followed by children working individually.*

🕐 *40 minutes.*

Key background information
During reading, children will create images of the fictional characters in their mind's eye; these can then be drawn on when they represent their perceptions of these characters in words and pictures. This activity will encourage them to visualise characters and to imagine them both within and beyond the bounds of the book.

Preparation
Make a copy of photocopiable page 137 and complete it for your own favourite fictional character from children's literature. You may need to reread the appropriate book in order to do this. When you have completed it, think about how you created the visual image and the information on the sheet.

Make a collection of different illustrators' versions of fictional characters with whom the children might be familiar

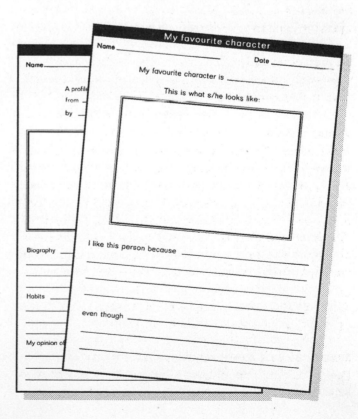

– Long John Silver, Alice and figures from mythology might be good starting-points. Photographs of television and cinema characters from such stories should also be included. Display this collection in your classroom a week or so before you intend to conduct the activity outlined below. Draw the children's attention to it, and try to convince them that there is no such thing as an 'official' version of a fictional character: each reader is free to compose their own image of the people that she reads about.

Resources needed
The required number of copies of photocopiable page 137.

What to do

Introduction
Ask the children to talk in pairs about their favourite characters from books that they have read or have had read to them. In order to stimulate the conversation, you could refer to characters from a book or story that you have recently shared with the children.

Ask them to close their eyes and to imagine what the character looks like, and what kind of person he or she might be if they were able to live a life outside the book that contained them. You could ask them to visualise what it would be like to live next door to such a person, or to go to school with them.

Development
Distribute the photocopiable sheets and show the children the one you have completed for your own favourite character. Talk through the decisions that you had to make in order to complete the sheet.

Ask them to do the same for their own character, reminding them that in order to do so, they should think about both what they have been told about the character in the text and what they can work out for themselves, using inference and imagination.

Conclusion
The children can share their responses, and discuss the decisions they have made about the character they chose. Encourage them to justify these decisions by referring to the text. This will be particularly important where children have made eccentric responses to the task (a three-legged Long John Silver or a male Alice, for example).

Suggestion(s) for extension
Children can use this format as a basis for creating their own fictional characters. They can also be encouraged to make a range of other representations of their favourite characters.

Suggestion(s) for support
Photocopiable sheet 138 provides a simpler format for this type of activity.

Either of the sheets can be enlarged to poster size and completed through shared writing. This would be appropriate for a group of children who have been reading a book or series together and who wish to make a joint report on a particular character.

Assessment opportunities
Children's responses to this activity might provide evidence both of 'careful' reading (characters who accurately reflect the information in the text) and of the use of inference and imagination.

Opportunities for IT
As part of the extension activities, children could use a word processor, desktop publishing program or graphics package to present and publish some of the documents suggested. The teacher, or more able children, could set up master pages for things such as passports and reports for children to complete. This means that children do not have to get involved with the format of their document but can concentrate on the information and the style of the writing.

Display ideas
Children's drawings of the characters, and examples of the other types of representation suggested above, can be displayed in your reading area alongside the books that inspired them and other illustrators' perceptions of these characters.

Other aspects of the English PoS covered
Speaking and listening – 1a, b, c, d.
Writing – 1a, b; 2a, b, c.

Reference to photocopiable sheets
Pages 137 and 138 provide suggested formats for this activity. Children can use either or both sheets, or design their own format.

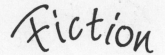
RELATIONSHIP DIAGRAMS

To create a pictorial record of the relationships between people in a story.

†† *Whole class.*

🕐 *Varying times throughout the reading of a class novel.*

Key background information

This is another activity involving the children in the creation of a visual record of their reading. In previous activities, children have been encouraged to make graphic representations of settings and characters. In this activity, they are helped to visualise the complex relationships between characters. It should be conducted at storytime and should involve the whole class; but the long-term objective is to encourage children to use this procedure in their independent reading of fiction, particularly novels.

Preparation

Read a good book which features plenty of characters and build up a visual record of the relationships between the characters in a manner similar to Figure 1, which is based on *Black Ships Before Troy* by Rosemary Sutcliff (Frances Lincoln, 1993). Explain to the children what you are doing, and tell them that they will be involved in a similar activity during the reading of the next class novel.

Resources needed

A large blank chart; one piece of card for each character in the story you are going to read; Blu-Tack; felt-tipped pens.

What to do

Introduction

Put up the blank chart where it can be seen by all the children. Remind them that the purpose of the activity is to help them to follow the course of the story by indicating how the characters are related to each other.

Development

As you tell the story, pause at a strategic point after each new character has been introduced, and invite one of the children to write the character's name on a piece of card and to stick it to the chart.

As the story unfolds, invite the children to group the cards under tentative headings. These might be 'children' and 'adults', 'friends' and 'enemies' of the central character, 'heroes' and 'villains', or any other categories that fit the context of the story.

In many cases, a family tree will be appropriate. The use of lines to indicate relationships between characters can be extended, as in Figure 1, by drawing labelled arrows between character names.

Conclusion

Remind the children at the end of the session that the chart as it stands can only reflect the story as it stands. Relationships will change, characters will move from group to group, and new groups may have to be formed.

Suggest to the children that they should start to use this strategy to map relationships in their independent reading, perhaps using their readers' notebooks to draft their own diagrams.

Suggestion(s) for extension

This type of work can feed into projects on story grammar, as suggested in the activity on page 36. Following this procedure for a few books (not for *all* the books you read with the class) and helping the children to apply it to their own reading, should raise the children's awareness of the complexity of the character types and the relationships between characters in fiction.

Suggestion(s) for support

Any sorting activity based on characters in books, or in media such as television soap operas or comic-book serials, will help children to clarify

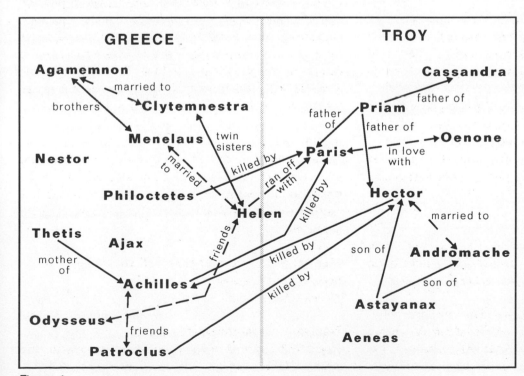

Figure 1

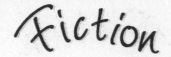
relationships in fiction. Soaps are particularly amenable to such activities. Children can collect photographs of all the characters, mount them on cards, and sort them according to multiple criteria: 'young' and 'old', 'those I like' and 'those I dislike', 'family groups', 'friendship groups', and so on.

Assessment opportunities

The children's interest in, and understanding of, a particular story can be monitored through their responses to this activity. Make a note of any children who identify less obvious patterns of relationship, or conceive of original ways of representing the relationships.

Opportunities for IT

Children could extend their work to the use of a branching database on the computer. They will need to 'teach' the database differences between different characters by posing questions which have a 'yes/no' answer. The computer then creates a key which can be used by another child to identify any item included within the programmed set of items. Children could use the characters in a television 'soap' or from a book they are reading. The creation of the key is an excellent language development activity. Different groups of children could create their own branching database and try it out with other groups.

Display ideas

The labelled chart makes a useful working display which can be altered from day to day. In many cases, it would be informative to make a copy of the chart in its early stages and to compare this with the chart as it stands at the end of the story.

Other aspects of the English PoS covered

Speaking and listening – 1a, b, c; 2a, b.

 THEMES IN FICTION

> *To prompt children to consider similarities between stories from different times and different cultures, and to speculate about the possible origins of such relationships.*
> †† *Whole class.*
> 🕐 *30 minutes.*

Key background information

This a discussion activity which can be included in storytime at the end of the day. You should try to conduct the activity on a regular basis, rather than as a one-off.

Note that there are many different levels of similarity that you might explore here. At one level, you can compare different versions of what is essentially the same story. For example the children could look at different versions of 'Beauty and the Beast' or 'East of the Sun, West of the

Moon'. At another level, you can look at stories which are distinct but which share related motifs. For example, *Krindlekrax* by Philip Ridley (Red Fox, 1992) might be compared with 'The Bakerloo Flea' from *Nasty!* by Michael Rosen (Puffin, 1984).

Preparation

Collect groups of books which clearly have related storylines. Display them in your book area and invite the children to read the stories and to try to spot the similarities between them. Include both novels and short stories that can be read at one sitting. Collections of folk-tales from different cultures are an excellent source of such stories. *World Tales*, edited by Idries Shah (Octagon Press, 1991), is a beautiful book containing many less well-known versions of familiar tales. *The Classic Fairy Tales* by Iona and Peter Opie (Oxford University Press, 1974) and the *Virago Book of Fairy Tales*, edited by Angela Carter (Virago, 1990), are also useful sources.

Resources needed

A selection of books with similar storylines, as described above.

What to do
Introduction

Select two or three of the shorter stories that you have displayed and read them out to the children. Some suggestions include: 'Cat Anna' from *Crack a Story* by Susan Price (Faber, 1990); 'Baba Yaga's Daughter' from *The Kingdom Under the Sea* by Joan Aiken (Puffin, 1973); 'The Baba Yaga' from the *Virago Book of Fairy Tales*; 'Cinderella'

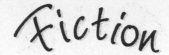

in any version; 'Donkeyskin' from *The Rose Fairy Book* by Andrew Lang (Dover Publications, 1969), and the 'Algonquin Cinderella' from *World Tales*; *East of the Sun, West of the Moon* by P.J. Lynch (Walker, 1994); 'The Enchanted Pig' from the *Red Fairy Book* by Andrew Lang (Dover Publications, 1969).

Development

Ask the children to identify the similarities and differences between the stories. As they do so, write these up on a chart or OHP transparency.

Try to get the children to offer a very brief summary of the plot elements shared by these stories. Often, the best way of expressing this is in the form of a problem which underlies the events of the narrative. For example, both 'Donkeyskin' and 'Cinderella' could be summarised thus:

X, who is rich, falls in love with Y, who is poor. Social conventions and/or accidents of fate keep them apart.

When an effective summary has been agreed on, it can be written out on a card and displayed alongside the stories it relates to. If you carry out this activity two or three times a week, you will soon build up a collection of theme cards which the children can use for storytelling games.

Conclusion

Ask the children to consider why stories written in different parts of the world and at different times often share common patterns. Why, for example, is the motif of the three brothers or three sisters so prevalent? What is so universally fascinating about buried treasure, men transformed by witches into animals, evil step-parents, children lost in forests, and impossibly difficult tasks completed with magical assistance? There are no definitive answers to these questions, of course; but the children might come up with some interesting suggestions.

Remind them to be on the look-out for stories which share plot patterns, so that they can go on contributing to the collection of theme cards.

Suggestion(s) for extension

Themes, characters and settings are all elements in *story grammar*, the study of the ways in which these elements combine to form narrative. When children are familiar with this kind of work, they can use drama and storytelling games to explore ways of creating new stories by combining characters and settings from a range of existing stories.

One way to stimulate this is to challenge the children to create their own adventure or fantasy board game, using a story map (see 'Story map' on page 32) or a combination of story maps to make up a board. The children can be given responsibility for writing the game manual and for selecting characters and settings.

Suggestion(s) for support

Some children might find it difficult to envisage the underlying shape of a story, concentrating instead on the 'surface' events. Try to overcome this by telling related stories during a sequence of storytimes, and by including overt references to earlier stories in your discussions. For example, you might make creation myths the topic for one week's storytelling, 'Rule of Three' stories (stories featuring three brothers, sisters, tasks, wishes and so on) the topic for another, quests the topic for a third, trickster stories the topic for a fourth, and so on.

Assessment opportunities

This sort of discussion will enable you to assess how aware the children are of the underlying themes of stories, and how well they can relate their reading to earlier reading and to experiences in real life.

Opportunities for IT

Children could design and publish their own adventure game. The whole class can be involved firstly in discussing and agreeing the theme, locations to be visited and the characters to be met. A master plan is needed which links the adventure together in the form of a flow chart (similar to those in the

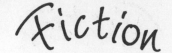
'Rotary story' activity) and shows how the links between the various pages work. The children will then need to work out puzzles or problems to be solved at each location.

They can work in pairs or small groups with a word processor, or DTP package, to write specific chapters of the adventure. If two pages are left blank for each chapter there will also be space for illustrations. It is important to spend some time looking at adventure-style books, the language used and the style of the writing. Children can then try to write in a similar fashion, emphasising the description of the locations and the characters. One group of children could act as the editors, making sure that the storyline is compatible with the plan and that different groups know what pages the reader of their section should turn to next.

An alternative to creating a paper book would be to use a multimedia authoring package. The same plan and writing would be needed but the final game could be played 'on screen', with the software offering children the choices and taking them to the next part of the adventure when appropriate.

Similar adventure games can also be written using the list-processing aspects of LOGO (Longman) to create a branching adventure game.

Display ideas
Collections of related stories from different parts of the world and from different times can form a display in your reading area, together with the children's written reflections and drawings related to these themes.

Other aspects of the English PoS covered
Speaking and listening – 1a, b, c, d; 2a, b.

MIXING THE INGREDIENTS

To identify particular aspects of a story style and combine them in order to create new stories.

†† *A group of independent readers and writers.*

🕓 *Open-ended.*

Key background information
This activity extends the children's awareness of different fictional genres, and provides a link between reading and writing. It is quite challenging, and would suit a group of accomplished readers and storytellers.

Preparation
Set up a large chart based on the illustration in Figure 1. Fill it in for a story that the class are all familiar with, then

Type of story	Setting	Specific places	Characters	Events
Western				
School				
Science fiction				
Fairy tale				
Thriller				

Figure 1

encourage them to continue recording information on the chart as they hear more stories or read them independently. Draw up a chart template on paper and issue copies of this record sheet to your selected group. Ask the children to fill them in independently.

Resources needed
Photocopiable sheets 131 and 132 (Story starters), writing materials.

What to do
Introduction
Ask the children to share and discuss the record sheets that they have compiled. Hand out the story-starter sheets and ask them to anticipate how the columns on the chart might be filled for each of the anticipated continuations. Invite the group to give an oral performance of the continuation of one or more of these stories, and record this on tape.

Development
Ask the children to think about how the predictability of each of the genres might be undermined. For example, you might try mixing ingredients from each of the columns so that characters from Western stories are placed in settings from science fiction stories, while characters from traditional fairy stories show up in the Wild West, or typical events from fairy stories start happening to people in traditional school stories.

Using the story-starter sheets again, invite the children to retell their continuations, this time deliberately shuffling the ingredients so that the expectations of a listener expecting the patterns of a traditional genre would be thwarted. Again, this should be recorded on tape.

Conclusion
Ask the children to listen to the two stories, or sets of stories, on tape and to evaluate the language play that they have

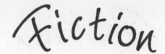
engaged in. What is the value of predictable genres to the reader? What is the value of the type of scrambling and shuffling of story elements that they have been experimenting with? Are there times when they personally prefer one type of story process to the others?

If the children want to publish the stories that they have created orally, make arrangements for them to do this.

Suggestion(s) for extension
The children might be interested in devising the sort of story grammar game suggested in 'Themes in fiction' on page 36.

Encourage the group to look out for published stories in which genre conventions are broken – *The Stinky Cheese Man and Other Fairly Stupid Tales* by Jon Scieszka and Lane Smith (Puffin, 1993) is an entertaining example – and to consider using this sort of play in their own creative writing.

Suggestion(s) for support
Preface the activity by reading to the group a story in which the type of 'story mixing' described above occurs. Read out one of the story starters and complete the next stage yourself, demonstrating how the expected ingredients can be replaced with others. For example, Buck Moose's story might continue:

In the street outside the saloon a spaceship stood, its landing lights still revolving and the sun blood red on the titanium shell of its fuselage. As Buck watched, the landing ramp descended with a quiet electronic hum, and seven sad, little men, bearing between them a glass coffin, came sobbing and struggling down its slope.

Assessment opportunities
Note the children's awareness of underlying patterns in fiction, and their ability to manipulate these patterns in their own storytelling.

Opportunities for IT
Children could publish their oral stories using a word processor or desktop publishing package.

Display ideas
Completed stories can be published and displayed alongside notices inviting other children to read them and to compare them with more conventional tales.

Other aspects of the English PoS covered
Speaking and listening – 1a, b, c; d; 2a, b; 3a, b.
Writing – 1a, b, c; 2a, b, c, d, e; 3a, b, c.

Reference to photocopiable sheets
Photocopiable sheets 131 and 132 can be used for the 'Rotary story' activity and for prediction, as well as 'mixing it'.

DESERT ISLAND BOOKS: A CATALOGUE

To encourage children to use books which are of special importance to them and to reflect on why they find these books so appealing. These books can then be used to start a bibliographical database.

†† *Whole class, working in small groups.*

🕐 *An initial lesson of about 30 minutes, then open-ended follow-up work.*

Key background information
This activity is based on the popular 'Desert Island Books' idea, which is in turn based on the radio programme *Desert Island Discs*. The children are encouraged to select a small number of books which are of special interest to them, then record and organise both bibliographical information about each book and a succinct summary of the book commending it to other children in the class.

Preparation
Select four or five books that you would like to have with you if you were marooned on a desert island. Record bibliographical details of the books on one side of a large index card, and try to summarise the appeal that each book has for you in 50 to 100 words on the other side. Familiarity with the critical and concise reviews found in journals such as *Books for Keeps* would be very helpful, and would also provide a range of models for the children's own book reviewing.

If you have access to a simple database program and sufficient terminals for the children, familiarise yourself with this so that bibliographical information can be recorded on disk rather than on cards. If your access to a terminal is restricted to the usual one or two per class, small-group sessions in which the children transfer their data on to disk

READING

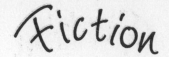

can follow the whole-class lesson outlined below. Alternatively, the whole lesson can be done with one small group at a time, with the teacher or a child who has good keyboard skills 'scribing' responses directly on to disk.

Some time before the planned lesson, explain to the class that they are going to start to build a database of their favourite books so that they will be able to share their interests and enthusiasms. Explain the 'Desert Island Books' idea, and ask them to start thinking about which of the books that they like would fall into this category.

The day before the lesson, remind the class about this idea and ask them to have their nominations ready for the next day. They should try to bring in at least one book, but not more than two. Note that their choices need not be confined to fiction.

Resources needed

Your own prepared index cards, the books on which your index cards are based, an enlarged copy or OHP transparency of one of the cards, notebooks for drafting, four of five blank index cards for each child in the class, a box for storing index cards in.

What to do

Introduction

Show the children your own desert island books and talk to them about how you first encountered the books and why they are special for you. Read favourite extracts from one or two of the books to them. Divide the class into groups of four and allow them 15 or 20 minutes to share their own books in a similar way.

Title: The BFG
Author: Roald Dahl
Publisher: Puffin
publication 1984
0-14-031597-7

INDEX CARDS

Development

Show the children your index cards and the enlargement of one of them. Indicate the different categories of bibliographical information (title, author, publisher, place of publication, date, ISBN number) and discuss the different uses of these types of information.

Distribute the index cards and ask the children to fill one in for a book of their own choice, following the format you have displayed. When this has been done, read the recommendations that you have written for each of your books, and suggest ways in which the children might write similar pieces for their chosen books. It is important to emphasise the brevity of the recommendation: the children should be discouraged from attempting to write a summary of the entire plot. Instead, they might be asked to focus on:
▲ a particular episode that they found exciting;
▲ a character that they sympathised with or found particularly interesting or disagreeable;
▲ any aspect of the book that related to their own experiences;
▲ the range of emotions that they experienced while reading the book, with particular attention to how they felt at the end.

The children's recommendations can be written in notebooks before being redrafted on to the cards.

You might encourage the children to quote short extracts from their books. A limit of 50 to 100 words should be suggested, but need not be too strictly adhered to.

Conclusion

Allow the children time to share each other's work before discussing how the data might be organised into a catalogue. The most obvious model for a collection of fiction records will be alphabetical arrangement by author. You could explore ways of subdividing such an arrangement by genre, as is the practice in some public libraries – in which case, children can discuss the possible categories that the book collection could be divided into.

If you have access to a computer database, make arrangements to plan a demonstration of how to encode the data on the cards, and how it might be retrieved using a range of field names.

Tell the children that the extra index cards are a reminder that this procedure is open-ended and that the database should be updated throughout the year.

Suggestion(s) for extension

In many classrooms, there are groups of children who share enthusiasms for particular authors or genres. A recent survey in a vertically-grouped Year 5 and 6 class revealed clear blocks of support for the following types of reading experience: Roald Dahl; Terry Pratchett's *Discworld* novels; Enid Blyton; Scholastic's *Point Horror* series; Mary Norton's *Borrowers* books; spin-offs from various adventure games.

Groups with such preferences can be helped to prepare presentations which provide the whole class with an account of why these enthusiasms have developed. Presentations might include personal accounts of individual readers' experiences, extracts being read aloud, information about authors, and dramatic interpretations of scenes from books.

Suggestion(s) for support
In any class, there are bound to be one or more children who have no enthusiasm whatsoever for books. Broadening the scope of this activity to include other forms of print media (magazines, manuals, comics, and so on) might help to draw such children into the activity. Alternatively, you could try to get them to create a card for an imaginary 'desert island book' that has not yet been written for them. This could be based on some other type of media form (a film or TV programme), or on some activity that the children in question find interesting.

Assessment opportunities
Knowledge of bibliographical conventions can be assessed. The writing of the recommendations of particular books will provide evidence of children's appreciation of literature and their ability to convey their feelings in concise language.

Opportunities for IT
Before the children fill in the data record cards on their desert island books, discuss how to write the information under each of the headings. Information such as the order of the author's name (surname or forenames first), how to write the ISBN number (use of spaces, dashes and slashes) and if the book is to be placed into a category from a pre-determined selection (fiction, non-fiction or a more detailed

analysis such as adventure, horses, schools) will need an established format. This is important to make sure that the final database is useable and gives consistent results from any search. You might want to include the name of the child writing the card, and age or gender.

Once the children have completed these cards they can enter the data on to a computer database. The headings (fieldnames) should match those on the card and it is helpful to make sure they are in exactly the same order. Some software will allow you to select a range of 'tokenised' items, so that when the children enter the category of book they are given the set of categories from which they can choose. This ensures that only the agreed categories are used. If the children are to include their summaries on the database, the software needs to have the ability to include 'free text'. Not all databases used in schools have this facility.

If the number of computers is limited, children can take it in turns to enter their data. If they work in pairs, the observer can read the data to be entered and check for spellings and accuracy. If more than one computer is used, and the datafiles are to be merged into a single datafile for interrogation, it is absolutely essential to create identical databases to ensure they are merged correctly.

Once the data has been entered, children can use the datafile to search for information. Depending on their previous experience, children may need to start with simple questions such as 'How many people have included books by Roald Dahl?' or 'How many books are about schools?' Children could also create graphs of the most popular types of books or authors. If information on the gender of the author or the writer of the card is included, it becomes possible to look for connections between gender of author, or reader, and the type of books recommended.

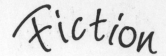

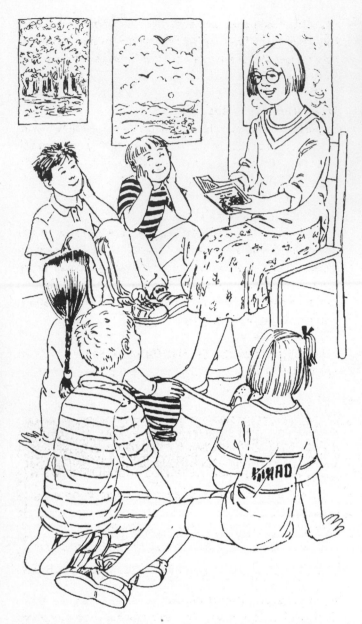

SCHEHERAZADE'S DIARY

To identify moments of climax and turning-points in stories and use these to plan a read-aloud programme for a chosen audience.

†† *Two small groups, with children within the groups working in pairs.*

⏱ *45 minutes for the initial lesson, then open-ended follow-up work.*

Key background information

This activity is based upon the stratagem used by Scheherazade, narrator of *The Arabian Nights*, to escape execution by postponing the conclusion of each story that she told until the following night. Each group of children is given the task of preparing a collection of short stories to read aloud to another group (or to any other audience). The idea is then to identify a point in each story at which it would be most suspenseful to postpone the narrative. This activity is most suitable for independent readers who want to practise more effective oral reading, and is a good way of creating co-operative reading links between classes of different ages.

Preparation

A few weeks before the initial lesson, adopt Scheherazade's strategy yourself at storytimes: telling short stories up to a critical point, postponing the conclusion until the next session, and allowing yourself enough time after this to take another story up to a similar point. If the children do not comment on what you are doing, draw their attention to this rhythm, and invite them to discuss its use in media such as comics and television serials.

Resources needed

Storybooks and collections of short stories that lend themselves to the approach outlined above, an edition (or a collection of editions) of *The Arabian Nights*, photocopies of two short stories (one story per group and one copy of the designated story for each pair of children). If possible, try to select stories with which both groups are unfamiliar.

What to do

Introduction

Remind the children of the strategy you have been using at storytime, and explain to them that the purpose of this session is to start work on a compilation of stories that they will be reading to a chosen audience, using the Scheherazade technique to sharpen the attention of the listeners. If they are unfamiliar with the story of Scheherazade, share it with them; then show them your editions of *The Arabian Nights*, and discuss some of the stories that they may have heard. They may be interested to learn that there is no 'authorised version' of this collection, and that some of the well-known stories, such as that of Aladdin, are relatively recent additions.

This activity also provides an ideal opportunity to talk about the wider use of databases outside school, and can obviously be linked to those in the public library, or to CD-ROMs the children may use. Look at the accuracy of information. This is particularly relevant when children cannot find the answers to questions about their own book due to wrongly entered data.

Display ideas

The early stages in the development of the database can be supported with a display of the books which are featured, together with copies of the children's recommendations and illustrations based on the stories. Instructions for how to add information to, and retrieve information from, the database should also be included.

Other aspects of the English PoS covered

Speaking and listening – 1a, b, c; 2a, b.
Writing – 1a, b, c; 2a, b, d, e.

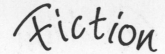

Fiction

Development

Distribute the photocopies, asking the children to read the story and to agree with their partners on a point at which a reading aloud might be most effectively suspended. This point can be marked with a straight line across the page or between words. When this has been done, pairs within each group can compare where they have drawn their lines and their reasons for doing so.

One child from each group can then be selected to read the story aloud to the other group, up to an agreed suspension point. When this has been done, both groups can discuss how each story might end before listening to the rest of the tale. They can then evaluate the effectiveness of the chosen suspension point and offer alternatives.

Conclusion

Allow the pairs of children to select their own storybooks and short story collections. During the rest of this session, and in subsequent sessions, they can work on creating a sequence of stories to be read aloud to their chosen audience. Figure 1 shows one possible format for planning this sequence.

Suggestion(s) for extension

This is a useful activity to offer to outstanding readers who wish to work individually. In this case, the teacher can act as a response partner, commenting on the effectiveness of the suspense points, and of the overall programme, before the reading aloud is begun.

Monday March 16th	'Cat Anna' from *Crack-a-Story* by Susan Price To page 6 'get them and eat them'
Tuesday March 17th	Finish 'Cat Anna' 'The Alien at 7b' from *The Ghost at Codlin Castle* by Dick King-Smith To page 46 'brown feathers lay on the ground'
Wednesday March 18th	Finish 'The Alien at 7b' 'Horrorgram' from *The Screaming Field* by Wendy Eyton To page 92 'She held out her hand'.
Thursday March 19th	Finish 'Horrorgram' 'Birthday Girl' from *In Black and White* by Jan Mark To page 69 'and she sat up'.
Friday March 20th	Finish 'Birthday Girl' 'Owning Up' from *Dracula in Sunlight* by Chris Powling Whole story.

Figure 1

Children can also be encouraged to create audiotaped serialisations of favourite novels using this idea, though in many cases the suspense points will correspond with the chapter structure.

Suggestion(s) for support

Beginning readers, who are building a repertoire of favourite stories, can be encouraged to read two or three of these to a partner or small group, having identified appropriate suspense points beforehand.

Assessment opportunities

Note the reader's ability to identify turning-points in the narrative, and the author's use of rhetorical devices such as repetition and altered sentence structure to signal these points. The extended activity also allows the teacher to monitor individual children's progress in reading aloud and in selecting appropriate texts for a specific audience.

Other aspects of the English PoS covered

Speaking and listening – 1a, b, c, d; 2a, b; 3a, b.

READING RESOURCES SURVEY

To make a critical survey of available reading resources.

†† *Small groups, reporting to the whole class.*

🕐 *40 minutes for the initial session, then open-ended follow-up work.*

Key background information

Over the last few years, children's reading resources have been subjected to a lot of critical scrutiny arising from social changes and developments in theories of reading. This activity attempts to engage the children themselves in such scrutiny. Some of the issues arising from this activity might be considered controversial, and it is advisable to inform and involve parents and other school community members in the project.

In the lesson plan outlined below, the issue of gender roles has been selected in order to provide a focus. (*Language, Literacy and Gender* by Hilary Minns, Hodder & Stoughton 1991, provides an excellent review of issues and strategies in this area.) Other issues relevant to your own teaching environment can also be explored through the same process.

Preparation

Collect as wide a range of historical and contemporary children's reading material as you can, and display it in your classroom alongside a notice inviting the children to browse and discuss this material. Your collection might include:

▲ disused reading schemes and other types of school book (school stock cupboards usually have a rich variety of these);

▲ old children's books rescued from junk shops;

▲ favourite childhood books lent by parents, grandparents and other adults in the community;

▲ old comics and annuals.

Devote a few minutes at regular times to whole-class discussion of this material. Ask the children to compare the historical and present-day material, and help them to compile a list of the major differences that they notice. The children are likely to focus on such aspects as the more sophisticated styles of illustration and typography that are available now, and on obvious features of content, such as changes in costume and everyday technology. You should also draw their attention towards:

▲ the depiction of gender roles in text and illustration;

▲ the depiction of people from different cultures;

▲ the relationships between adults and children.

Inform the children that they are going to take part in a survey of classroom reading resources, and ask them to start thinking about what should be provided to make reading an enjoyable and informative activity for everybody in the class.

Organise groups to consider different aspects of the books, as suggested above.

Resources needed
See above.

What to do
Introduction
Help the children to draw up a list of criteria for book provision which would be fair both to boys and to girls. They might consider:

▲ how males and females are depicted in words and pictures – are particular personal qualities and activities disproportionately attributed to either gender?

▲ the relative number of male and female main characters in books;

▲ the relative number of male and female authors.

When they have done this, help them to design a record sheet similar to the one illustrated in Figure 1. (This is based on an example in *Language, Literacy and Gender*.)

Book record

Title

Author

Publisher

Date

Main characters

How are boys/men depicted in this book?

How are girls/women depicted in this book?

Comments

Figure 1

Development

Allocate sections of the book collection to each pair of children and allow them time to scan these books and record their findings. It is important that different interpretations of the gender roles presented in literature should be discussed within and between the pairs of children.

Conclusion

The group should share their work with the rest of the class, some of whom might want to dispute their opinions of particular books. Talk to the children about what might be done to address any concerns that they have. Writing to publishers and authors might be an appropriate response to such concerns.

Suggestion(s) for extension

This work should be extended to include other issues in children's literature, and should be used to inform and encourage continuing evaluation of new books and other reading resources coming into the classroom. The children might also research the opinions of parents and other adults, including writers and publishers, by designing questionnaires and writing letters.

Suggestion(s) for support

Children can be helped to appreciate the issues involved in this type of evaluation by comparing a small number of samples of literature which reflect different social values more vividly. Children's reading schemes from the 50s and 60s, for example, usually show very clearly-defined roles for males and females. Discussion of how and why modern-day schemes differ from these should help to make children more aware of this issue. The presentation of such material should be handled with a great deal of sensitivity. Many children will have attitudes which differ from those which you believe to be desirable, and you will need to be able to handle potential conflict in ways which neither demean the child nor ingrain such attitudes even more deeply.

Assessment opportunities

Note the children's ability to scan reading material and to appreciate the social values reflected in text and pictures.

Opportunities for IT

Children could use the data they collect to create a database of the range of resources available to them. The data collection sheet may need to be altered to make the database more 'searchable'. A revised list of fields might include: title; author; author gender; publisher; date of publication; main female characters; main male characters; boys/men depicted (good/fair/poor) or other descriptors; girls/women depicted (good/fair/poor) or other descriptors.

Such information would enable searches based on female authors and women characters, or good role models, date of publication and male/female roles. The database could be updated as new resources are acquired or removed.

Display ideas

Children's writing about what they have discovered can be added to your initial display of reading materials.

Other aspects of the English PoS covered

Speaking and listening – 1a, b, c; 2a, b.
Writing – 1a, b, c; 2a, b.

A LETTER TO THE AUTHOR

To reflect on the content of a book by formulating questions and opinions to be communicated to the author.

†† *Whole-class introduction, followed by children working individually.*

🕐 *40 minutes.*

Key background information

Writing to the author of a chosen book makes children more aware of the processes by which books are created, and provides a channel for the expression of enthusiasm, uncertainty or reservations. It is essential that the children write only to an individually-chosen author whose work they feel strongly about. An imposed letter-writing task is unlikely to deepen the children's appreciation of a book, and it is also unfair to the writer receiving such letters.

This activity would fit well into part of the preparations for a book week with a focus on the works of a particular author.

Preparation

Try writing yourself to authors whose work you find interesting. This should not be fan mail, but an expression of curiosity about their work, containing genuine questions. Keep copies of the letters you send, and when you get a

Dear Roald,
     I enjoyed reading your book The BFG very much. I would like to know w

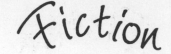

reply, share the original letter, the book or story it is based on and the author's reply with the children. Ask them to start thinking about who they would like to write to.

Resources needed
Writing materials.

What to do
Remind the children of the conventions for writing letters, using an enlarged version of your own letter or an OHP slide of it if necessary.

Discuss the types of questions that it would be useful to ask an author about his or her work, and stress that reference to particular characters and episodes is more likely to elicit a detailed response than generalised expressions of enthusiasm or disdain.

Allow the children time to redraft and proofread their letters with partners.

Some children may want to write letters to authors who are no longer alive. The writing of such letters can help to focus the children's feelings about particular texts. It can also lead to drama-related work in which pairs or small groups of children, who share a liking for a particular author, can try to write responses in role.

Suggestion(s) for extension
A similar procedure can be used for the exploration of other issues in children's fiction.

Suggestion(s) for support
This activity can be conducted as a part of a reading conference with individual children. Questions can be elicited as the teacher and child share a particular book, and the

teacher can act as a scribe for children who find independent writing difficult. Authentic contact with an author can act as a powerful motivation for children who are daunted by reading.

Assessment opportunities
Note the children's ability to identify relevant issues in their reading. The questions that children ask should provide evidence of imaginative involvement in fiction.

Opportunities for IT
This activity lends itself to the use of a word processor to draft and redraft the letters written. Older children could also be introduced to formatting commands to create the letter layout. They should be discouraged from positioning the address using spaces but should use the tabs or the right justify facility. Children could also explore the use of fonts and font sizes to make the letter easy to read.

Display ideas
Copies of letters and replies can be displayed together with extracts from, and illustrations of, the stories which inspired the correspondence.

Other aspects of the English PoS covered
Speaking and listening – 1a, b, c, d; 2a, b.
Writing – 1a, b, c; 2a, b, c, d, e; 3a, b, c.

A CLASS COLLECTION

To provide opportunities for summative assessment in a purposeful context, each child will contribute an extract read aloud from a favourite book to be recorded on a cassette for the purposes of promoting reading in younger classes.

†† *Each child will have an individual reading conference with the teacher.*

⏲ *15–20 minutes per child.*

Key background information
During this activity, the class as a whole will produce a cassette which promotes reading to a younger age group. The cassette will consist of extracts of fiction, non-fiction and poetry selected by individuals in the class which is being assessed.

Preparation
This activity should be planned half a term in advance. Inform the children at this time that they will be preparing the tape for a younger class over a period of weeks. Explain that the purpose of the cassette is to give the children to whom it is addressed a selection of approximately five-minute 'tasters' from fiction books. Encourage the children to be on the

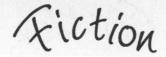

lookout for enjoyable material that could be included on the cassette. Remind them that they can contribute their own reading of any items that you read to them at storytime or at other times of the day. Put a 'signing-up' list on display so that the children can indicate when they have chosen something that they want to contribute.

Resources needed
A tape recorder.

What to do
Before the reading
Ask the child to explain why she has chosen the extract. Read it yourself and comment on anything that you find appealing. Encourage the child to read the piece silently, or aloud, as a rehearsal for the reading to be recorded.

During the reading
Provide appropriate help with the reading of difficult words or phrases, but allow the child sufficient time to demonstrate the use of her own resources before you step in.

After the reading
Play the tape back and allow the child to comment on her reading. Allow a second attempt if the child is dissatisfied with the quality of the reading.

Suggestion(s) for extension
Children who have chosen extracts which they are able to read confidently could be encouraged to make tape-recorded

books for their own listening collection. This could take the form of a single longer piece of work, or a variety of selections forming a personal anthology (which can form part of an assessment portfolio and be added to over the years).

Suggestion(s) for support
Children who have difficulty reading their chosen items can be assisted in the normal way by the teacher, who can then help them to select a more appropriate piece for independent reading. It is important that, having established a communicative purpose for this activity, the teacher ensures that each child is able to participate in the project.

Inability to select an appropriate text
Talk to the child about recent reading and/or listening experiences. If this fails to elicit an appropriate text, discuss the child's non-literary interests, and from what you learn of these, try to construct a text with the child that reflects these interests. This can be done through shared writing, with the teacher scribing the child's ideas. This text can then be rehearsed and read by the child.

Over-reliance on one strategy when reading aloud
This should be identified at the rehearsal stage. Help the child to appreciate the range of cues provided in the text by selecting a word with which the child is having difficulty and modelling strategies such as reading back, reading on and focusing on initial letters and word length in order to identify the word.

Lack of natural intonation in the reading
This can only be remedied by practice. You could try modelling appropriate intonation by reading the extract aloud yourself after the rehearsal phase and before the child attempts an independent reading.

Reluctance to talk about why the extract was chosen
Children often find it difficult to verbalise their preferences. You should model this process by sharing your own preferences in books the children are familiar with and talking about them. It might help children to become more fluent if they discuss their choices in small groups or with a reading partner before they sign up for the reading.

Assessment opportunities
A copy of the tape can be kept, with a note of the dates on which the extracts were read, as evidence of the child's reading interest and reading-aloud ability at that date. The discussion preceding the reading provides data about the child's preferences and sense of the purpose of reading, as well as the strategies used by the children to decode difficult parts of the text while 'rehearsing' for the reading. The discussion that follows the reading should give some idea of the child's level of critical awareness.

Opportunities for IT

Children could use an art package or graphics software to design and print the cassette sleeve for their personal anthology. The teacher, or some of the more able children, could design a grid of the correct size which could be used as a master document for children to start their design. This would ensure the final inlay would actually fit the cassette case. Children could add text, rotating it and selecting appropriate fonts and font sizes, to ensure that the information fits on to the inlay. Children could print a copy to fit into their cassette case and another for a class display.

Display ideas

Personal anthologies can be illustrated and used as a feature of the listening area.

Other aspects of the English PoS covered

Speaking and listening – 1a, b, c.

READING CONFERENCE

To enable the teacher and child to make a summative assessment of reading experiences and to make plans for further development.

†† *Individual conversations between each child and the teacher.*

🕐 *20 to 30 minutes per child.*

Key background information

This activity attempts to provide a summative evaluation of a child's reading over the course of a term or a school year. It requires a large commitment of time for each child from the teacher, and so is only feasible if the other children in the class are being supervised by an assistant.

Preparation

Before each conference, ask the children to have ready a collection of material related to the work they have done since the last assessment. This might include a reader's notebook, an annotated list of books read, and any other forms of writing or illustration stimulated by reading. The child should also bring along a book that she is currently reading. The place in which the conference is held should be physically comfortable, and there should be reasonable freedom from interruptions.

Resources needed

A notebook and tape recorder.

What to do

Talk to the child about her reading over the period of time in question. Try to ascertain what the child has found enjoyable, and what she hasn't liked. You should also try to gauge the range of reading, and of activities related to reading, that the child has experienced. Encourage the child to engage in an evaluation of any material that she brings to the conference.

A list of questions that might help the discussion is given below, but it is important that the session should not turn into an interrogation.

▲ Do you like reading? If so, what do you like about it?
▲ How good a reader do you think you are?
▲ How do you choose a book?
▲ What books have you enjoyed reading recently?
▲ What did you particularly enjoy about them?
▲ What stories do you enjoy listening to?
▲ Have you any favourite authors or illustrators?
▲ Who is your favourite character, and what do you like about him/her?
▲ How would you recommend a favourite book to a friend?
▲ What do you do when you come across a word you don't know?
▲ What would you like to read next?
▲ What can we do to make reading more enjoyable for you in the future?

At some point in the session, ask the child to read aloud from her current book, and make a record of the strategies that she is using. Pay particular attention to any deviations from the printed text. These can be classified according to whether they maintain the meaning of the text, change it or destroy it. Try to determine whether the child is using contextual and graphophonic clues constructively or not. This process will be easier if you record the reading on tape and afterwards play it back to support the notes you have made during the reading itself. A simple miscue analysis procedure, such as that suggested in *A Question of Reading* by Cliff Moon and Bridie Raban (David Fulton, 1992) will help you to do this more systematically.

Talk to the child about her plans for further reading, suggesting authors, titles and types of literature if needed.

Suggestion(s) for extension

The reading conference can form a part of the process of portfolio assessment, in which teacher and child are jointly responsible for maintaining a collection of records of the child's achievements over time.

Suggestion(s) for support

Try to keep the focus on positive achievement, even with children who show little interest in reading. Consider the wide range of reading experiences that the child brings to the conference, including forms of reading that the school might not have initiated or sanctioned. It is also important that you demonstrate your own enthusiasm for reading during the course of the session, as well as before and after it.

Other aspects of the English PoS covered

Speaking and listening – 1a, b, c; 2a.

Information books

The purpose of the activities in this chapter is to develop children's information retrieval skills and to enhance their appreciation of the distinctive language of information texts. Many of the activities are applications of the work of Lunzer and Gardner on DARTs or 'directed activities related to texts' and of the Exeter Extending Literacy Project on the use of writing frames to scaffold children's writing in non-fictional genres. *Learning from the Written Word* by Lunzer and Gardner (Oliver and Boyd, 1984) and *Developing Non-fiction Writing: Working with Writing Frames* by Maureen Lewis and David Wray (*Primary Professional Bookshelf* series, Scholastic 1995) are good sources of background information.

The procedures outlined will help children to formulate overall purposes for reading information texts, to translate those purposes into specific questions to direct a search of the texts, and to compare what they find in the texts with previous background knowledge. Children are urged to make predictions both before and during their reading, and to highlight key words and phrases in texts as a preliminary to taking notes. Discussion is an essential element of each procedure, enabling children to make both their background knowledge and their interpretations of material from the texts explicit. Links with writing and with other parts of the curriculum manifest themselves in activities which direct children to make their own information books, and to respond to information books through drawing and other forms of representation.

A READ-ALOUD PROGRAMME

To foster appreciation of information books and to extend children's familiarity with the distinctive language patterns of these books and the way in which they are organised.

†† *Whole class.*

🕐 *15 to 30 minutes.*

Key background information

Many of the difficulties that children experience in comprehending information books has been attributed to their lack of familiarity with the grammatical and discourse patterns of this type of writing (see *The Language Demands of School Learning* by Katharine Perera for a detailed account of this issue). This activity will help to introduce children to these patterns by incorporating information books into a daily read-aloud programme.

Preparation

Make a display featuring your favourite information books and ask the children to contribute their own favourite information books to it. Make sure that the text of the books is of interest to the children in your class and is at an appropriate level for them. Information books that have been created by the children themselves as part of their topic work should also be included.

Resources needed

Information books.

What to do

When the children are familiar with the display, select from it any book that you think will be of interest to the children, and read it aloud to them as part of the 'listening diet' that you provide at storytime.

When locating the passage that you want to read, demonstrate the use of the contents page and textual signposts such as headings and subheadings. Show how further information about items in the passage can be located by using the index. Once these procedures have been demonstrated a couple of times, they can then be carried out by the children: tell the class what you want to read about, and invite individual children to find you the relevant passage using these features.

As you read aloud, encourage the children to form mental images of the objects, events and processes described in the text. Some children might like to draw sketches and doodles. Afterwards, these visualisations can be compared; and you can encourage the children to question and discuss the content of what you have read, without turning this part of the session into an interrogation of their attentive abilities.

Inform the children that you wish to make the reading-aloud of information books a regular part of the school day, and invite them to look for passages in their own reading that they think would be of interest to the rest of the class. Your own reading-aloud of such material should be aimed at encouraging the children eventually to read aloud themselves.

It is useful to hold read-aloud sessions in the school library, where you can demonstrate the use of the book catalogue and familiarise the children with the classification system and the layout of the books on the shelves. Again, inviting a child to find a particular book, or a book on a particular subject, will provide the class with practical demonstrations of library skills.

Suggestion(s) for extension

Many of the activities from the chapter on fiction which seek to extend the range of children's reading, and to develop a personal response to fiction, can be adapted as strategies to deepen their appreciation of information books. The oral retelling of passages that children have read from information books is highly recommended, as well as the procedures outlined in 'Introducing a reader's notebook' on page 15, 'Desert island books: a catalogue' on page 39, 'Scheherezade's diary' on page 42, 'A letter to the author' on page 45 and 'A class collection' on page 46.

Suggestion(s) for support

Children who are reluctant to read aloud to the whole class can be encouraged to do so with a small group of people

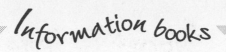

with whom they feel comfortable. If children do not contribute 'favourite books', you could discuss this during your individual reading time with the child, and make suggestions for appropriate reading based on the child's personal interests.

Assessment opportunities

This routine activity will enable you to monitor the children's appreciation and comprehension of information books, as well as their skill at reading aloud.

Display ideas

See above. A tape-recording of the children reading their favourite chunks from information books can be added to the display.

Other aspects of the English PoS covered

Speaking and listening – 1a, b, c; 2a ,b; 3a.

LIBRARY ACTIVITIES

To familiarise the children with library layout and classification.

†† *Small groups working under supervision in the school library.*

🕐 *20 to 30 minutes per activity.*

Key background information

This section outlines a set of activities that can be used on a regular basis with small groups of children in order to familiarise them with the organisation of books in the library. The activities can be carried out under the supervision of older children who have been given responsibility for library maintenance.

Preparation

At the start of the school year, take small groups of children into the library and give each child a card with the name of a book written on it. These should include fiction, poetry and folklore items as well as information books. Ask the children to locate the books, and make notes on how they go about this task. This simple assessment activity will help you to designate appropriate groups for the different activities.

Resources needed

Books and other library resources; a colour- and number-coded wall index of the library classification system should be on display.

What to do

These activities should be spread over several sessions. Each one should begin with the children making themselves comfortable in the library, and the teacher or supervisor reading out a story, poem or information book extract,

preferably one chosen by the children. The activities are outlined below in approximate order of difficulty, and assume a library organised according to a Dewey-based colour-coded system.

▲ Place a heap of books, both fiction and non-fiction mixed together, on the table. Ask the children to sort them into story and information book sets, and then to indicate on which particular shelves they belong.

▲ Draw the children's attention to the letter on the spine of each fiction book and invite them to speculate on its function, explaining this if necessary. Then ask the children to put these books into their proper places on the shelves. The problem of how to place authors such as Ashley, Ahlberg and Anderson should be discussed.

▲ Information sources can be sorted into book and non-book items. Point out the number and colour coding on the spines of non-fiction books, and draw the children's attention to the wall index. Ask the children to return the books to their proper places. In most schools, the Dewey system is followed and folklore and poetry books are placed among the information sources. Point this out to the children and explain the rationale behind it.

▲ Before the children come into the library, the supervisor can put a selection of books in the wrong places on the shelves. Each child is then given a shelf space to search, and incorrectly filed items should be returned to their proper places.

▲ Demonstrate the use of the wall index, then invite children to nominate a topic that they would like to find a book about.

'carpet', 'carpenter', or even 'scarecrow' depending on what is included in the database and whether the search is set up to look for words 'that start with car' or 'include car'. This type of database could be a permanent resource in the library if enough computers are available. It could be set up on an older type of computer which is no longer in everyday use. Alternatively, the datafile could be included on each computer in the school, and searches undertaken and results printed out before individual children go to the library.

Other aspects of the English PoS covered
Speaking and listening – 1a, b, c; 2a, b; 3b.

Topics which are not named as such on the guide can be searched for under related categories (for example, for 'eagles' look up 'birds').

▲ Repeat the previous activity, but the children can now search the subject index card file or database in order to scan the range of titles available and select a particular item that they would like to find.

Suggestion(s) for extension
The skills developed through these activities will be extended as the children apply them to authentic research tasks.

Suggestion(s) for support
Support can be provided during information read-aloud time (see previous activity) and library browsing time, and when children are working on their own projects.

Assessment opportunities
Observation of how the children go about these tasks will enable you to assess their growing awareness of the organising principles of the library, and their ability to use these principles to guide their own information searches.

Opportunities for IT
Children could use a database of Dewey reference numbers which has been created by the teacher or other children. Such a database could just include the Dewey number and the classification of the book. This would enable children to find out where a book on 'cars' might be found. It will also extend children's use of databases, particularly in defining the search questions. A search for 'car' might also bring up

IDENTIFYING CURRENT KNOWLEDGE

To guide children's reading of information texts by making explicit what they know about a topic to be investigated, and what they would like to find out.
†† *Whole class, small groups, then whole class again.*
🕒 *Two sessions of approximately one hour each.*

Key background information
These sessions will help children to pose questions about a topic, so that they have a purpose to guide their reading. Without such a purpose, children's reading of information books can be aimless and uncritical as their unfocused attention wanders over the text.

The best time to carry out the sessions is when the children are just about to start on a new topic. In the first session, you and the children will create a 'knowledge map' and a list of questions connected to the topic. In the second session, the list of questions will be sorted and those which can be most appropriately pursued through reading will be identified.

Preparation
The day before this activity is due to take place, tell the children that they are going to make a map of all that they know about the given topic, and then tabulate everything that they would like to find out. This might prompt them to bring to mind all of their prior knowledge and any questions they might have about the topic.

In between the two sessions, draw up neat versions of the knowledge map and the question list which will have been produced in the first session. With regard to the latter, ask yourself which ones can be most appropriately answered by reading information books and which by other means (such as experiment, asking somebody, storytelling).

Resources needed
Writing materials.

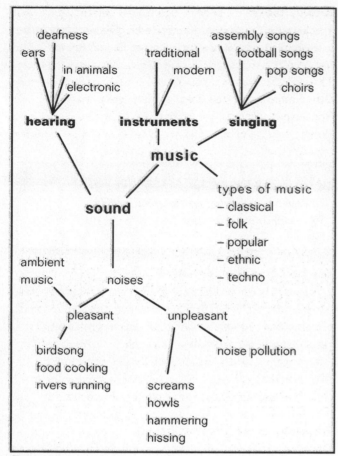

Figure 1

What to do
Session One
Introduction
Write the name of the topic in the middle of a large piece of chart paper, or at the centre of the board, or on an OHP transparency (either of the latter two options is preferable, as this activity will involve erasing and relocating ideas). Ask the children to contribute any words or phrases connected to this central theme. Write these down on either side of the central word or phrase. When the children's stock of ideas is exhausted, add any of your own that have not yet been offered, explaining their meanings if necessary.

Show the children how the ideas that they have provided can be formed into related groups connected to the central theme (see Figure 1).

Development
Organise the children into pairs or groups, and ask them to copy the diagram so far and then to extend it so that all the terms contributed have been grouped according to meaning. When this has been done, allow the children to compare the different ways in which they have grouped the ideas.

Through discussion with the children, construct from these different formats an agreed way of representing the children's current knowledge about the topic. The complexity and scope of the completed diagram will, of course, vary widely according to the age and experience of the children.

Conclusion
Ask the children to work in their groups again to study the diagram and to ask each other as many *genuine* questions (that is, those to which they genuinely do not know the answer) connected to the topic as they can. Fluent writers can act as scribes to jot these questions down. When the children have come up with as many questions as they can, ask them to share these with the class. As they do so, write them down on a large chart so that the children will be able to read through them at leisure.

Inform the children that in the next session, you will be returning to the questions in order to select those which will form the basis for their exploration of the topic and the reading arising from it. In the meantime, they should browse through the chart and question list with a view to developing them further.

Session Two
Introduction
Display a 'tidied-up' version of the knowledge map and the list of questions to the children and ask them if they want to add to either of these. Explain that the knowledge map is to be extended throughout the topic as answers are found to selected questions.

Development
Explain to the children that the questions they have generated lend themselves to different ways of searching for answers, and that some questions might not be answerable at all. If you teach older children, you could ask them to suggest categories for sorting the questions, based on how they might be answered. This is a challenging task, and if the children cannot do it, you could suggest the following categories:
▲ Questions that can be answered by asking somebody.
▲ Questions that can be answered through reading. (See Figure 2.)

Type of question	Example
Ask somebody for the answer/Do a survey	What is the most popular type of music in our school? What songs did adults like when they were children?
Experimental	Do people with big ears hear better? Do young children hear better than adults?
Unanswerable, except by a story	Who was the first person to invent a musical instrument?
Unethical	How loud would you have to shout to deafen someone?
Find the answer by reading	Who invented the saxophone? How do string instruments differ from country to country?

Figure 2

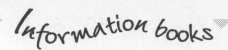

▲ Questions that might be answered by designing and carrying out an experiment.

▲ Questions that nobody is likely to be able to answer (sometimes these questions might be 'answered' in a provisional way by making up a story that supplies the answer).

▲ Questions that it would be unethical to investigate.

Conclusion

When the questions have been sorted, highlight those which are amenable to being answered through reading, and rewrite these on a separate chart. Ask the children to identify which of them they would particularly like to pursue. (This will help you to plan research groups.)

Remind the children that the knowledge map should be added to as the topic progresses and the answers to the questions are found.

Suggestion(s) for extension

As a prelude to subsequent topics, children who have become accustomed to this procedure and are good at working independently can go through this process without the support of the whole-class introduction. It is a particularly useful routine for helping children who want to research a specialist area to organise their work.

Suggestion(s) for support

Children who are reluctant to contribute to whole-class discussion can be encouraged to talk about their knowledge of a topic, and pose their questions about it, during their reading time with you.

Assessment opportunities

Note the children's ability to connect ideas, to recognise areas of potential enquiry, and to recognise the different ways of finding answers to questions.

Display ideas

The knowledge map and the table of questions will form a working display that can be added to and annotated as the topic progresses.

Other aspects of the English PoS covered

Speaking and listening – 1a, b, c; 2a, b; 3b.
Writing – 1a, b, c.

RELEVANT OR NOT?

To develop skimming and scanning skills.
†† *Pairs or small groups.*
🕑 *45 minutes.*

Key background information

This activity builds on children's skimming and scanning skills, and provides a playful context for them to develop the ability to sort textual information into that which is relevant to their reading purposes and that which is not.

Preparation

Read the exemplar text on photocopiable page 139. This may be used as an OHP or enlarged to make a script big enough for all the children in the group to see. If you are attempting this sort of activity for the first time, the page may be duplicated for each pair of children in the group. It is better practice, however, to use the sheet as a starter activity and to prepare a similar text yourself based on a topic that the children are actually covering.

Resources needed

A prepared text related to your current topic, or photocopiable sheet 139, reproduced as an OHP or enlarged, one copy of the text for each pair of children in the group, a felt-tipped pen or OHP pen. Photocopiable page 140 can also be used if appropriate.

What to do
Introduction

Discuss the title of the exemplar text with the children and ask them to suggest who might use this text and what their purposes might be in doing so. What kind of information might such a reader be expecting to find? Read the text aloud to the children.

Development

Ask the children to identify any portion of the text which does not seem useful in relation to the purposes identified during the introduction session. The children's responses here will depend on the purposes identified, but there should be general agreement that at least some of the sentences are irrelevant. Some children might disagree with judgements about what is irrelevant and what is not, and these

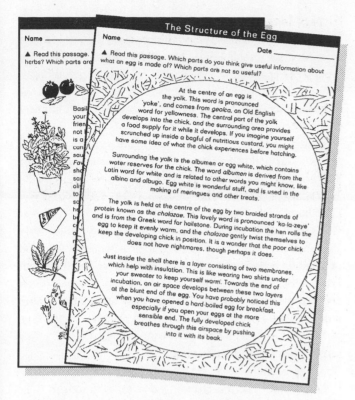

The Structure of the Egg

Name _____

▲ Read this passage. Which parts do you think give useful information about what an egg is made of? Which parts are not so useful?

At the centre of an egg is the yolk. This word is pronounced 'yoke', and comes from *geolca*, an Old English word for yellowness. The central part of the yolk develops into the chick, and the surrounding area provides a food supply for it while it develops. If you imagine yourself scrunched up inside a bagful of nutritious custard, you might have some idea of what the chick experiences before hatching.

Surrounding the yolk is the albumen or egg white, which contains water reserves for the chick. The word *albumen* is derived from the Latin word for white and is related to other words you might know, like *albino* and *albugo*. Egg white is wonderful stuff, and is used in the making of meringues and other treats.

The yolk is held at the centre of the egg by two braided strands of protein known as the *chalazae*. This lovely word is pronounced 'ka-la-zeye' and is from the Greek word for hailstone. During incubation the hen rolls the egg to keep it evenly warm, and the *chalazae* gently twist themselves to keep the developing chick in position. It is a wonder that the poor chick does not have nightmares, though perhaps it does.

Just inside the shell there is a layer consisting of two membranes, which help with insulation. This is like wearing two shirts under your sweater to keep yourself warm. Towards the end of incubation, an air space develops between these two layers at the blunt end of the egg. You have probably noticed this when you have opened a hard-boiled egg for breakfast, especially if you open your eggs at the more sensible end. The fully developed chick breathes through this airspace by pushing into it with its beak.

contentions should be discussed fully. Mark these portions of your text with a felt-tipped pen or OHP pen.

When this has been done, give each pair of children either a copy of the text or a copy of a similar text that you have prepared yourself. Allow them time to go through the text, crossing out portions which they think are irrelevant.

Conclusion

The whole group should compare their findings, and any disagreements should be discussed. Help the children to agree on the wording of an edited version which serves the reader's purpose more efficiently (i.e. one which contains little or no irrelevant information).

Suggestion(s) for extension

Present children with a variety of texts dealing with the same subject-matter. Both instructional and information text can be used, and some children may like to collect their own examples. Help them to identify what it is that makes the texts different from one another. One factor will probably be that some texts contain more information than others. Discuss how the quantity of information that readers need depends on their purpose and their interests.

Some children might also enjoy preparing texts containing irrelevant or semi-irrelevant chunks. These can be edited and word-processed, and used as a resource for other groups of children doing this activity.

Suggestion(s) for support

The point of this activity can be clarified if the 'irrelevance' of certain portions of the text is exaggerated. See photocopiable page 140 for more glaring alternatives to the given text.

Assessment opportunities

Note can be made of the children's ability to match text content to readers' purposes. Their spoken comments on why a particular sentence might be judged relevant or irrelevant will be informative in this respect.

Opportunities for IT

Some children might also enjoy preparing texts containing irrelevant or semi-irrelevant chunks using a word processor. These can then be edited and used as a resource for other groups of children undertaking this activity.

Other aspects of the English PoS covered

Speaking and listening – 1a; 2a, b.

Reference to photocopiable sheets

Photocopiable sheet 139 provides a text containing information which might be of relevance to somebody who wants to learn about the inside of an egg; it also contains peripheral information of less relevance to this purpose. This text, minus its irrelevancies, can also be used for sequencing, deletion, labelling and modelling activities. The text on photocopiable page 140 incorporates information which is glaringly irrelevant, and would make a useful introduction to this type of activity for younger or less experienced readers.

UNDERLINING KEY WORDS

To develop children's note-making skills by searching information texts for words which will help them to memorise the important information in the text.

†† *Small groups, working in pairs.*

🕐 *40 minutes.*

Key background information

This activity arises from earlier work in which children identify purposes of reading. The key idea is that only parts of any information text will relate directly to the reader's purpose, and efficient readers attend most directly to those relevant parts, rendering the rest of the text to some extent redundant.

This activity will only help the children if it is carried out on a regular basis. The process of identifying key portions of text is quite a complex one, and you should expect some difficulties the first few times the children try this.

Preparation

Type out or prepare photocopies of two portions of text relevant to your topic. One of them will be used as a demonstration text and should be enlarged to poster size. The other will be given to the children for them to evaluate, so there should be enough copies for each child to have one of her own. The text should be about one page in length, with a print density appropriate to the reading level of your

group. Alternatively, sheets of acetate can be paper-clipped to actual book pages.

Resources needed
Texts prepared as above, felt-tipped pens.

What to do
Introduction
Ensure that the children have each formulated a question to consider when reading the text. Bobbie Neate in *Finding Out About Finding Out* (Hodder & Stoughton, 1992) suggests that looking at the title and sub-headings and considering the words *who, what, why, how, where, when* in relation to them might help here.

Explain to the children that they are to read the text carefully; and whenever they come across a word or phrase that seems particularly relevant to their question, they should underline it. Use your poster text to demonstrate this process. Underline the first relevant items yourself, talking through the process with the children as you do so. Then encourage them to help you to identify other words and phrases. Limit yourself to ten or a dozen items.

Development
Distribute the text extracts or the information books and acetates. Remind the children that they should underline only a limited number of items. Suggest that they should select the ones that would enable them to recall information relevant to their questions, even if they did not have the text in front of them.

Allow the children to work through the task individually, but make sure that pairs of children compare their responses at regular intervals. When they have gone through the process independently, they should be encouraged to try to come to an agreement on what the best ten or so items are in relation to a particular question. Intervene with specific suggestions only if the children seem frustrated by the task.

By talking to the children as they work, ensure that they are not just underlining at random or selecting words for their curiosity value.

Conclusion
The group as a whole should compare and justify their choices. Ask the children to write their selected words and phrases on a piece of paper or in a notebook. Tell them that in a day or two's time they will be returning to these notes and writing up a brief response to their questions without the aid of the original text.

Suggestion(s) for extension
See extension for 'Relevant or not?' (page 54).

Make sure that the children do actually return to their notes in order to make a fuller written response. When this has been done, the children can compare their own writing with the original text. This is not to check that they have 'got it right', but to highlight the differences between the original text (with all its redundancies) and their own more focused writing.

When exploring texts on an unfamiliar subject, it might be useful to ask children to underline and list all the unfamiliar words that they find, and then to try to derive their meanings from the context. When the children's hypotheses have been checked using a dictionary or with the teacher, the list can be used as a glossary.

Suggestion(s) for support
Help the children to formulate a question based on the text, using the technique suggested by Neate (see above). When this has been done, conduct the entire activity as you did for the introductory session. You may need to use this communal approach several times before children are confident enough to conduct the activity independently.

Assessment opportunities
The underlinings made by the children will give some indication of how well they have discriminated between crucial and peripheral information. Their extended writing will provide evidence of how well they are able to use the notes that they have made.

Display ideas
Texts with different patterns of underlining can be displayed side by side, together with the questions related to them and the books from which they were extracted.

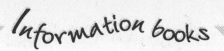
Other aspects of the English PoS covered
Speaking and listening – 1a, b, c; 2a, b; 3b.
Writing – 1a, b, c; 2a, b, c, d; 3b, c.

Reference to photocopiable sheets
Any of the photocopiable sheets referred to in this chapter can be used as a rehearsal for this activity, but it is best to use texts related to authentic current concerns.

UNDERLINING FOR PARTICULAR PURPOSES

To develop scanning and note-making skills by searching texts for particular purposes.

†† *Groups or whole class, working in pairs.*

🕐 *40 minutes.*

Key background information
This activity is a development from the previous one. Instead of highlighting words and phrases to get the gist of the text, the children now underline phrases and sentences in different colours in order to separate out different kinds of information in the text.

Preparation
As for 'Underlining key words' on page 55.

Resources needed
As for 'Relevant or not?' on page 54; each pair of children will also need a set of coloured pencils or felt-tipped pens.

What to do
Introduction
Display your poster text, and ask the children to study the heading and any subheadings and illustrations in order to predict what the text might be about. Read it through with the children and discuss the content. Identify two or three different types of information that the text presents; then read through the text again and, in collaboration with the

children, underline in different colours, phrases and sentences which relate to these types of information.

Development
Distribute photocopies of your second selected text to the children. Ask them to make predictions about the overall content (as above), then help them to identify the different types of information presented. Allow the children time to work in pairs, underlining portions of text appropriately. As with the previous activity, it is helpful to stipulate a maximum number of words to be underlined in relation to each type of information.

If the children find some portions of the text difficult to understand, they could underline these sections in a specific colour.

Conclusion
Ask the children to compare their marked-up texts and to discuss any differences they find.

Suggestion(s) for extension
If a text is 'rich' enough, it can be used on different occasions in relation to different information goals.

Suggestion(s) for support
With inexperienced children, the entire session can be conducted as a shared reading activity.

Assessment opportunities
As for 'Underlining key words' on page 55.

Opportunities for IT
Topical resources might be taken from a CD-ROM. The text could be word processed and copies printed out for children.

Display ideas
Multiple copies of the text can be displayed, each marked up differently in relation to different information focuses.

Other aspects of the English PoS covered
Speaking and listening – 1a, b, c; 2a, b; 3b.
Writing – 1a, b, c; 2a, b, c, d, e; 3a, b, c.

Reference to photocopiable sheets
The following pages can be used for the purposes of this activity, though again it is better to use texts which relate to your current work. Suggested information focuses are given for each page.
Page 139: The structure of the egg – technical vocabulary, irrelevant information, word derivations.
Page 143: Onchlids – appearance, diet, habitat, peculiarities, portions of text which suggest that this is an imaginary animal.
Pages 147 and 148: Acid rain – arguments for and against the control of acid rain.

MODELLING (GRAPHIC OUTCOMES)

To reflect on a text in order to create a pictorial representation of the information in it.

†† *Whole class or group, working as individuals.*

🕐 *40 minutes.*

Key background information

Modelling is a technique that many children find both challenging and enjoyable. It is also invaluable to the teacher in providing a visible representation of the child's understanding of a particular text.

Preparation

Select a text relevant to your current topic, and try to make a graphic representation of the information that it provides. This can be a drawing or set of drawings, or some more schematic format such as a graph, pie chart or flow diagram. Try not to make your drawing too 'artistic', as this can inhibit some children and give the impression that the session is focused on art rather than on reading. Add labels if you feel this is necessary, but try to use as few words as possible. When you have done this, enlarge both the drawing and the text so that the whole class can focus on them.

Select a second text for the children to work on, making sure that this one lends itself to graphic representation, and make sufficient copies for each child or pair of children. Remove all illustrations from the copies.

Resources needed

Selected texts, drawing materials.

What to do

Introduction

Present your drawing to the children and ask them to interpret it. Then present them with the corresponding text. Read it through together, and ask them how well they think you have expressed the information it contains. Discuss any alternative possibilities that the children can think of. Explain that they are now going to draw information themselves.

Development

Distribute the copies of the second text. Read through this with the children if this is necessary, explaining any unfamiliar vocabulary. Allow the children time to work individually, stressing that there is no correct solution to the task, and reminding them of the range of options available to them.

Conclusion

Encourage the children to compare their responses with those of their partners, and to share any particularly interesting responses with the class.

Suggestion(s) for extension

This activity should be carried out at regular intervals with a variety of kinds of text. When planning future topics, make a bank of amenable texts for the children to work on in this way. Ensure that the children have experience of a range of possible responses, both schematic and pictorial.

Suggestion(s) for support

The entire activity can be carried out as shared reading using an enlarged text, but with the children making individual responses. Some children will be reluctant to share their drawings because of their poor opinions of their skills in this field. It is important to stress to such children that it is the expression of ideas that matters, rather than technical skill. This point should also be made to children who spend too much time on the aesthetic aspects of their drawings. Try to model this approach by joining in with the activity, making rough sketches rather than careful works of art.

Assessment opportunities

Check the children's drawings to see how accurately their ideas are expressed and to assess creative responses. This activity will also enable you to spot any misinterpretations of the text.

Display ideas

A display of the original text, with and without its original illustrations and surrounded by the children's drawings and diagrams, will reinforce the idea that texts are open to many representations and interpretations.

Other aspects of the English PoS covered

Speaking and listening – 1a, b, c; 2a, b; 3b.

Reference to photocopiable sheets

Any of the photocopiable pages in this chapter can be used for this activity.

IDEA PATTERNS

To help children to make notes and relate ideas from their reading.

†† *Small or large groups, with the children working individually or in pairs.*

🕐 *Open-ended.*

Key background information
This activity is a direct follow-up to the activities on pages 51 to 57, and will be most effective if children have had ample experience of engaging with texts in the ways suggested.

Preparation
Read any information text that you find interesting; and as you do so, jot down the ideas conveyed by the text and try to relate them to each other by drawing arrows between them. Tony Buzan in *Use Your Head* (BBC, 1974) suggests that the best way of doing this is to write a central idea in the middle of a piece of paper, and to visualise and record related ideas radiating out from this. You will probably find that you need to erase and relocate words and phrases several times.

Select books or extracts that will provide reading at an instructional or independent level for the group you intend to work with.

Resources needed
Selected texts, writing and drawing materials.

What to do
Introduction
Refer the children back to any work that they have done related to 'Identifying current knowledge' on page 52. This will involve displaying and discussing the topic knowledge

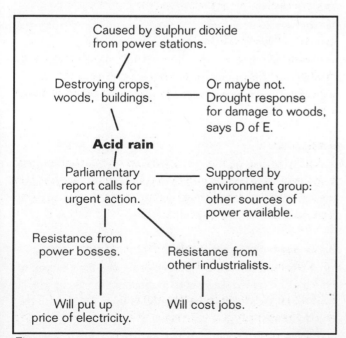

Figure 1

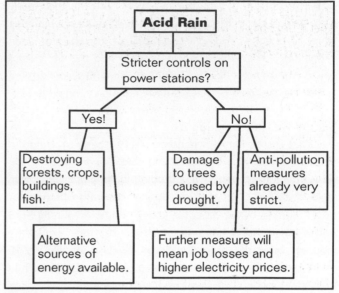

Figure 2

map and the table of questions. Explain to the children that they are going to record their own patterns of the ideas that they meet in texts related to their current topics of interest. Show the children the pattern that you have prepared, read aloud the text it was created from, and talk through the decisions that you have made in selecting words and phrases and placing them on the charts.

Development
Distribute copies of the selected text. Ask the children to consider the title and any illustrations, and to anticipate what they might learn from reading the text. Then ask them to read independently, and to underline a set number of words and phrases related to key ideas. Drawing rough sketches, as in 'Modelling (graphic outcomes)' on page 58, might also help.

When the children have done this, ask them to list the words and phrases that they have selected, and to rearrange these to make an arrowed diagram. The use of coloured pens and labelled arrows can help the children to clarify relationships between ideas. While they are doing this, provide any support that is needed, but try to find the time to do the same thing yourself.

Conclusion
Allow the children time to compare and discuss their responses. Show them your own response. Look at the topic knowledge map again, and try to agree on how what has been learned from the reading might be incorporated into this map.

Suggestion(s) for extension
Once children are accustomed to this activity, it can be incorporated into their routine note-making strategies. (Some older students use the technique quite effectively for taking lecture notes.)

As an alternative to the radiating patterns that many children find fascinating, you could provide prepared matrices which direct the children's attention to hierarchies of ideas in the text, or to opposing arguments and the viewpoints which create them. Figures 1 and 2 on page 59 show patterns based on the 'acid rain' texts from 'Role play' on page 68.

Suggestion(s) for support
Conduct the activity as a shared reading session. Help the children to identify key words and phrases, and write these down on cards. When the reading is finished, invite the children to sort through and rearrange the cards on the floor or a tabletop. Allow them time to experiment with different patterns, perhaps encouraging them to place what they believe to be the more important cards centrally. Try to encourage the groups to agree on a pattern, which can then be copied, expanded, illustrated and displayed.

Assessment opportunities
Note the children's ability to select salient points and to see how they are related.

Display ideas
Idea patterns can be displayed alongside other material related to the topic. As well as providing a vivid picture of the content of a text, they also show how individual readers reconstruct this content in different ways.

Other aspects of the English PoS covered
Speaking and listening – 1a, b, c; 2a, b; 3b.
Writing – 1a, b, c; 2a, d, e; 3b, c.

Reference to photocopiable sheets
Any of the photocopiable pages in this chapter can be used for this activity.

DIAGRAM LABELLING

To develop comprehension of a text by helping children to match key ideas in the text with elements of a visual representation.

†† *Small group.*
⏱ *40 minutes.*

Key background information
In this activity, children are encouraged to 'read' a diagram carefully and then to search a text for clues to how the diagram and its captions should be matched.

Preparation
Prepare or select a diagram of an object or process related to your current topic, and make photocopies of a text relevant to this theme. Delete all captions and labels, and prepare a

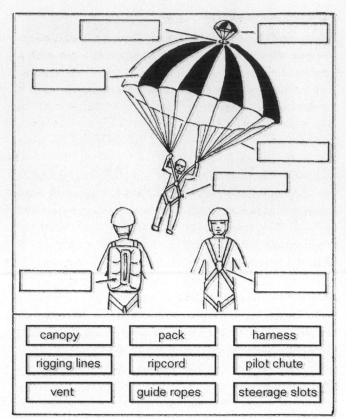

canopy	pack	harness
rigging lines	ripcord	pilot chute
vent	guide ropes	steerage slots

Figure 1

set of cards bearing appropriate labels for the blank spaces or arrows. The diagram and cards should be large enough for your selected group to see and handle them comfortably, and should be suitable for class display once the labelling task has been completed. Figure 1 shows an example.

Resources needed
The diagram and labels.

What to do
Introduction
Show the children the visual support material that you have prepared, and encourage them to talk about their own knowledge of the topic in question. Explain that they are going to produce a completed diagram with help from a related text.

Development
Distribute copies of the text and read it through with the group, making reference to the diagram where appropriate. Allow the children to sort through the labels themselves and to discuss where they should be placed.

Conclusion
When all of the labels have been placed, ask the children to show the completed diagram to the rest of the class and talk through the task with them, justifying their choice for the position of each label.

The children's diagram can then form part of a class display.

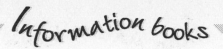

Suggestion(s) for extension

If you want the activity to be more challenging, include related but redundant labels, so that the children have more labels than spaces. Alternatively, preparing two or three fewer labels than are required provides the children with the challenge of composing their own labels for the empty spaces. A further step is to withhold all of the labels and ask the children to write their own.

Suggestion(s) for support

Display the diagrams and the labels so that they are all clearly visible to the children. Conduct the activity as a shared reading session. When you reach a part of the text related to a particular label, ask the children to identify the appropriate label and to attach it to the correct part of the diagram.

Assessment opportunities

Note the children's ability to scan the text for specific items of information, and their ability to co-ordinate their reading of the text with their reading of the diagram.

Opportunities for IT

Some software, like *My World* (SEMERC), has been specifically written for this type of activity. Commercial files are available, and teachers can also create their own. Similar work can be undertaken using a drawing package. The teacher could draw the diagram and produce a set of labels to be placed around the edge of the drawing. The diagram or drawing to be labelled could be scanned in and imported into the software. Alternatively, suitable drawings or photographs might be taken from CD-ROMs. Children could then place

these labels in the appropriate places, or even use the drawing facilities to draw lines linking the labels to the correct parts of the diagram. Final solutions could be printed out for display.

Display ideas

The completed diagram should be displayed, alongside other visual material related to the same topic.

Other aspects of the English PoS covered

Speaking and listening – 1a, b, c; 2a, b; 3b.

Reference to photocopiable sheets

Photocopiable page 141 can be used if it fits in with your topic. Some other photocopiable texts might also lend themselves to diagrammatic representation.

CONSTRUCTING A TIMELINE

To develop children's awareness of time relations in information texts.

†† *Groups of children working individually.*

🕒 *Two 40-minute sessions.*

Key background information

This activity combines labelling and graphic modelling, and is appropriate for texts which have a chronological element.

Preparation

Select or prepare a text, related to your current topic, which describes a process or chain of events occurring over a specific period of time. This might include an account of a historical period or the life story of an individual.

Draw a large timeline representing the period covered by the text, and prepare a set of labels, mounted on card, which relate to the main events within that period.

Resources needed

See above; examples of timeline illustrations from published books; the text on photocopiable page 142, with labels corresponding to events within the story cut out and mounted on card (see below).

What to do
Session One

Read the first and last paragraphs of page 142 with the children, explaining if necessary that it is a piece of fiction in the form of an information text. Invite them to speculate on the content of the intervening paragraphs before distributing copies of the entire page.

Show the children examples of timelines from published texts, and explain how this device helps the reader to visualise

---

The parachute

Name _____ Date _____

If you jump out of a plane your body will fall towards the Earth. Within 12 seconds, it will be falling at a speed of 54 metres per second. A person hitting the ground at this speed would be killed instantly. The job of a parachute is to slow the body down so that it reaches the ground at a safer speed of about 7 metres per second.

The parachute does this job by providing the parachutist with an enormous extra skin in the form of a canopy. This canopy effectively expands the surface area of the parachutist so that air resistance to his or her fall is hugely increased, and the speed of the fall is therefore reduced.

The canopy of the parachute is the umbrella-shaped expanse of nylon fabric that floats above the parachutist, attached to his or her body with rigging lines. When not in use, the canopy and rigging lines are folded away inside a pack which is fastened to the parachutist's body by a harness. The pack is held shut with securing pins to which the ripcord is attached.

When the parachutist pulls the ripcord, the pack opens up and releases a small pilot chute. When this opens, it pulls out the main canopy and rigging lines. As the canopy fills with air, the parachutist's rate of descent decelerates rapidly. The harness protects the body from shocks while this happens. When the parachute is fully open, the parachutist can direct it to the ground by operating guide ropes which control steerage slots in the canopy.

historical processes. Draw a line on the board or on a piece of chart paper, and mark it with a scale representing the 20 years covered by the text. Make labels related to the events within this text (for example: 'international scientific research landing'; 'abandonment of research station'; 'passage of Comet Malachite'; 'first freighters leave Earth'; 'death of Earth's last rainforests'; 'death of lunar rainforest'; 'discovery of lunar rainforest'; 'decision of United Nations to exploit rainforest') and invite the children to place these at the appropriate points on the timeline (see below). Ask them to justify their decisions to place labels in particular positions.

Session Two

Before presenting your topic-based text to the children, discuss its content in relation to their previous work, and explain that they are going to complete another timeline related to this new text. Read it through with the children and resolve any difficulties before proceeding.

Present the children with the new timeline and related labels, and allow them time to arrange the labels to show the order of events within the text. Check that the labelling task has been completed satisfactorily, and discuss any differences in opinion as to where particular labels should go.

As with the diagram labelling activity, the children can present the completed work to the rest of the class.

Suggestion(s) for extension

When children have become accustomed to this type of activity, they can be set the task of drawing their own timelines and writing their own labels. It is advisable to limit the number of labels the children can make, so that they approach the text with the intention of seeking out the crucial events. This constraint should help to develop their note-making skills.

The Forests of the Moon

The emergence of a rain forest amongst the craters and dust seas of the moon was first noticed in 1999 by Cynthia Rainstone, an amateur astronomer working from her garden shed. Ms Rainstone's discovery was reported two years after the passage through the Earth's exosphere of Comet Malachite, and astrobiologists have speculated that the forests grew from spores deposited by the comet.

Computer-enhanced images of the new forest revealed that within a year of the emergence of the first trees, the canopy had reached a height of 50 metres, and that the foliage was densely populated by a wealth of species whose behaviour and physical characteristics appeared to be completely different from those typical of terrestrial fauna.

Scientific interest in this new ecosystem was, of course, intense: and seven years after Ms Rainstone's discovery, the first international expedition landed on the moon to carry out explorations of the forest. The scientists were not, however, the first people to arrive. Two years earlier, a fleet of space freighters had been sent out secretly from Earth by Hackco, the multinational logging company; and by the time the scientists arrived, they had already cleared an extensive area of the forest, shipping the high quality timber back to Earth.

An emergency delegation of scientists appealed to the United Nations to suspend the logging operation until a full scientific survey had been made of the forest. At its first meeting, the scientists revealed that fruits discovered in the forest contained the full spectrum of human nutrients, as well as compounds with versatile healing properties and the power to raise levels of intelligence and good-naturedness among subjects who had volunteered to eat them. The forest creatures which had been examined all appeared to be non-aggressive and intelligent. Moreover, the capability of the trees to grow rapidly in a very thin atmosphere and with almost no water merited intensive and prolonged research.

The argument over who, if anyone, had the rights to the forest raged for ten years, and during this time the last of Earth's tropical rain forests vanished. It was this event which eventually swayed the opinions of the decision makers. The moon was declared open for commercial exploitation, and the scientists were granted a square mile 'protected research zone'. Within a year of the decision being made, seven of Hackco's rivals had sent their own freighters to the moon. In 2019, the last of the trees in the lunar forest was felled. Two years earlier, the research zone had been abandoned, its trees and the creatures who dwelt within them having succumbed to the pollution caused by the lumberjacks.

Comet Malachite is expected to return in approximately ten thousand years.

Suggestion(s) for support

As with the previous activity, shared reading can be used to support understanding of the original text, and the labels can be placed (with the teacher's support) during the actual reading. The use of illustrations might help some children to identify appropriate labels.

Assessment opportunities

The accuracy with which the labels are matched to the timeline will present evidence of the children's understanding of the text. If they are creating their own labels, this will provide evidence of their ability to scan the text and make notes based on selected information.

Opportunities for IT

Commercial timeline software is available for some computers. However, similar work can be undertaken using a drawing package or word processor. The timeline could be drawn using a drawing package, and children could use the mouse to drag the labels to the appropriate positions. The completed timeline could be printed out for display purposes. Children could use the same software to make up their own timelines, for other children to sequence in the same way.

Display ideas

The timeline can be displayed alongside other forms of written and graphic response to the information provided on the activity sheet.

Other aspects of the English PoS covered

Speaking and listening – 1a, b, c; 2a, b; 3b.
Writing – 1a, b, c; 2a, b, c, d; 3a, b, c.

Reference to photocopiable sheet

Photocopiable page 142 can be used for the introductory activity.

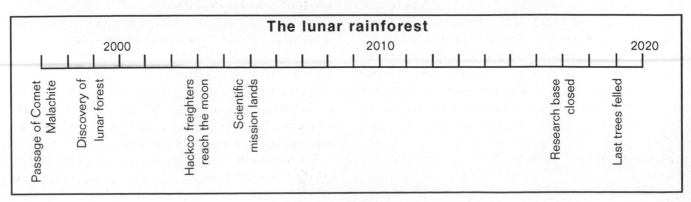

The lunar rainforest

2000   2010   2020

- Passage of Comet Malachite
- Discovery of lunar forest
- Hackco freighters reach the moon
- Scientific mission lands
- Research base closed
- Last trees felled

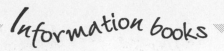
TABULATING INFORMATION

To develop scanning and note-making skills, and to encourage children to compare information from different sources.

†† *Small or large groups, working in pairs.*

🕐 *40 minutes.*

Key background information

This activity requires children to compare and classify information, preferably from a range of sources. If done regularly, it is an effective way of encouraging them to scan text for specific items, and to compare what different texts have to say about these items. It follows on from the underlining activities 'Relevant or not?' on page 54 and 'Underlining key words' on page 55, and can be carried out in combination with these activities.

The completed chart can be used by other children as a source of condensed information, and as a resource for writing up notes into more extended prose.

Preparation

Select a text, or preferably a range of texts, related to your current topic and involving some form of classification and comparison. Texts which present comparative information on types of creatures, people, places, things and ideas are best suited to this activity. Extracts from periodicals can also be used, as well as encyclopaedias and other information texts on CD-ROM.

If you want to combine this activity with underlining, you will need to make photocopies of the samples of text, or prepare acetate sheets to cover the printed pages.

Prepare a poster-sized matrix similar to the one shown in Figure 1, with headings to focus the children's attention on the relevant items of information. Prepare smaller versions of this chart for each pair of children to work on. Display the large chart in the classroom some days before the activity, alongside the range of relevant books and other sources.

Resources needed

See above.

Information \ Instrument	piano	guitar	sitar	flute	violin	mbira
Origin/ History						
Made from						
Played by						
Outstanding Players						

Figure 1

What to do

Introduction

Draw the children's attention to the large chart, and ask them how many of the cells they can fill in without recourse to the texts. Allow them to look at the texts and work with the children on completing the first line of the chart, using the texts as a resource to find new information or to check any contributions that they have made orally. Emphasise that one of the objectives of the activity is for the children to compare different sources of information.

Development

Distribute copies of the matrix and allow the children time to read the texts that you have provided and to complete their charts. If you are using photocopies, remind them of their work on underlining and encourage them to use this technique in order to highlight relevant information. While they are doing this, provide support and try to make sure that children are not simply copying chunks of information on to the chart. If this is the case, help them to locate the word or phrase that carries the crucial information.

Conclusion

Pairs of children should compare their completed table with those of other pairs. Any differences in the children's work, and any discrepancies between sources of information, should be discussed and agreement reached on how the large version of the chart should be completed. When this has been done, the completed chart can be displayed and presented to the rest of the class. If appropriate, it can also be used as a resource for more extended writing.

Suggestion(s) for extension

When children are accustomed to this type of activity, they can devise their own chart formats and headings.

Suggestion(s) for support

Prepare a set of labels bearing appropriate responses for each of the cells in the table. As the portion of text related to each line in the table is read, help the children to locate the appropriate label and to place it in its proper cell.

The difficulty of the task can be controlled through your selection of source materials and the complexity of the matrix.

Assessment opportunities

The children's responses to this task will provide evidence of their ability to scan text for selected ideas and to organise those ideas into a different format. Critical awareness of sources of information might also be evident in their responses to discrepancies between different sources.

Opportunities for IT

Some of the texts to be scanned could be presented to children on the computer screen itself so that they have experience of reading from a computer screen. If the text is taken from a CD-ROM, children can use the linked words to move to other resources offering more information. Other texts to be used might be taken from CD-ROMs and printed out or pre-processed using a word processor.

Display ideas

The completed chart can be displayed and used as suggested above.

Other aspects of the English PoS covered

Speaking and listening – 1a, b, c; 2a, b; 3b.
Writing – 1a, b, c; 2a, b, c, d, e; 3a, b, c.

INTRODUCING WRITING FRAMEWORKS

To introduce children to the use of writing frameworks for the restructuring of factual material derived from non-fiction texts.

†† *Whole class or smaller groups, working in pairs.*

🕒 *30 minutes.*

Key background information

Children will read a non-fiction text and transfer key information to a comparison/contrast matrix. This activity is suitable for children who need help in the structuring of their non-fiction writing.

A writing framework is simply a sequence of open-ended sentences. In order to complete these sentences, the children have to reflect on their background knowledge and on what they have learned from the text. This is a well-established procedure, but it has recently been the subject of research by the Exeter Extending Literacy Project. *Developing Children's Non-fiction Writing: Working With Writing Frames* by Maureen Lewis and David Wray (*Primary Professional Bookshelf* series, Scholastic 1995) contains a wealth of practical information about the use of a variety of frameworks.

Preparation

Reproduce photocopiable pages 143 and 144 and complete the activity yourself. Seek out examples of authentic non-fiction texts, relevant to the work that the children are doing, which might lend themselves to this approach. Devise a writing framework appropriate for the text you have selected, or use the framework on page 144 if this suits your purposes.

Resources needed

Selected texts, and photocopiable pages 143 and 144 reproduced on a scale large enough for all the children in the group to see.

What to do

Introduction

Read through the passage on photocopiable page 143 and discuss whether onchlids are real animals or not. Show the children photocopiable page 144 and explain how this framework is to be completed. Work through this with the children, scribing their responses and using underlining as appropriate.

Development

Distribute the texts you have selected, and ask the children to predict what they are likely to be about (from the titles) before reading and discussing them. Distribute the framework sheets and ask the children to complete them, using underlining if necessary, and then to compare their completed

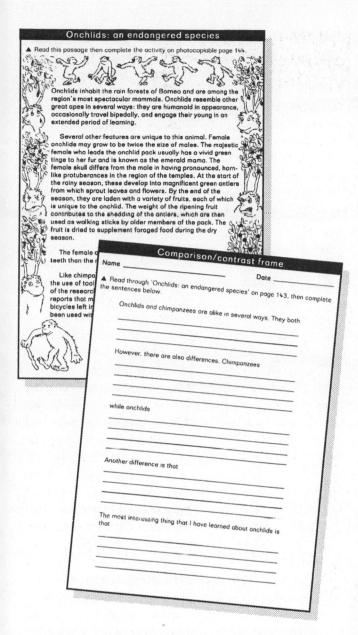

Onchlids: an endangered species

▲ Read this passage then complete the activity on photocopiable page 144.

Onchlids inhabit the rain forests of Borneo and are among the region's most spectacular mammals. Onchlids resemble other great apes in several ways: they are humanoid in appearance, occasionally travel bipedally, and engage their young in an extended period of learning.

Several other features are unique to this animal. Female onchlide may grow to be twice the size of males. The majestic female who leads the onchlid pack usually has a vivid green tinge to her fur and is known as the emerald mama. The female skull differs from the male in having pronounced, horn-like protuberances in the region of the temples. At the start of the rainy season, these develop into magnificent green antlers from which sprout leaves and flowers. By the end of the season, they are laden with a variety of fruits, each of which is unique to the onchlid. The weight of the ripening fruit contributes to the shedding of the antlers, which are then used as walking sticks by older members of the pack. The fruit is dried to supplement foraged food during the dry season.

The female o...
teeth than the...

Like chimpa...
the use of tool...
of the research...
reports that m...
bicycles left in...
been used wit...

Comparison/contrast frame

Name _____ Date _____

▲ Read through 'Onchlids: an endangered species' on page 143, then complete the sentences below.

Onchlids and chimpanzees are alike in several ways. They both
_____
_____

However, there are also differences. Chimpanzees
_____
_____
_____

while onchlids
_____
_____
_____

Another difference is that
_____
_____
_____

The most interesting thing that I have learned about onchlids is that
_____
_____
_____

sheets with another pair of children. It should be emphasised that the frameworks are always open to amendment and extension by the children, and should not be allowed to become a constraint on their writing.

Conclusion

Make arrangements for the children to work with response partners in redrafting and proof-reading their work. Encourage them to talk about the sequence of tasks that they have completed, and to try to identify in what ways the procedure might have been useful. Explain that in future sessions, similar procedures will be used on a variety of texts.

Suggestion(s) for extension

Children can provide suggestions for the restructuring of the framework sheets, and can help to suggest texts for future investigation. Note that the framework becomes redundant as soon as children are able to incorporate the structure into their independent writing.

Suggestion(s) for support

The entire activity can be carried out orally, with suitably enlarged fact and framework sheets, with the teacher or a helper supporting the reading and scribing responses on to the framework sheet. By amending the framework as you compose and revise the text, you can remind the children that they have the freedom to do this when they are working with frameworks independently.

Assessment opportunities

Note children's ability to identify salient features of the text to include in the framework sheet, and to complete the sheet without recourse to verbatim copying.

Opportunities for IT

Some children could undertake this activity using a word processor. A file containing the framework could be created by the teacher and children can develop their editing and redrafting skills by completing the framework on the computer itself. Final copies could be printed out for display purposes.

Other aspects of the English PoS covered

Speaking and listening – 1a, b, c; 2a, b.
Writing – 1a, b, c.

Reference to photocopiable sheets

Photocopiable pages 143 and 144 are provided as a demonstration activity. Alternative writing frameworks are provided for 'Sequencing' (below) and 'Role play' on page 68.

SEQUENCING

To encourage children to reflect on the structure of ideas in an information text.
†† *Whole class working in small groups.*
🕐 *40 minutes.*

Key background information

This activity is similar to the sequencing activity in the Fiction chapter (see page 16). However, with information texts, the ideas will not necessarily be organised chronologically. This means that children have to focus on the alternative ways in which ideas might be structured in the text.

Preparation

Cut photocopiable page 145 into separate paragraphs and explore different ways of reconstructing the text. You will probably find that there are two or three acceptable ways of organising the six chunks. Consider how you would argue for one arrangement over another.

Select a text related to your current topic, photocopy it and cut it up into six to eight chunks, then mount these on card. Produce enough copies for each group of three or four

children to have a set each. Photocopiable page 145 can be used with the class as an introductory activity, if relevant to your current work.

Resources needed
See above.

What to do
Introduction
Remind the children of any narrative sequencing work that they have done, and tell them that they are going to attempt some similar work with an information text. Discuss the content of the text with the children before distributing the cards, so that their background knowledge is activated.

Development
Distribute the sets of cards and allow the children to read them and to try out different ways of arranging them. Encourage them to read through the suggested arrangements aloud in order to decide whether they sound right.

If children have made arrangements which are clearly wrong, point out clues which will enable them to correct this. These clues might include chronological markers, pronouns referring back to items in earlier sentences, and sentence connectives like 'however', 'consequently' and 'although'. The use of words like 'another' and 'also' will suggest connections with earlier sections. Opening paragraphs usually contain a topic sentence which sets the scene for the whole piece.

Conclusion
Invite each group to read out their agreed ordering of the chunks, and to justify their decisions. Try to achieve a consensus between the groups as to what the order should be. When this has been done, show the children the published order of the chunks, and compare this with their own agreed version.

Suggestion(s) for extension
The task can be made more difficult by increasing the number of chunks, by cutting texts into sentences rather than

paragraphs, and by choosing more complex texts. Providing a text that is more open to alternative arrangements will mean that the readers have to focus more closely on the grammatical structure of the sentences to justify their choices.

Suggestion(s) for support
With inexperienced readers, the first few times they attempt this activity it is helpful for them to work with texts that they have created in collaboration with the teacher (through shared writing).

The best way of supporting children who are beginning to work with unfamiliar texts is to sit with a group and to try out two or three alternative arrangements with them, thinking aloud as you do so and making explicit reference to the organisational features mentioned above.

Assessment opportunities
Listening to the children's conversations as they manipulate the chunks should give you an insight into their awareness of the organising features of text. Watch out for children who make alternative arrangements as good as, or better than, the published order.

Opportunities for IT
Some children could use a word processor to re-order the information. The original text can be typed on to the word processor and then the order of the various chunks moved around. Save this version as a master copy. Children can then use the 'cut' and 'paste' commands or the mouse to drag portions of the text into different locations. Other groups of children could use the same software and commands to re-sequence the text which could be checked against the original. Copies of the text could be printed out at each stage and used for work away from the computer. The children should also be introduced to the 'load' and 'save' commands so that they can return to work at a later date.

The recovery of the Thames: expository frame

Name _____ Date _____

▲ Read through 'The recovery of the River Thames' on page 145 and fill in this sheet.

Preliminary notes

Dangers	Improvements

Before my reading, I knew that _____

I have now learned several things more about the Thames.
Firstly _____

Another thing I learned is that _____

The most int

The recovery of the River Thames

By 1960, one of the most important rivers in Britain was on the brink of death. The River Thames, which flows through London, was so polluted that few organisms could survive in it. Factories along its banks poured waste into its waters, adding to the pollution caused by raw sewage. The river was a health risk to people who lived near it.

Another danger associated with the Thames was that of flooding. The water level rises rapidly whenever there is a high tide. If strong winds occur at the same time, there is a real danger of the river bursting its banks. The communities living alongside the Thames had long been threatened by the devastation that a serious flood can cause.

Recently, there have been changes for the better. The water is getting cleaner as the old docks and factories close down. The surviving factories now have to obey stricter anti-pollution laws.

New sewage works have also opened, so there is less dumping of poisonous filth into the river. The water is much cleaner now, and supports a wider variety of water birds, fish, plants and other wildlife.

The general public have become more aware of environmental issues. Groups of walkers and wildlife enthusiasts have successfully campaigned for better footpaths along the river, so that everybody can enjoy its improved scenery.

The danger of flooding has also receded in recent years. A magnificent tidal barrier has been built across the river at Woolwich. It consists of movable sections which are usually lowered to let water traffic pass. But whenever there is a flood risk from tidal surges, the sections are raised from the river bed to form a protective wall.

Display ideas

As with narrative sequencing, this activity can be incorporated into an interactive display. Appropriate texts can be displayed in a shuffled order on a sequencing board for children to work with.

Other aspects of the English PoS covered

Speaking and listening – 1a, b, c; 2a, b; 3b.

Reference to photocopiable sheets

Photocopiable page 145 can be used as an introduction to this activity. The published order of the paragraphs is not necessarily the 'best' arrangement. The other photocopiable texts related to this chapter could also be used, and might provide opportunities to discuss different principles of text organisation. For example, the text of 'Forests of the moon' on page 142 is chronologically organised; while in 'The structure of the egg' on page 139, the account starts at the centre of the egg and works outwards.

GENERATING QUESTIONS

To develop personal responses to information texts.
†† *Whole class working in small groups.*
🕒 *30 minutes.*

Key background information

This activity reverses the traditional model of comprehension work by encouraging children to formulate their own questions about a text. In order to do so, they have to reflect on what they have learned from reading and what they still need to know.

Preparation

Select a short text, or a selection of texts for the different groups, based on a current theme of interest to the children. This might relate to your current topic, to current issues in the news, or to the children's interests outside school. It is essential that the children should be able to read the material fairly easily within the first ten minutes or so of the lesson, so there should be a careful matching of the level of reading material to the children in each group.

Resources needed

See above. If you decide to work from the children's personal interests, you could enlist their help by asking them to bring into school reading materials related to these interests. These materials might include manuals, magazines and other media as well as conventional information books. Approaching the activity in this way is much more difficult than providing the class with one topic to discuss, though it may be possible to organise groups based on shared interests.

What to do

Distribute the texts and ask the children to read them through, and then to make up four or five questions arising from the material to which they would really like to know the answers. Individual children should write their questions down and then exchange them with a partner. The children could try to answer each other's questions in their groups, or suggest sources of information from which answers might be derived.

To conclude this session, suggest some possible ways in which the questions might be pursued:
▲ as the basis for planning a programme of further reading;
▲ as part of a letter to the author;
▲ as an enquiry to another authority on the subject, or to a more open source of information such as the Internet or *The Guardian*'s 'Notes and Queries' column.

Suggestion(s) for extension

The practice of generating questions can be incorporated into the children's general reading strategies. It is a particularly useful practice for children to apply to their own written work at the end of a topic or scheme of work, encouraging them to reflect on what they have learned and what they would still like to discover.

Suggestion(s) for support

Incorporate the asking of questions about information texts into your read-aloud programme (see 'A read-aloud programme' on page 50).

Before the reading of a particular text, write the words *who*, *what*, *where*, *when*, *how* and *why* on a chart or on the board. Read the text with the children and model the process of generating questions based on these stimulus words as you do so.

Assessment opportunities

The type of questions that children ask can give you an insight into their personal and creative responses to their reading, as well as providing more straightforward evidence of their comprehension and appreciation of the given texts.

Display ideas

Children's questions before and after reading can be displayed together with a copy of the material on which the questions were based, their tentative answers and their ideas for further research. The technique can be combined with the modelling of graphic outcomes, and this can be incorporated into the display.

Other aspects of the English PoS covered

Speaking and listening – 1a, b, c; 2a, b; 3b.
Writing – 1a, b, c.

ROLE PLAY

To develop children's personal responses to the issues raised by information texts.

†† *Whole-class introduction followed by small-group work.*

🕐 *Open-ended.*

Key background information

This activity aims to explore social and political issues raised by information texts, and to examine the motives of particular parties involved in these issues.

Preparation

Select a text or a range of texts related to a current issue. These might include extracts from newspapers and magazines as well as information books. Enlarge them so that the whole class can read them, and duplicate a copy for each small group of children. Photocopiable pages 147 and 148 can be used if appropriate.

Resources needed

See above.

What to do

Introduction

Talk to the children about the issue involved and ask them to express their opinions on it. Display the texts, read them aloud to the children, and prompt further discussion. Explain to the children that they are going to use the texts to devise role-play activities related to the issues involved.

Development

Working in small groups, the children can develop role-plays using choices from the following frameworks. These scenarios are based on the texts on pages 147 and 148.

▲ A conversation between the committee chairman and the five persons named in the newspaper report.

▲ A conversation between two people in Britain in 100 years' time, after reading the history book extract.

▲ A panel discussion or phone-in in which one group play the characters involved, giving responses to questions prepared by another group.

▲ Newspaper or television interviews. The group can work in pairs, with one person being a reporter and the other one of the six characters. After a specific amount of time, the character becomes a reporter, and the reporter assumes the role of another character.

▲ A legal tribunal, in which each character has to state his or her case and then answer questions.

▲ A television news slot, in which a reporter presents a summary of the issues, members of the public are asked for their views, and key figures are interviewed.

▲ A set of television or cinema adverts sponsored by the

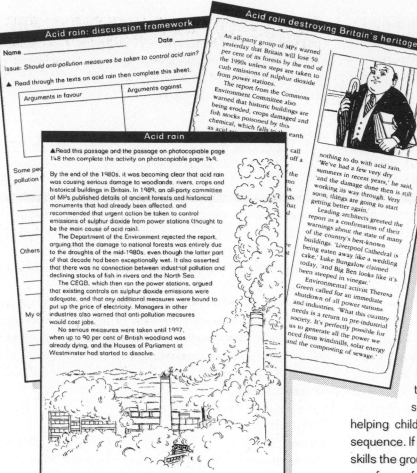

Acid rain: discussion framework

Name _____

Date _____

Issue: *Should anti-pollution measures be taken to control acid rain?*

▲ Read through the texts on acid rain then complete this sheet.

Arguments in favour	Arguments against

Acid rain destroying Britain's heritage

An all-party group of MPs warned yesterday that Britain will lose 50 per cent of its forests by the end of the 1990s unless steps are taken to curb emissions of sulphur dioxide from power stations.

The report from the Commons Environment Committee also warned that historic buildings are being eroded, crops damaged and fish stocks poisoned by this chemical, which falls to the earth as acid rain...

nothing to do with acid rain. 'We've had a few very dry summers in recent years,' he said, 'and the damage done then is still working its way through. Very soon, things are going to start getting better again.'

Leading architects greeted the report as a confirmation of their warnings about the state of many of the country's best-known buildings. 'Liverpool Cathedral is being eaten away like a wedding cake,' Luke Bungalow claimed today, 'and Big Ben looks like it's been steeped in vinegar.'

Environmental activist Theresa Green called for an immediate shutdown of all power stations and industries. 'What this country needs is a return to pre-industrial society. It's perfectly possible for us to generate all the power we need from windmills, solar energy and the composting of sewage.'

Acid rain

▲Read this passage and the passage on photocopiable page 148 then complete the activity on photocopiable page 149.

By the end of the 1980s, it was becoming clear that acid rain was causing serious damage to woodlands, rivers, crops and historical buildings in Britain. In 1989, an all-party committee of MPs published details of ancient forests and historical monuments that had already been affected, and recommended that urgent action be taken to control emissions of sulphur dioxide from power stations (thought to be the main cause of acid rain).

The Department of the Environment rejected the report, arguing that the damage to national forests was entirely due to the droughts of the mid-1980s, even though the latter part of that decade had been exceptionally wet. It also asserted that there was no connection between industrial pollution and declining stocks of fish in rivers and the North Sea.

The CEGB, which then ran the power stations, argued that existing controls on sulphur dioxide emissions were adequate, and that any additional measures were bound to put up the price of electricity. Managers in other industries also warned that anti-pollution measures would cost jobs.

No serious measures were taken until 1997, when up to 90 per cent of British woodland was already dying, and the Houses of Parliament at Westminster had started to dissolve.

CEGB, the Department of the Environment, heritage and environmental groups.

▲ An enactment of a demonstration, with speeches, slogans and banners, in which groups campaign for an end to acid rain, or for the preservation of their jobs.

▲ A short play in which the issues are presented in a way understandable to a younger audience.

All of these options could be recorded on cassette or videotape, or in photographic form.

Conclusion

Help the children to evaluate their work, perhaps using recordings of their presentations. Discuss ways in which their concerns regarding these issues might be addressed in the world beyond the classroom.

Suggestion(s) for extension

This activity could be extended into a more ambitious dramatic presentation for an assembly or parents' evening. It could also lead to extensions in language and artwork in the form of letter-writing and the development of campaign literature such as brochures, posters and hand-outs.

Suggestion(s) for support

Underlining, patterning and sequencing activities will help the children to get to grips with the opposing ideas in the text.

The notes developed in these activities can then be worked into dialogues between the different people involved (for example, a power worker, a forester and an MP who has both a power station and endangered buildings in his constituency). These dialogues can be represented as cartoons, produced through shared writing if necessary, and used as blueprints for the drama activities outlined above.

Assessment opportunities

This activity will provide evidence of the children's ability to appreciate opposing ideas, and of the fluency with which they can express either their own point of view or an assumed one.

Opportunities for IT

Children could work in groups at the computer to write, redraft and organise their role-playing situation. The word processor is a good tool for helping children to structure their argument into a logical sequence. If one pupil, or an adult helper, has good keyboard skills the group's original ideas can be typed on to the screen as a form of brainstorming activity. These ideas can then be sequenced into a framework for more extended writing on each point. Alternatively, children could write the script for a short play or interview using the techniques outlined in 'Tabulating information' on page 63.

Display ideas

A photographic, video and audio record of the presentations can be displayed alongside relevant texts.

Other aspects of the English PoS covered

Speaking and listening – 1a, b, c; 2a, b; 3a, b.
Writing – 1a, b, c; 2a, b, c, d, e; 3a, b, c.

Reference to photocopiable sheets

Photocopiable pages 147 and 148 are suitable for this activity, and can also be used for sequencing, underlining, tabulation, patterning and modelling. A writing frame (see the activity on page 64), designed to enable children to produce a 'discussion document' on this issue, is included on page 149.

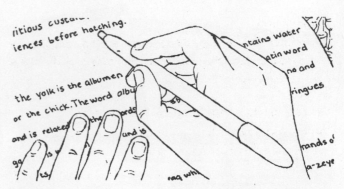

DELETION

To help children to focus on selected emphases in information texts, and on vocabulary selection.

†† *The whole class or groups, working in pairs (or small groups).*

🕐 *20 to 40 minutes.*

Key background information

As with the deletion activities for narrative prose, the aim of this activity is for children to reconstruct a passage by reflecting on their background knowledge and on the content of the remaining text. Two crucial principles should be borne in mind: alternatives for some or all of the deleted items should be possible, and the prepared passage must be open-ended enough to promote discussion. If these are neglected, the activity can become an unsatisfying gap-filling exercise.

Preparation

Select a text, or a range of texts, matched to the different reading abilities of your groups (some of the photocopiable texts may be suitable for this purpose). Make deletions based on those aspects of the text that you want the children to focus on. These might include technical vocabulary, key concepts, or particular parts of speech. Leave the opening paragraph intact and delete no more than 10 per cent of the words in the passage. Make a copy of the text for each pair of children, and one large copy so that you can demonstrate the procedure to the whole group.

Resources needed

See above.

What to do

Introduction

Talk to the children about the subject matter of the texts, so that their background knowledge is activated. Display the text and read through it with the children. Help them to identify suitable candidates for the first two or three deletions, prompting with intonation and directing their attention to available clues. Point out that clues to a particular item might occur later in the text, so it is important to read the whole text first and to scan forwards and backwards when discussing each item. Emphasise that there might be more than one suitable candidate for each space.

Development

Distribute the texts and allow the children plenty of time to discuss them. While they are working, remind them (if necessary) of the principles outlined in your introduction.

Conclusion

Ask each pair of children to compare their reconstruction of the passage with that of another pair, and to discuss any

differences. Different versions can be read aloud to the class and evaluated by the children. When this has been done, show the original text to the class and talk about any differences between it and the versions they have made.

Suggestion(s) for extension

This is a versatile activity that can be extended in many ways. The restoration of deleted phrases, paragraphs, headings, captions from illustrations and labels from diagrams will all help children to focus on selected concepts and aspects of written language, as long as the principles mentioned above are borne in mind.

Suggestion(s) for support

Support can be provided by controlling the length and difficulty of the text, and the number and frequency of deletions. The task can be made easier if initial letters are left intact, or if the words deleted are supplied on a separate part of the sheet. If this is done, it might be useful to provide more words than spaces, so that children have greater scope for discussion.

The activity can be conducted as a shared reading with less experienced readers. The teacher should read the passage aloud and use 'voice pointing' (slightly exaggerated intonation) in order to indicate clues in the language patterns of the text. All responses can be given orally, and the children can then be invited to select appropriate words written on cards to fill the gaps in the text.

Assessment opportunities

This activity will provide evidence of the children's ability to use semantic and syntactic information to identify words. If initial letters are provided, evidence of phonic knowledge will also be available. The children's discussions will enable you to assess their ability to consider alternative solutions based on their appreciation of language patterns.

Opportunities for IT

Some children could undertake this activity on the computer. The original text could be produced using a word processor and children could type in the missing words, perhaps using a bold or italic style to highlight the places where the insertions have been made. These can be printed out and used for display purposes.

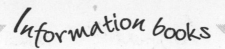

Display ideas

Alternative versions of the reconstructed text can be displayed alongside the original text and other visual material related to the subject matter.

Other aspects of the English PoS covered

Speaking and listening – 1a, b, c; 2a, b; 3b.
Writing – 1a; 2a, d, e; 3b, c.

MISSING PERSONS

To raise children's awareness of the social values embedded in texts.

†† *Whole-class introduction, followed by work in small groups.*

🕐 *30 minutes for the introductory session, then open-ended follow-up.*

Key background information

This activity gives the children an opportunity to reflect on changing social values by making a survey of the ways in which particular groups of people have been depicted in information books.

Preparation

Collect a range of information books on a single topic. This can be a broad topic such as food or the weather, or something more specialised such as Greek life or how machines work. It is important that you include out-of-date as well as contemporary material, and that it is suitable for a range of ages.

Resources needed

Books, writing materials, formats for collecting and displaying information, summary sheets.

What to do

Introduction

Inform the children that they are going to carry out a survey of information books, focusing initially on illustrations, in order to assess how they represent, or fail to represent, certain groups of people. Show the children a format for conducting a simple content analysis of illustrations, and use a short text in order to demonstrate how the spaces should be filled in. (Figure 1 provides one format for recording this.)

Development

Distribute the books, ensuring that each group receives a good range of styles, and the recording sheets. Within the groups, the children should work individually. If they are working with densely-illustrated books, ask them to focus on the larger illustrations. If some of the books are very long, it might be appropriate to focus on particular chapters.

Conclusion

Ask each group to pool their findings and to complete a summary sheet. Discuss the findings as a whole class. It is important to emphasise that some forms of omission are perfectly understandable in the context of the author's purpose, while others are more serious. For example, it is common to find books on Ancient Greece which omit the role of slaves in that culture, or books on the history of science which omit the role of women. Ask the children to share any findings on how more recent books differ from older ones.

Suggestion(s) for extension

This activity can be extended into a survey of the content of books as a whole, rather than just the illustrations. It can also lead to some interesting follow-up work in the form of report writing, letters to authors and illustrators, and the type of role-play activities outlined in 'Introducing writing frameworks' on page 64.

Suggestion(s) for support

The completion of the content analysis and summary sheets can be conducted through shared writing, with the teacher acting as scribe.

p18 **Subject:** American food
Text/text summary: Hamburgers are one of the most popular foods in America.
Content of illustration: A girl at a drive-in serving hamburgers to a family in a car.

p35 **Subject:** Indian food
Text/text summary: People in India like hot food. Special spices are added to food.
Content of illustration: A woman grinding spices by a wood-burning stove.

Figure 1

Assessment opportunities

Note the children's ability to scan the books and to make concise notes. Their awareness of the issues raised by the activity can be assessed during discussion, though some children might prefer to keep their opinions to themselves.

Opportunities for IT

Children could use the computer to create a report on each of the books surveyed. A master page for a report on each book could be created so that the reports are written to the same framework. This might best be achieved using a desktop publishing package so that children are restricted to writing within the frame provided for each section of the report. This ensures that the reports are concise and will all fit on to a single side of paper. It might also be possible to include example pictures by scanning them into the computer and then placing them into the report.

Display ideas

A range of books can be displayed, perhaps ordered by publication date, alongside the children's record sheets and written comments.

Other aspects of the English PoS covered

Speaking and listening – 1a, b, c; 2a, b.
Writing – 1a, b, c; 2a, c, d, e.

WRITING AN INFORMATION BOOK

To integrate children's skills in the reading and the writing of information texts, and to provide the teacher with evidence of the development of these skills.

†† *Children working individually within co-operative groups. Each child will be responsible for producing one book, but will be assisted by partners in redrafting and proof-reading the book.*

⏲ *1 hour for the introductory session, then open-ended follow-up.*

Key background information

This activity will be extended over several sessions. It should be initiated early in the term, perhaps a week or two into the study of a topic, when children have had the chance to decide on a personal area of interest within that topic.

Preparation

Decide on your own area of interest within a topic and prepare a mock- up of an information book on this theme. This should consist of:

▲ a preparatory sketch of the cover, including a blurb or summary of content, cover illustration, title design, picture and brief biography of the author;

▲ introductory pages (title page and bibliographical information);

▲ a list of contents;

▲ an outline of the chapters, with headings and sub-headings, spaces for illustrations and captions;

▲ a glossary;

▲ an index (to be completed when the book is finished).

Ask the children to identify areas of interest within the topic that they would like to pursue, and organise pairs or groups of three or four based on these choices.

Resources needed

Your mock-up book, book-making materials or home-made books, a range of published books and other materials related to the topic, access to a word processor, drawing materials.

What to do
Introduction

Tell the children that during the following weeks they will be making their own books about their chosen area of interest, and that the objective of the first session is to produce a mock-up which will be the blueprint for these books.

Show the children your mock-up book and a range of published texts related to the topic on which it is based. Indicate each feature of the published text, and show the children how you have incorporated these features into your mock-up book. Explain the choices you have made in identifying chapter sequence and content, headings and subheadings, illustrations and glossary entries.

Development

During the remainder of this lesson, the children should work on preparing their mock-up books. These should be shared at the end of the session and suggestions made for amendment and extension.

Subsequent sessions should be devoted to putting together the actual books. The preceding sequence of activities, incorporating the identification of current knowledge, question-setting and a range of procedures for note-making and reconstructing information from books, can be used to create the children's own texts. Throughout this procedure, the children can work co-operatively as editors and proof-readers.

When the books have been completed, ask the children to give them a proper classification number and a colour-coded label.

Conclusion

The completed books should be shared with the class and displayed in the school library. At the end of the year, selected books or photocopied sections of them can be added to the children's assessment portfolio.

Suggestion(s) for extension

Books can be produced in dual-language editions, as audio books, and as big books for younger audiences to share.

Suggestion(s) for support

This sequence of work can be carried out as a co-operative effort, with children taking responsibility for different parts of the task – for example, illustrating, indexing, writing the glossary, making notes, writing up the chapters. In this case, however, it will not be as easy to use the activity as a summative assessment of a range of information skills.

Children who are beginner writers can be supported through shared writing.

Assessment opportunities

The procedure outlined above can involve the whole range of skills mentioned in this chapter. Observation of the processes the children go through while making their books, and the quality of the final product, will enable you to assess how well they have integrated these skills.

Opportunities for IT

Children could put their book together using a range of IT tools. The books can be created using either a word processor or desktop publishing package; an alternative approach would be to create an electronic book using a multimedia authoring package.

If children are using a word processor the writing can be undertaken at the computer with drafting and editing taking place either at the screen or on paper back at a desk. Children will need to discuss the page layout, the position and use of pictures, the size and style of text that is appropriate for the intended audience for the book. Pictures can be included by either drawing them with an art or graphics package, scanning pictures drawn by the children themselves, using commercial clip art or pictures taken from CD-ROMs. Children may wish

to restrict the line lengths, or justify their text to remove the ragged righthand margin. They will also need to be shown how to 'force' a new page to make chapters, or leave spaces for pictures. This would be an ideal place to introduce page numbers and even headers and footers with more able pupils.

Part of the editing process will be to ensure that all spellings are correct and children could be introduced to a spell checker, the way it works and its limitations. On more sophisticated word processors it is even possible to check for correct grammar and this will pick up the correct use of things like 'their' and 'there'.

If an electronic book is to be created children will need to be shown how to use authoring software. Many children will have already seen such books on CD-ROM, and smaller versions on disk, and will understand how to move around the book. If they have not seen this type of resource before, try to show them examples before starting. Children will usually need some support for their first attempts, and organising computer sessions when there is parental or other help available is a good idea.

In writing such a book each page is linked to the previous and next page by an arrow or other picture (often called an icon). It is usually also possible to get back to the title or contents page in order to go to a different section altogether. This initial structure could be set up by the teacher in advance so that children have only to make the links to each new page as they write the book.

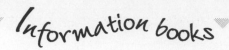
The book can include text, which is entered, edited and formatted in the same way as with most word processors. However, the text is usually placed into a frame which can be moved around the page to create the desired format. Pictures can be added from scanned photographs, children's drawings or other illustrations, directly from art or computer drawing packages, from commercial clip art collections or from CD-ROMs.

It is even possible for children to read the story and to include their own voices as each new page appears on the screen or as children click on the words. This is accomplished using a microphone linked to the computer which digitally records the children's voices. Other sound effects can be recorded and added in a similar way, so that when the reader clicks on the word 'dog' you hear it bark. If sounds are added the files created can be very large so unless you have a hard disk to store the book on it may not fit on to a floppy disk. The final story can also be printed out (minus sound effects of course) so that children can make a hard copy to keep.

Display ideas
Children's completed books can be displayed in the library. A photographic or video record of the stages involved in making the books would provide a useful resource for children in subsequent years, and serve as a demonstration to parents of the work done in the school.

Other aspects of the English PoS covered
Speaking and listening – 1a, b, c; 2a, b; 3b.
Writing – 1a, b, c; 2a, b, c, d, e; 3a, b, c.

 # LIBRARY RESEARCH

To provide an opportunity for children to demonstrate their level of competence in deriving information from books.

†† *Small groups of four to six children in the library, observed by the teacher.*

🕐 *30 minutes.*

Key background information
This activity mirrors the set of library games outlined at the beginning of the chapter, and is aimed at finding out how effective these and subsequent activities have been in developing the children's skills in using information books. The activity is best carried out at the end of a term or half-term, in preparation for the topic which is to follow after the break.

Preparation
Prepare a set of questions or information tasks, written on individual cards, which are related to the topic to be studied during the next term or half-term. These should be of a fairly

general nature. (For example: 'Find three ways in which Ancient Greek civilisation affects the way we live today' or 'What are the advantages and disadvantages of motor transport?') Ensure that the questions are at a suitable level for your children, and that the library contains adequate resources to enable the questions or tasks to be addressed.

Resources needed
Question cards; appropriate books.

What to do
Take each group into the library separately and give each child a card. Explain that you want them to try to answer the question or to perform the task on the card without help, using the organisational resources of the library and of the books themselves.

Observe the children as they work; note their ability to use the classification system and subject index, and features of the books such as the contents page and index, to guide their search.

The children can convey their findings to you orally, or in note form.

Suggestion(s) for extension
The work that the children do in the course of this activity should form part of the basis for the knowledge map which is constructed as a preliminary activity for the next class topic (see 'Identifying current knowledge' on page 52). Books that the children have found, and notes that they have made, can form part of an initial stimulus display to arouse interest in this topic.

Suggestion(s) for support
Intervene only if the children show signs of frustration or confusion. Support should be offered in the form of prompt questions and reminders about the function of information organisers and signposts in the library, and in the books themselves. If this activity takes place after a term or half-term in which the children have been engaged in the kind of tasks outlined in this chapter, such prompts should help to develop their library skills. An assessment of what children are able to do with teacher support is as important as an assessment of what they are able to do independently.

Assessment opportunities
Notes made during this activity will enable you to plan appropriate tasks for the children in future lessons.

Display ideas
See above.

Other aspects of the English PoS covered
Speaking and listening – 1a, b, c; 2a, b; 3c.
Writing – 1a, b, c; 2a.

Poetry

Children seem to have a natural urge to explore the field of poetry. Play involving the rhythms and sonorities of oral language develops very early in children, and an appreciation of rhyme and alliteration has consistently been acknowledged as a robust predictor of later reading ability.

In this chapter, children are encouraged to appreciate published poetry, widening the range of their interests from the comical and frightening poems that most children seem to revel in to a wider scope of emotions and issues. This involves the production of class and personal anthologies, the planning of an eclectic programme of performance and display, and the establishment of a prominent place for poetry in class discussion.

The poetic potential of ambient language is also examined; the rhythmic qualities of speech and print extracts and of phonological phenomena like rhyme, alliteration and onomatopoeia are used to foster curiosity and delight in language, and to forge links between the reading process and the arts of music, drama and dance.

READING

CREATING A PLACE FOR POETRY

To stimulate children's interest in poetry by involving them in a programme of reading and sharing favourite poems.

†† *Whole class.*

🕐 *30 minutes.*

Key background information

This is a planning and attention-focusing activity which should take place as early in the school year as possible. Storytime at the end of the day might be a good time to conduct this activity.

The initial stimulus is made up of your own collection of poetic material, so it is a good idea to start considering this some months in advance, perhaps keeping a notebook to record linguistic 'found objects' that strike you as poetically appealing.

Preparation

Make a collection of your favourite anthologies and write out large versions of your favourite poems on chart paper. Try to make sure that at least some of these are likely to appeal to the children that you teach. Do not confine yourself to published poems: items such as song lyrics, nursery rhymes, slogans, jingles and fragments of memorable language that have struck you as having a poetic quality should also be included. Visual material related to all these items, including photographs, objects and pictures of poets, might also be useful. Display this material in the classroom a day or two before the session begins, and draw the children's attention to it.

Resources needed

A collection of poems and related items.

What to do

Conduct a reading-aloud session in which you share your favourite poems with the children. Invite them to give their responses to the poems, before telling them what it is about the poems and the qualities in them that appeal to you. Show them the supporting material that you have collected and explain its connection to the words you have read aloud.

Ask the children to share any poems that they know with the class. At some point, it is likely that somebody will raise the question as to what counts as a poem and what does not. Ask the children for their own opinion on this, stressing that it is a question with no simple answer, though some reference by you to the idea of intense or memorable language might be helpful.

Explain to the children that you would like them to help plan some ways in which poetry can be shared by the class throughout the year. Suggest that they can help in the following ways:

▲ Planning work on an *ad hoc* basis with partners to present favourite poems to the class, perhaps accompanied by music or various types of illustration.

▲ Identifying an area for the display of poems selected, illustrated and handwritten by the children.

▲ Contributing to an illustrated class anthology.

▲ Making a collection of poems on audiotape, including examples collected from the school community in a variety of languages and dialects.

▲ Keeping a record of poems in their personal journals, which can be shared at set times during the week.

▲ Keeping a notebook of fragments of interesting language.

▲ Writing to contemporary poets whose work they enjoy.

▲ Contributing library books to a permanent but changing display of published anthologies.

▲ Selecting poems on an individual basis to memorise and recite.

▲ Keeping an eye open for photographs, drawings and snippets of writing related to poems on display in anthologies or on walls.

▲ Keeping an eye open for poetry or verse in various places: newspapers, advertising sites, graveyards, on television, on walls.

Make a list of the ideas suggested by the children and make sure that the practicable ones are built into the routine life of the class as soon as possible.

Suggestion(s) for extension

Many of the activities in the rest of this chapter present extensions of this basic activity.

Suggestion(s) for support

Children who are not interested in poetry, or who have had their interest dulled by ridicule or previous teaching experiences, might be encouraged to participate if the teacher demonstrates an interest in the whole range of poetic language rather than just its bookish manifestations. Popular

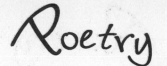

songs and chants, graffiti, jokes in verse and playground games are all sources that should be explored.

Assessment opportunities

Children's contributions to the activities outlined above can be recorded. Written work and other graphic materials can be added to a portfolio of favourite poems compiled by the teacher with the child's help.

Opportunities for IT

A word processor could be used for any of the activities involving the presentation of poetry. Children could experiment with a variety of fonts or fomats in presenting their favourite poems in an interesting or different way. They could, for example, include a picture or use a picture as a background to the poem so that the text overprints the picture.

Using a multimedia authoring package children could present an electronic anthology of their favourite poems. These could include text, pictures, speech (children reading the poem) and even sampled music. Pictures can be scanned from photographs, magazines or from children's own drawings. They can also be created using an art or drawing package. This work takes time to complete and put together and could be extended over a whole project on poetry.

Other aspects of the English PoS covered

Speaking and listening – 1a, b, c, d; 2a, b; 3a, b, c.

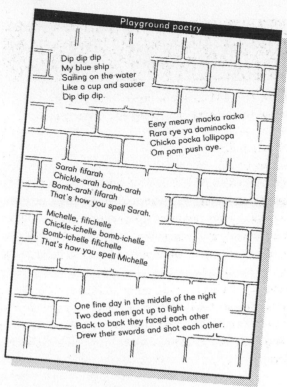

Playground poetry

Dip dip dip
My blue ship
Sailing on the water
Like a cup and saucer
Dip dip dip.

Eeny meany macka racka
Rara rye ya dominacka
Chicka pocka lollipopa
Om pom push aye.

Sarah fifarah
Chickle-arah bomb-arah
Bomb-arah fifarah
That's how you spell Sarah.

Michelle, fifichelle
Chickle-ichelle bomb-ichelle
Bomb-ichelle fifichelle
That's how you spell Michelle

One fine day in the middle of the night
Two dead men got up to fight
Back to back they faced each other
Drew their swords and shot each other.

as a child, especially if these are likely to be unfamiliar to the children.

Selecting from these sources, make poster-sized copies of individual playground rhymes and A4 copies of a selection of such rhymes.

Resources needed

See above. Photocopiable page 150 can be used to complement your own findings. A home-made blank book is needed for the anthology.

What to do
Introduction

Explain to the children that they are going to carry out some research into a particular way in which children have used language through the ages. If you were able to prepare a tape, play this now. Otherwise, show the children the posters and lead them in a group choral reading of the texts. Include both familiar and unfamiliar rhymes in these recitations. Suggest to the children that one of the objectives of the research should be to publish an anthology of such rhymes, including those which their parents and grandparents chanted when they were young.

Development

Hand out the A4 rhyme selections and allow the children time to read and discuss these. They should try to sort the rhymes into their own categories, based on discussion of where and when the rhymes are likely to be recited; for example, nonsense rhymes, insults, dipping games and so on. Ask them to identify rhymes that they have not encountered before, and draw their attention to regional and historical variations in rhymes that they are familiar with.

PLAYGROUND POETRY

To compile a class anthology of contemporary and historical playground rhymes and songs through reading and research.

†† *Small groups or the whole class divided into small research groups.*

🕐 *A starter lesson of about 45 minutes followed by open-ended research.*

Key background information

This activity will enhance children's awareness of playful uses of language and of patterns of continuity and change in the oral traditions of the playground. It can easily be built into a topic on a historical theme.

Preparation

Try to read *The Lore and Language of Schoolchildren* by Iona and Peter Opie (OUP, 1959), *The People in the Playground* by Iona Opie (OUP, 1993), and any other sources of playground oral traditions that you can find. You should also try to record on tape (or at least transcribe) some examples of your pupils' own traditional rhymes and songs before the lesson; and remember to include ones that you used yourself as a child, especially if these are

The children can then select a rhyme from the sheet or from their own repertoire to write out and illustrate. This work can be annotated with information on the context in which the rhyme is normally used.

Conclusion

Set the children the task of asking their parents, grandparents and other adult friends for rhymes that they recited as children, and for information about when and how the rhyme was used. Rhymes from different parts of the world will be of particular interest, as will regional variants of British rhymes. These can be written up, illustrated and annotated in subsequent lessons, and added to the anthology. Children who speak languages other than English can contribute dual-language versions of rhymes.

Suggestion(s) for extension

Fluent readers can be given chapters of the background information books (see above) to comb through independently. To focus their explorations, you could ask them to look for unfamiliar variants of familiar rhymes, or for rhymes of a particular kind.

The research could be extended by encouraging the children to write to schools in different parts of the country, or different parts of the world, explaining the project and asking for contributions to add to the anthology. This would provide a wealth of opportunities for a range of purposeful reading and writing activities, including the use of e-mail.

Suggestion(s) for support

The entire lesson could be conducted orally, with the teacher guiding less able readers through a shared reading of the poster texts.

The children could also be set the task of recording (on tape) appropriate rhymes popular among different age groups in the school. These could be collected in the playground, or, more manageably, in a quiet corner of the school.

Assessment opportunities

Observations of oral reading, handwriting and research skills.

Opportunities for IT

The anthology of playground poetry could be extended by including poems from schools around the country or across the world. If the school has access to electronic mail through CAMPUS or the Internet it is possible to post messages asking for examples of poetry. These will arrive as ASCII text and so can be included in a word processed anthology of playground poetry.

Display ideas

As well as being included in the anthology, individual rhymes can be mounted and displayed alongside appropriate playground photographs, both contemporary and historical.

Other aspects of the English PoS covered

Writing – 1a, b, c; 2a, b, c, d; 3a, c.
Speaking and listening – 1a, b, c; 2b; 3a, b.

Reference to photocopiable sheet

Photocopiable page 150 provides a selection of appropriate rhymes to kindle interest.

NURSERY RHYMES

To create a classroom anthology of nursery rhymes, through reading and research.

†† *Whole class, or the class divided into research groups.*

🕐 *An initial lesson of about 45 minutes, followed by open-ended research.*

Key background information

The purpose of this session is to enhance children's awareness of nursery rhymes and of patterns of continuity and change in these traditions. The activity might form part of a topic on a historical theme.

Preparation

Read through *The Oxford Dictionary of Nursery Rhymes* edited by Iona and Peter Opie (Oxford University Press, 1992), *Mother Goose Comes to Cable Street* by Rosemary

Tones and Andrew Mann (Puffin, 1980) and any other sources of traditional and modern nursery rhymes that you can find. Make a display of nursery rhyme collections, and in the week before the lesson takes place, ensure that the children have plenty of opportunities to browse through it.

Resources needed
See above. Photocopiable page 151 provides a starter selection of nursery rhymes. A home-made blank book is needed for the anthology. The following books might also feature in your display, alongside the two already mentioned:

No Hickory No Dickory No Dock by John Agard and Grace Nichols (Puffin, 1992).

The Helen Oxenbury Nursery Rhyme Book selected by Brian Alderson (Collins, 1990).

Traditional Scottish Nursery Rhymes selected by Norah and William Montgomerie (Chambers, 1990).

Fee Fi Fo Fum, based on the Opies' collection, illustrated by Raymond Briggs (Picture Puffin, 1969).

Pop Goes the Weasel by Robert Crowther (Walker, 1987).

Mother Goose by Tomie De Paola (Methuen, 1984).

What to do
Introduction
Ask each child to select a favourite nursery rhyme that they would like to read aloud and to talk about. Allow them time to do this, then read aloud a favourite rhyme of your own, and share with the children anything you think they might find interesting about the history of these rhymes (*The Oxford Dictionary of Nursery Rhymes* is an excellent source book for such information). Explain to the children that the purpose of the lesson is to begin work compiling a class anthology of nursery rhymes, including examples to be collected from outside the school.

Development
Discuss with the whole class the design of a suitable format for collecting nursery rhymes from family and friends, together with information about the context in which each rhyme was learned and recited. As with the playground poetry project on page 77, the research can be extended by corresponding by post or e-mail with schools in other parts of the country and the world. If you have decided to do this, compose with the class an appropriate covering letter at this point. The layout of the anthology should also be agreed before compilation begins.

Conclusion
The children can write out and illustrate their chosen nursery rhymes. These can be mounted and included in the anthology.

Suggestion(s) for extension
As with the playground poetry project, fluent readers can be given chapters of the resource books to comb through independently. To focus their explorations, you could ask them to look for unfamiliar variants of familiar rhymes or for rhymes of a particular kind.

Suggestion(s) for support
Poster-sized copies of selected rhymes can be made and used for shared reading. These can then be cut up into lines or stanzas and sequenced by the children. When they have gained sufficient confidence to read their chosen rhymes independently, the children can write them out and illustrate them for inclusion in the class anthology.

Assessment opportunities
The teacher will be able to observe handwriting skills and reading fluency in the course of this activity.

Opportunities for IT
The anthology could be written using a word processor or desktop publishing package. As in 'Playground poetry' on page 77, electronic mail could be used to extend the collection of nursery rhymes from around the country or the world. Children could use an art package to create their own illustrations for inclusion in the anthology, or could draw them and use a scanner to make a digital version which can be included with their writing. As an alternative to a printed anthology, an electronic book of the poetry using a multimedia authoring package can be created.

Display ideas
As well as publication in the anthology, individual rhymes can be displayed alongside photographs, children's artwork and traditional and modern published illustrations.

Other aspects of the English PoS covered
Speaking and listening – 1a, b, c; 2a, b; 3a, b.
Writing – 1a, b, c; 2a, b, c, d, e; 3a, b, c.

Reference to photocopiable sheet
Photocopiable page 151 provides a 'starter collection' of nursery rhymes.

RIDDLES

*To read and attempt to solve some traditional riddles.
To compile a riddle collection, including ones that the
children have written themselves.*

†† *Whole class or small groups.*

🕐 *45 minutes, then open-ended follow-up.*

Key background information

Riddles are a literary form with a long history and a wide
scope. They are found in such early English texts as *The
Exeter Book* (c. 940) and in the oral traditions of cultures
throughout the world. Their appeal is perhaps based on a
universal love of wordplay and fascination with metaphor.

Spelling riddles are traditional word games in verse form,
which require readers to focus closely on the letter patterns
in given words in order to identify a hidden word.

Riddles were once very popular in children's comics and
periodicals, so this activity could fit into a topic on either
word games or the media. The
purpose of this activity is to further
the children's enjoyment of these
dimensions of language, and to
engage them in deriving meaning
from writing which is deliberately
puzzling and ambiguous. It could
also be built into a programme
of spelling activities.

Preparation

If you are not already familiar
with this field, read up on the
history and scope of traditional
riddles. Prepare a poster-sized
version of photocopiable
sheet 152 if you are working
with a small group, or
duplicate sufficient copies for
a larger group. The
photocopiable page gives
examples of both traditional
riddles, which conceal the
identity of an object, and spelling riddles that conceal the
spelling of a particular word. Collect a variety of jokes which
rely for their impact on wordplay, and other examples of
traditional and spelling riddles.

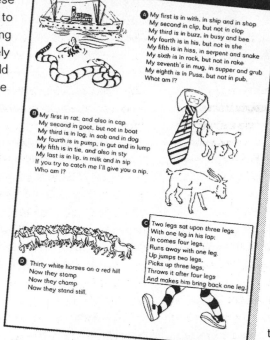

Resources needed

See above. A good resource for jokes is *The Ha Ha Bonk
Book* by Janet and Allan Ahlberg (Puffin, 1982); and for
riddles, *The Exeter Book of Riddles* by Kevin Crossley-Holland
(Penguin, 1993). Old comics or annuals featuring riddles
would also be a valuable resource, together with examples
of other old-fashioned and modern word games.

What to do
Introduction

If looking at traditional riddles, start off by telling the children
some jokes of the sort: 'What dog keeps the best time? *A
watch dog.*' Invite them to tell their own jokes. Discuss how
such jokes rely for their impact on the double or multiple
meanings of certain words. Proceed to more involved
conundrums of the type: 'I have a face but no eyes, a voice
but no mouth; what am I?' *A clock.* Encourage the children,
working individually or in pairs, to make up their own jokes
and share them with the class.

If looking at spelling riddles, present your collection of
word games to the children and allow them time to play the
games and talk about them. Work through the conventions
of one or two of the spelling riddles with the group, then
leave them to work independently on the rest.

Development

Distribute the copies of photocopiable page 152 if you are
working with a whole class, or display the poster-sized version
if you are working with a small group.
Read through one of the traditional
riddles with the children, and help them
to work it out. Discuss how the
traditional riddles work in a similar
manner to the jokes that you have
shared. Be sure that the children
understand how spelling riddles work
before asking them to complete the
spelling puzzles on the activity sheet.
Allow the children plenty of time to work
out both types of riddle.

Let the children suggest answers to
spelling riddles, and work with them on the
composition of new ones, trying as far as
possible to use their ideas for the clue words
and the rhyming couplets. Then allow
enough time for the children to write their
own riddles.

When this has been done, a discussion of
the different ways in which the riddles are
related to each other (for example, by
apparent age, by structure, by level of
difficulty, and so on), should afford an opportunity for you to
talk to the children about the historical and cultural scope of
riddles.

Conclusion

Share the riddles with the rest of the class. These can be
collected to make a class anthology. Invite children who have
not participated in this activity to make up their own examples
of riddles, and to try to collect various types of riddle from
whatever sources they have access to and add these to the
anthology.

Suggestion(s) for support

The riddles on photocopiable page 152 can be recited as a group reading before discussion. The riddle frameworks on this page can be completed by children working in collaboration with the teacher or a more able peer.

When working with spelling riddles, obviously the shorter the target word and the shorter the clue words, the easier the riddle will be. By working in a group with a riddle enlarged to a size that all the children can see, you can help the children to build the target word by colour-coding the letters in each of the clue words given.

Suggestion(s) for extension

Fluent readers might be interested in reading and attempting to solve longer riddles translated from Anglo-Saxon poetry. (Showing the children the original text alongside the translation should enhance their awareness of historical change in the English language.) They might even be inspired to try writing riddles in more involved verse forms for themselves. *A Selection of Anglo-Saxon Poetry* (Faber) features many such examples.

If any of the children are particularly interested in this verse form, they can be challenged to write spelling riddles for the longest words that they can think of.

Assessment opportunities

Note the children's appreciation of the multiple meanings of words and their ability to use this aspect of language creatively. Evidence of the appreciation of metaphor and the ability to use it might also be noted. Working on spelling riddles will highlight children's ability to identify spelling patterns.

Opportunities for IT

Children could use a word processor to originate and edit their riddles. They could then use the formatting facilities of the word processor to present the riddle in an interesting way. The riddle collection could be created using a word processor or desktop publishing package. However, a more entertaining approach would be to use a multimedia authoring package. If children work in pairs to research or write a riddle, the electronic anthology could begin with a list of 'authors'. By clicking on the author's name their riddle would be presented on screen. The framework could be set up in advance by the teacher and over a period of time each pair of children could be allowed time to write their riddle on to the page, altering the text styles and the page layout to suit the length of their riddle. They could even add illustrations scanned from their drawn pictures or created using an art package.

Each riddle could have its answer hidden on another page which is linked to the riddle page. Children would be presented with a riddle and asked to guess the answer. They could then click on a symbol which would give them the answer. Children could be recorded speaking their riddle, and its answer, and the recording could be stored with the written text so that the computer speaks the riddle as well as presenting it in a textual format. Clues could be provided in a similar way so that clicking on a clue symbol would provide more information to help the solver.

Display ideas

The children's own riddles can be published in an illustrated book, or displayed alongside traditional riddles and pictures of the objects represented by the answers to the riddles.

ask them to read out the words that they have come up with. Write these words out on the board or chart, then compose as short a sentence as you can using the words that have been offered. Ask the children to repeat the process with the same words, incorporating any other alliterative words that they can think of.

Other aspects of the English PoS covered
Writing – 1a, b, c; 2a, b, c, d, e; 3a, b, c.
Speaking and listening – 1a, b, c; 2a; b; 3a, b.

Reference to photocopiable sheet
Photocopiable page 152 provides a starter collection of riddles. The answers are given below.
Spelling riddles: A – hibiscus; B – agouti.
Traditional riddles: C – a man on a stool holding a leg of lamb, which is stolen by a dog; D – teeth and gums.

ALLITERATIVE WORD WEBS

To focus children's attention on the initial letters of words, and to explore the phenomenon of alliteration.
Whole class, working individually, in pairs or in groups.
10 to 15 minutes.

Key background information
In this activity children will brainstorm ideas for words beginning with a particular letter or blend of letters, and then attempt to compose stories, poems or tongue-twisters incorporating these words. This is a valuable task to set on a daily basis, perhaps during the first ten or fifteen minutes of the school day.

Preparation
Seek out any written materials which rely on alliteration for their effectiveness. These might include tongue-twisters, poems or extracts from poems, snippets of stories, proverbs, and political or advertising slogans. Share these with the class and ask them to try to describe what is distinctive about these pieces of speech or writing.

Resources needed
Notebooks and writing materials.

What to do
Write an initial letter or blend of letters on the board or on a chart, and around it write a number of words which begin with the same letter or blend (as shown in Figure 1). Ask the children to write out as many words as they can that begin in the same way. Allow about five minutes for this activity, then

Suggestion(s) for extension
Ask the children to collect examples of alliteration from their reading and from environmental print. Discuss the different effects produced by alliteration of particular letters or letter blends.

Suggestion(s) for support
Provide materials for the children to scan for appropriate words: simple dictionaries, stories, poems, comics and adverts.

Assessment opportunities
Phonic knowledge and vocabulary can be assessed through children's contributions to the word web. Creativity and sensitivity to the possibilities of alliteration can be assessed through their compositions.

Opportunities for IT
Children could publish their collection of tongue-twisters and alliterative material using a word processor or desktop publishing package.

Display ideas
A collection of tongue-twisters, poems and other alliterative material composed by the children can be displayed alongside published material of the same type.

Other aspects of the English PoS covered
Speaking and listening – 1a, b; 2a.
Writing – 1a, b; 2d; 3c.

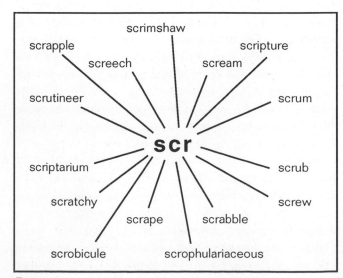

Figure 1

ALLITERATIONS LOST AND FOUND

To enhance children's appreciation of alliteration and general interest in the phonology of language.

†† *Selected groups working individually or as partners.*

🕓 *20 minutes.*

Key background information
The ability to appreciate alliteration has been identified as an important indicator of reading ability. In this activity children will restore a text from which selected initial letters and blends of letters have been deleted, and discuss the effects produced by alliteration.

Preparation
Select two poems in which alliteration plays a part, preferably on a theme related to current topic work. Prepare a copy of each poem in which the initial letter or letter blend of the alliterated words has been deleted.

Resources needed
Poems prepared as above, and other intact alliterative poems to read aloud. Suggested poems: 'Grim and Gloomy' by James Reeves and 'The Whales Off Wales' by X.J. Kennedy, both in *Wordspells*, selected by Judith Nicholls (Faber, 1987); 'Midnight Snow' by Gareth Owen, from *My Granny is a Sumo Wrestler* (Lions, 1994); and 'Working in Winter' by John Mole, from *Catching the Spider* (Blackie, 1990).

What to do
Before reading the intact poems aloud, discuss their titles and ask the children to think about what the subjects of the poems might be. Ask them to listen out for any special 'sound effects' in the poems.

Read the poems aloud to the children, and ask them to share their immediate responses. If nobody draws attention to the alliteration, emphasise this aspect with a rereading, relating it to such familiar phenomena as tongue-twisters.

Hand out the amended poems and ask the children to read them both silently and aloud, and to discuss what the missing words might be. Given the clues provided by the theme, rhyme and metre of the poem, it should not be too difficult to identify the original words. When this has been done, encourage the children to read the poems aloud in their restored versions, and then to play about with the sound of the words by substituting alternative initial letters and blends, and savouring the effects.

Suggestion(s) for extension
Children can seek out other poems in which alliteration features, as well as collecting tongue-twisters and other sayings which demonstrate this aspect of language. Research outside the classroom might turn up old advertising slogans (Graded grains make finer flour), proverbs (Many a mickle makes a muckle), idioms (Bed and breakfast), similes (Right as rain), nicknames (Dirty Den) and a wealth of tabloid newspaper headlines (Leamington elects loony left leader). Children might enjoy playing substitution games with these items.

Fluent readers might enjoy the dense use of alliteration by poets like Gerard Manley Hopkins and Dylan Thomas. 'Inversnaid' by the former and 'Fern Hill' by the latter would make good introductory reading to their less accessible work.

Suggestion(s) for support
Conduct this activity as an immediate follow-up to the 'Alliterative word webs' activity on page 82. Make enlarged versions of the poems and read through them with the children, using oral cloze and voice accentuation to highlight the deletions.

Assessment opportunities
Observe children's ability to suggest appropriate letters and blends, to create new words by substitution, and to appreciate the effects of this type of language play.

Other aspects of the English PoS covered
Speaking and listening – 1a, b, c; 2a, b; 3b.

RHYME COLLECTING

To enhance children's phonological awareness, and to encourage them to reflect on the use of rhyme in media texts, particularly for the purposes of advertising.

†† *Whole class or small groups.*

🕐 *45 minutes.*

Key background information
In this activity, children will scan a variety of texts looking for examples of rhyme, and will discuss the popularity of rhyme in print media and in oral tradition.

Preparation
Collect as wide a variety of texts as you can (these should include newspapers, comics, magazines, greetings cards and, if possible, video and audiotapes of TV and radio adverts and trailers). Scan these yourself for examples of rhyme to make sure that the children will have enough data to work on. You should also collect examples from advertising hoardings, shop displays and public notices.

A week or so before the lesson, explain the objective of the lesson to the children and ask them to collect their own examples of 'environmental rhymes'.

Resources needed
See above.

What to do
Introduction
Present the children with two or three examples of advertising rhymes, and ask them to identify their sources. The children can then contribute their own examples, and talk about what they find appealing or unappealing about such rhymes.

Development
Give the group, or groups within the class, the collection of materials that you have made, augmented by whatever data they have brought in themselves.

Ask them to scan the material, cutting out or writing out on index cards any examples of rhymes that they find, and making a note of the context in which they find them.

This activity can form the basis of a discussion as to why rhyme is so popular as an 'attention attractor' and source of amusement. You could suggest that the children try sorting the rhymes into categories according to their purposes, structures or intended audiences.

Conclusion
Ask the children to select two or three examples of rhyming messages, translate them into non-rhyming equivalents, and then discuss how the two types of message differ. This could also be related to the children's experiences of rhyming and non-rhyming poetry.

Suggestion(s) for extension
Children who show a particular interest in this area can be helped to investigate the wide scope of uses to which rhyme has been put in everyday language. Apart from the long history of rhyme in advertising, the following areas might be looked into:
▲ epitaphs;
▲ rhyming proverbs from a variety of oral traditions;
▲ rhyming political slogans;
▲ the use of rhyming couplets by Shakespeare and other dramatists to close scenes in plays;
▲ rhyming mnemonics ('i before e except after c' and so on);
▲ cartoon strip stories with rhyming narrative;
▲ the use of rhyme in newspaper headlines, particularly in the tabloids.

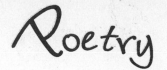
Children can also be encouraged to seek out examples of other types of phonological wordplay in these sources: for example, alliteration, assonance (vowel rhymes) and puns.

Suggestion(s) for support
If you are working with children who find it difficult to scan through material, go through a sample of the texts in advance and highlight examples of rhyme usage with a marker pen. The children can be asked to seek out the highlighted text and to identify what it is that these extracts have in common. When this has been done, they can then be given small expanses of unmarked text to scan through for themselves. The discussion activity can then proceed as outlined above. The 'translation' of rhyming into non-rhyming information can be conducted as a shared writing activity.

Assessment opportunities
Note the children's ability to scan text, to appreciate rhyme and to reflect critically on the influence of rhyme in persuasive text.

Opportunities for IT
Children could work with a word processor to translate the rhyming message into a non-rhyming version. They could mark and copy the original rhyme to the bottom of the screen where they can work on it, editing it and checking it against the original at the top of the screen to make sure it still gives the same message.

Children might also like to experiment with the speech facilities on some word processors so that they can listen to the original and edited version of their work. This will also create an opportunity to talk with children about the limitations of speech on the computer.

Display ideas
Examples of text from newspapers and magazines can be mounted and displayed in a matrix of the type shown below.

Other aspects of the English PoS covered
Speaking and listening – 1a, b, c; 2a, b; 3b.
Writing – 1a, b, c; 2d; 3a, c.

RHYMES IN THE PRINT MEDIA

Headlines	Adverts	Cartoons	Competitions

⬦ 💻 SAVOURING SOUNDS

To foster enjoyment of the phonological qualities of words and children's curiosity about these qualities.
†† *Whole class.*
🕐 *30-minute introductory session, then open-ended follow-up.*

Key background information
Phonological awareness, the realisation that spoken words consist of clusters of sounds that can be separated and recombined, has been identified by recent research as an important contributor to reading ability. The following sequence of activities looks at various ways of exploring the sounds of words in order to develop aesthetic appreciation of language as well as phonological awareness. The starting-point is an exploration of onomatopoeia, the way in which the sound and sense of certain words echo and reinforce each other.

Preparation
List as many onomatopoeic words as you can, and collect a selection of poems which emphasise onomatopoeia. Make a display of these and encourage the children to contribute to it. If the children are unfamiliar with the concept of onomatopoeia, a display in which words are grouped and illustrated according to such familiar categories as animal noises and watery sounds would be helpful.

Resources needed
Poems and words (as outlined above), written out, illustrated and displayed, with individual copies of poems for pairs of children, and sets of words copied on to cards for group sorting. Suggested poems: 'The Tin Can Band' by Margaret Mahy from *The Second Margaret Mahy Storybook* (Dent); a selection from *Noisy Poems* edited by Jill Bennett (OUP, 1989); 'Counting Out Rhyme' by Edna St Vincent Millais, from *Wordspells* edited by Judith Nicholls (Faber, 1993).

What to do
Hand out the collections of onomatopoeic word cards and invite the children to sort and group them freely: by origin (whisper, burp, spit, nag), by spelling pattern (whisper, wham, whirr, whippoorwill), or by sound quality (whisper, murmur, sigh, rustle).

Ask the children to extend the collection by contributing any words that they know which you might have omitted. Words from languages other than English are particularly valuable, as they demonstrate the universality of this phenomenon, and also highlight similarities and differences between languages. Any words that the children make up themselves to indicate environmental sounds that have not yet acquired dictionary status should also be welcomed. For

Extend the discussion to include other words, not necessarily onomatopoeic, that children simply like the sound of. Contribute one or two of your own and try to explain their appeal. Often this will have little to do with the actual meaning of the word. Encourage the children to represent these words graphically and then use them to make a display.

Suggestion(s) for extension

Independent readers who are particularly interested in this dimension of language can be helped to investigate the related phenomenon of *phonaesthesia*, the occurrence of the same consonant clusters in words of related meaning: slip, slime, slippery, slope, slump; crash, dash, rush, flash, gush. Though the sound and meaning relationship is not as obvious here as in clearly onomatopoeic words such as bang and groan, a connection is definitely suggested. Children can be encouraged to search dictionaries and thesauri for these word families, taking note not only of examples of the pattern but of exceptions also.

Suggestion(s) for support

Encourage children to brainstorm clusters of related onomatopoeic words, helping them by sharing poems and songs that feature this quality. The underlining of onomatopoeic words, the identification of shared spelling patterns, and compositional work with these words can all be done through shared reading and writing, with the teacher using enlarged texts and scribing the children's responses if necessary.

Assessment opportunities

This cluster of activities will enable you to observe the children's awareness of spelling-sound relationships, their ability to manipulate sound and word patterns, and their general interest in language.

Opportunities for IT

Children could use a word processor to enter their words and then use the font size and style to make them into expressive shapes. They may be able to experiment with the talking facilities of some computers to see if they can get the word processor to make the sound they want. This may mean adding extra consonants and vowels to the original spelling to make the computer give the right sound.

Children could also use an authoring package which allows speech files to be included. The onomatopoeic word can be spoken into a microphone which is linked to the computer. Using appropriate software the recorded sound can be edited and saved on to a disk. Children could then write the word on to the screen, alter its shape and style using the formatting facilities and then link it to a sound sample made with a microphone. Clicking on the word would then replay the sound linked to it. The format for such a presentation could

example, children might be encouraged to invent names for the sounds that computers make when they are saving data.

Encourage the children to make graphic representations of the words by writing them in expressive shapes and sizes and adding appropriate graphics (as shown in the illustration).

Show the children how selected combinations of the words can be repeated and modulated in varying rhythmic patterns to make 'concrete' or 'shape' poetry (where the poem's layout reflects its theme). Invite them to try this themselves.

Read the onomatopoeic poems aloud and ask the children for immediate responses. Hand out the copies of the poems and ask the children to read them silently, underlining the onomatopoeic words, and then to read the words aloud to each other.

be set up by the teacher in advance so that children are presented with a page with a frame for the word and another for the sound sample. Arrow symbols on each linked page would enable children to move backward and forwards through the sound samples.

Display ideas
See above.

Other aspects of the English PoS covered
Speaking and listening – 1a, b, c; 2a, b; 3b.
Writing – 1a, b, c; 2a, d, e; 3c.

NONSENSE

To deepen children's appreciation of nonsense poetry, and the relationships between sound and meaning in language.

†† *Whole class or small groups.*

🕐 *Four or five short sessions of 15–20 minutes each (which could be conducted at the ends of consecutive days or mornings), then open-ended follow-up.*

Key background information
This sequence of activities is connected to previous ones in this chapter, and will help to develop appreciation of phonology. As well as focusing on aspects of published nonsense poetry, it encourages children to experiment with sounds and meanings in their own writing.

Preparation
Collect as wide a range of nonsense poetry as you can. Make a display of it and draw the children's attention to it. Invite them to contribute to it from their own reading. Add any nonsense words that the children have encountered in their reading of poetry and prose, and any that they might have invented while doing the activities on alliteration and onomatopoeia.

Do the activity on photocopiable page 153, and make a note of the type of thinking involved in this activity. What aspects of phonology, meaning and grammar did you have to consider in completing the framework and the drawings?

Resources needed
Poems and words displayed as above and copied on to charts and cards, as for 'Savouring sounds' on page 85. Copies of photocopiable page 153. Suggested poems: 'Jabberwocky' by Lewis Carroll,

'A Quadrupremian Song' by Tom Hood, both in the *Book of Nonsense* selected by R.L. Green (Dent, 1956); 'My Last Nature Walk' by Adrian Mitchell, in *The Kingfisher Book of Comic Verse* selected by Roger McGough (Kingfisher, 1991); 'The First Men on Mercury' by Edwin Morgan, in *Strictly Private* chosen by Roger McGough (Penguin, 1988).

What to do
Hand out the nonsense word cards. Invite the children to group them in any way they like, read them to each other and exchange ideas about their meanings. These meanings could be illustrated and dictionary-style definitions written.

Read the poems aloud to the children and ask them to share their immediate responses. Hand out copies of the poems and allow the children time to read them silently and aloud to each other. Again, they can guess at possible meanings and illustrate words or passages from the poems.

Focus on the first stanza of 'Jabberwocky'. Read it aloud to the children and ask them to draw the scene depicted as you read it. Let them swap their drawings and talk about the different interpretations. When this has been done, read the rest of the poem to the children and discuss it.

Hand out copies of photocopiable page 153. Ask the children to read the stanza silently and to do the drawing, possibly amending the ideas that they had when first listening to the poem. Show them your own response to the completion activity and ask them to do this themselves. While the children are working on this, provide support for those who find it difficult to handle rhyme, metre and the coining of words.

Ask the children to compare their completions and drawings. Collect their responses to the activity and display them. Discuss similarities and differences between their responses, indicating the meanings suggested by word sounds and the different roles that the words are playing in the sentences. Terms like *noun*, *verb* and *adjective* might be used here if appropriate.

Suggestion(s) for extension
Help the children to compile an illustrated dictionary of the words that they have invented. (This links up with the 'Anti-scrabble' activity on page 123.) An anthology of favourite nonsense poems can be compiled.

Nonsense

Name _____

Date _____

▲ Read the verse below. How do you imagine the scene looks? Draw a picture of it in the box.

'Twas brillig, and the slithy toves
Did gyre and gimble in the wabe:
All mimsy were the borogoves,
And the mome raths outgrabe.

▲ Invent your own words to complete the verse, and draw a picture of the scene described in the box.

'Twas _____ and the _____
Did _____ and _____ in the _____
All _____ were the _____
And the _____

Suggestion(s) for support

Read through an enlarged copy of 'Jabberwocky', asking the children to visualise the scenes suggested by the words. Read the poem through again, pausing after each stanza to underline nonsense words and to allow the children to talk about their visualisations of these words.

Assessment opportunities

Note the children's readiness to experiment with language and to respond in individual ways to the stimuli presented.

Opportunities for IT

Children could compile a dictionary of nonsense words with their meanings using a word processor or desktop publishing package. Graphics could also be added to the dictionary if appropriate. This would give children an opportunity to look at the format of a traditional dictionary and the way in which styles are used to differentiate between the phonetic pronunciation of the word and its meaning. Children could be introduced to hanging indents to make the word stand out from the definition. In this sort of work children should be taught how to use tabs and reset margins rather than use the space bar to move text into desired positions.

Display ideas

See above.

Other aspects of the English PoS covered

Speaking and listening – 1a, b, c; 2a, b; 3b.
Writing – 1a, b, c; 2a, d, e; 3b, c.

Reference to photocopiable sheet

Photocopiable page 153 can be adapted for use with any of the other suggested poems.

SHAPING MEMORABLE LANGUAGE

To explore the different ways in which written language can be displayed on the page.

†† *Groups of two or three children working at the word processor.*

🕐 *30 minutes.*

Key background information

This activity attempts to engage children in making links between their own experiences of memorable oral language and the lineation and typographical patterns of printed poetry.

Preparation

Well in advance of this activity, ask the children to make a written and tape-recorded collection of short, intense snippets of oral language. This might include jokes, quarrels,

anecdotes, diatribes, tributes, insults and the speech patterns of market vendors and street preachers. Display and discuss this material. Also ensure that the children have had experience of reading poetry set out in a variety of visual patterns, including those in which the shape of the poem is used to reinforce meaning. *Madtail, Miniwhale*, a collection of shape poems selected by Wes Magee (Puffin, 1991) is a useful resource.

Before the lesson itself, ask each group to select one item from the display. When this has been done, type that item into a file on the word processor and give it an easily-recognisable name.

Resources needed
The display of examples of oral language, computers/word processors, tape recorders, poetry books.

What to do
Explain to the children that the purpose of the activity is to explore ways in which their samples of speech can be reshaped on the page to make patterns that emphasise rhythm and provide a blueprint for performance.

Discuss how the arrangement of poetry into lines and blocks of print affects the reading of the poem. Ask the children to read their selected pieces to each other, concentrating on the rhythm of the sentence patterns, how these are paralleled by punctuation, and how the modulation of these patterns affects the impact of what is said.

Demonstrate how the word processor commands can be used to shape the selected sample in the following ways:
▲ manipulation of the line patterns;
▲ emphasis on words and phrases through the use of bold and italic script;
▲ setting lines into blocks or stanzas;
▲ dragging or cutting and pasting words and word groups from one location to another;
▲ gradations in the sizes of letters, words, phrases, lines and stanzas.

Allow the children plenty of time to explore the possibilities, and try to ensure that each reshaping of the piece is accompanied by a recitation which reflects the effects of the new pattern. Alterations to the actual vocabulary and syntax of the original sample should be discouraged, but not necessarily forbidden.

When a final pattern has been decided on, it can be printed out, performed and recorded.

Suggestion(s) for extension
Encourage the children to make a collection of as many different visual arrays of poetry as they can find. Incorporate these into reading-aloud sessions involving the whole class, and discuss how the shape of the text on the page can inform the performance and the interpretation of the poem.

Suggestion(s) for support
The activity can be carried out as a class session, in which a selected item is discussed and the children's suggestions for its rearrangement are scribed by the teacher on the board or on a large sheet of paper. A class recitation should follow each redrafting.

Assessment opportunities
Make observations of the children's interest in links between typographical patterning and the manner in which the piece is read.

Opportunities for IT
Although children should be shown how to use the formatting commands such as 'centre' and 'justify', in this activity they may need to position individual words using the space bar in order to achieve the desired effect. More able children might like to explore the extra facilities offered by a graphics package in which text can be bent, twisted, and shaped in ways which are not possible on a word processor.

Display ideas
The poems can be displayed alongside their prose origins, appropriate illustrations and audiotapes of the children's reading.

Other aspects of the English PoS covered
Speaking and listening – 1a, b, c, d; 2a, b; 3a, b.
Writing – 1a, b, c; 2b; 3a, b, c.

WRITTEN RESPONSES

To help children to explore their responses to poetry through the use of the written word.

†† *Whole class or groups, working individually and then as pairs.*

🕐 *20–30 minutes.*

Key background information

This set of procedures, which can be used with any poem, is intended to stimulate children's thought through the process of writing. It is important that the teacher does not convey the impression that the purpose of writing about poetry is to tease out some secret hidden meaning, or simply to show how well the writer can remember what the poet has said.

Preparation

Select a poem that you think might appeal to the children. Make a copy for each child. The poem should preferably evoke an air of mystery, or suggest an ambiguous mood, or

lend itself to multiple interpretations. Most of the poems suggested below have been extensively anthologised: 'The Song of Wandering Aengus' by W.B. Yeats, 'The King of China's Daughter' by Edith Sitwell, 'The Listeners' by Walter de la Mare, 'Calico Pie' by Edward Lear, 'By St Thomas Water' by Charles Causley, 'The Secret' by John Mole (from *Catching the Spider*, Blackie 1990), 'Voice' by Alvie Ollivierre (in *Can I Buy a Slice of Sky*, edited by Grace Nichols, Knight 1991), 'And I Wait Patiently!' by Raymond Wilson (from *To Be A Ghost*, Puffin 1993).

Resources needed

Copies of the selected poem, writing materials.

What to do

Read the title of the poem to the children and ask them to write down any words and phrases that come into their heads. Putting the title at the centre of a piece of paper and arranging the associated ideas in a pattern around it is a good way to stimulate and represent this. Read the poem to the children, and ask them to extend the web as you do so.

When the reading is over, allow the children five or ten minutes to write their own immediate responses to the poem in any way that they choose. Pairs of children can then exchange these notes and compare them.

Hand out the copies of the poem, and ask the children to read the poem to themselves, both silently and aloud, and then to annotate the poem in any way that appeals to them: underlining key words and phrases; writing questions about aspects that they find puzzling; experimenting with alternative words, word order or title; writing a continuation; and other possibilities.

When this has been done, the children can read and discuss each other's responses.

Suggestion(s) for extension

The basic procedure outlined above can be extended in a number of ways:

▲ If the poem is by a living poet, children can write an appreciation of the poem and/or a set of questions addressed to him or her.

▲ Children can write a critical review of the poem.

▲ Children can rewrite the poem from a different point of view, or in a different genre (story, report, conversation), and discuss what has been gained or lost in this process.

▲ The children can work in pairs or small groups, annotating the poem for a presentation which might involve choral and alternating voices, music, sound effects and movement.

▲ Children can work on a word-processed version of the poem, exploring lineation and typography, as in 'Shaping memorable language' on page 88.

▲ Children can make a large, handwritten copy of the poem on a chart which might also include illustrations, written responses and other related pieces of writing.

It is important that these activities are presented to the children as options that they can choose to explore in relation to poems that they have enjoyed and selected themselves. The imposition of the activity or the poem is likely to be demotivating.

Suggestion(s) for support
Any of the above procedures can be conducted regularly as a shared writing activity, with the whole class or a small group, as a support for later independent work.

Assessment opportunities
These activities will enable you to assess the children's understanding and appreciation of a particular poem, as well as a range of writing skills.

Opportunities for IT
Many of the writing activities could be undertaken at the computer.

Display ideas
The children's handwritten poetry posters can be displayed in the class library. These should preferably include different interpretations of the same poem to demonstrate a range of responses.

Other aspects of the English PoS covered
Speaking and listening – 1a, b, c, d; 2a, b; 3a, b, c.
Writing – 1a, b; 2a, b, c, d, e; 3a, b, c.

GRAPHIC RESPONSES

To encourage children to respond to narrative, imagery and emotions in poetry through drawing and other forms of graphic representation.

†† *Whole class or groups, working individually or optionally in pairs.*

🕐 *20–30 minutes.*

Key background information
In this activity, children are encouraged to keep a graphic record of their responses to selected poems. Though this does provide opportunities to develop artistic skills, such development should not be seen as the main objective of the activity.

Preparation
Select a poem that you think will appeal to the children, and make a copy for each child. It should preferably tell a story, or present vivid imagery.

Resources needed
Copies of the poem, scrap paper, sheets of A3 paper, pencils.

What to do
Tell the children the title of the poem and ask them to draw any ideas suggested by this title on scrap paper. Distribute the sheets of A3 paper and ask them to fold it twice so that the paper is divided into four sections.

Establish a mood of concentration by asking the children to close their eyes while you read the poem aloud, and to 'draw their feelings' about it inside their heads. When the reading is over, ask them to transfer these mental images either on to the scrap paper or on to the A3 sheet. Stress that the poem is open to free interpretation, and that the objective is not to produce an accurate graphic counterpart of the objects and events that it depicts. (Though if children want to respond in this way, they can do so.)

Distribute the copies of the poem, and ask the children to read them both silently and aloud before developing the responses that they made during your reading aloud. The children can be encouraged to exchange and comment on each other's drawings, but many children might prefer to keep them to themselves.

Suggestion(s) for extension

The children can make their own books and start to build up a personal anthology of handwritten and illustrated poems.

Children can collaborate in producing a poster of the poem, illustrated with their own drawings and/or collage materials.

Ask the children to focus on the colour or colours suggested by the poem. Using paint or printing materials, they can then try to represent these colours abstractly or in recognisable images.

Narrative poems can be used as the theme for a frieze or comic strip.

Suggestion(s) for support

Children who are reluctant to commit themselves to paper might be less inhibited if this work were presented as an activity to be done in a private journal. It may also help if you present them with a range of other children's responses to the poem. Technical skill should be de-emphasised, and any sharing of the work made voluntary.

Opportunities for IT

Children could use an art package to explore the use of colour and in particular the representation of those colours in abstract shapes. On more sophisticated computers children can experiment with a range of colours and shades, mixing them and creating new colours. This activity requires access to a colour printer.

Display ideas

Any of the ideas presented above could lend themselves to display. If a poem has been interpreted by a range of illustrators ('Jabberwocky' is a good example), the children will probably be interested in displaying this range of illustrations alongside their own.

Other aspects of the English PoS covered

Speaking and listening – 1a, b, c; 2a, b.

ROLE-PLAY

To help children to explore issues presented by selected poems.

†† *Whole class, working in small groups. The activity should take place in the hall or another space where the children have freedom to move about.*

🕐 *30 minutes.*

Key background information

By involving children physically as well as mentally in poetry, drama and role-play, you can develop their sensitivity to the issues explored by the poet. For the purposes of illustration, the following activities all relate to Allan Ahlberg's poem 'The Boy without a Name' from *Heard It in the Playground* (Puffin, 1991).

Preparation

Prepare one copy of the poem for each group of children. Some days before the session, read the poem aloud to the class and engage them in any of the response and discussion activities that have been suggested earlier in this chapter. Put a copy of the poem on display, and tell the children what type of drama activity you are planning for them.

Poetry

Resources needed

Copies of the poem, any simple props or items of costume suggested by the content of the poem.

What to do

Divide the class into groups of three or four and allocate a space for each group. Distribute the copies of the poem, read it aloud and recap any activities that have been done with it so far. Each group then re-enacts any classroom or playground episodes mentioned in or suggested by the poem. Below are some possible activities:

▲ One child assumes the role of the boy without a name. The boy then describes his experiences to the other children, who ask questions.

▲ Each child takes a turn to assume the identity of one of the other children or adults mentioned in the poem. The other group members interview them about their behaviour towards the boy without a name.

▲ The last two activities are repeated, but now the characters are looking back on the episodes from the time frame of the poem. They reminisce about different episodes referred to in the poem.

▲ One child assumes the role of the poet, another the boy. The poet goes back in time and talks to the boy in the playground.

▲ The children plan a performance of the poem for one or more voices. The recitation is accompanied by an enactment of the poem.

When the children have had sufficient time to rehearse these activities, they take turns to present them to the rest of the class. After the presentations, groups should exchange ideas on how the activity might be extended

Suggestion(s) for extension

Groups of children who are particularly fond of one poet's work, or who have collected a set of poems on a theme of mutual interest, can be helped to plan an extended dramatic presentation of the poems, perhaps incorporating music and graphics.

Suggestion(s) for support

Children who find it difficult to become involved in drama activities can take part in the session as listeners, questioners and advisers.

Assessment opportunities

The success of this type of activity can be judged by the children's level of commitment and the liveliness of the debate stimulated by the presentations.

Display ideas

Photographs of presentations can be displayed alongside the stimulus poems and other related material.

Other aspects of the English PoS covered

Speaking and listening – 1a, b, c; 2a, b; 3b.

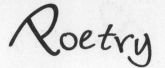
SEQUENCING

To develop children's awareness of the ways in which ideas are organised and presented in poetry.

†† *Whole class or groups, working in pairs.*

⏱ *20–30 minutes.*

Key background information
This activity is easier for the children if the selected poem has a clear narrative structure. *Algernon and other Cautionary Verses* by Hilaire Belloc (Red Fox, 1992) provides a good selection of such poems. Once children are accustomed to the procedure, poems with non-narrative organisation can be introduced.

Preparation
Select a poem that you think the children will find interesting. Cut it into six to eight segments and paste each segment on to a card. Make a set for each pair of children.

Resources needed
Segmented poems.

What to do
Hand out the card sets and ask the children to reconstruct the original poem. When the pairs of children have arrived at a tentative solution, they should compare this with that of another pair, reading their version of the poem aloud to assess its coherence. When this has been done, show the children the original version of the poem. If you are using a non-narrative poem, it is more likely that alternative sequences will have been developed. Through discussion, try to evaluate these with the children.

Suggestion(s) for extension
This activity can be used as a preliminary to any of the activities with intact poems outlined earlier in this chapter. The difficulty of the sequencing task can be increased by choosing poems with non-chronological organisation.

Suggestion(s) for support
A group of children can work on this activity with the teacher or another fluent reader, who can read aloud the suggested sequences and ask the others in the group to comment on the relative coherence of each.

Assessment opportunities
Note the children's ability to use textual signals such as connectives and pronouns to sequence the text, as well as their grasp of the overall structure of the poem.

Opportunities for IT
This activity can also be carried out using a word processor. The poem is prepared on the computer by the teacher

beforehand and then cut into sections and the order altered. If children have not used these facilities before they will need to be shown how to mark and move text. Children can then use the 'cut' and 'paste' commands to move the sections of the poem around to create a new sequence. The final result can be printed out for further discussion or display.

Display ideas
Poetry can be added to the resources you set out on the sequencing board mentioned in 'Sequencing: unfamiliar text' on page 16.

Other aspects of the English PoS covered
Speaking and listening – 1a, b, c; 2a, b; 3b.

DELETION

To develop children's use of a range of textual cues in reading.

Whole class or groups, working in pairs.

30 minutes.

Key background information
This activity requires children to restore words, phrases or longer segments of text deleted from a poem. As with the reconstruction activities mentioned in earlier chapters, the deletions that you make will be determined by the learning outcome that you are seeking for the particular children you are working with. You might want to focus on selected vocabulary, rhyme, or metrical pattern. The aim is not to try to guess the original words, but to reflect on the intact portions of text and to exchange ideas on alternative ways of reconstructing the poem.

Preparation
Select a poem that you think might appeal to the children you are working with, and make selected deletions of words and phrases, based on any of the principles outlined above. Leave enough of the opening lines intact to enable the children to construct a context for the poem and an overall idea of the poem's meaning. Do not make more than ten deletions in the whole poem. Make a copy of the poem for each pair of children.

Resources needed
Copies of the poem.

What to do
Discuss the title of the poem with the children and ask them to make predictions about its content. Read the opening lines aloud and discuss how the rest of the poem might progress.

Hand out the copies of the poem and explain the task to the children. Allow them to work in their pairs, intervening

only if frustration becomes evident. When children have arrived at a tentative completion of the poem, ask them to read this aloud to another pair of children for comparison and evaluation. At the end of the session, read the original poem to the children, and discuss any differences between this and their versions.

Suggestion(s) for extension
Like sequencing, this activity can be used as a preliminary to any of the activities with intact poems outlined in this chapter. An interesting variant is to give the children an intact poem with selected words and phrases highlighted, and to ask them to suggest alternatives which preserve, or perhaps amend, the meaning and metrical pattern of the original. If you can obtain a poet's earlier drafts of published work, this is ideal material for this kind of activity.

Suggestion(s) for support
Conduct the activity as shared reading with an enlarged text, using heightened intonation to highlight deletions. Alternative suggestions for restorations can then be incorporated into your reading, and evaluated by the group.

Assessment opportunities
Note the children's ability to use clues provided by meaning, syntax, rhyme and metre.

Opportunities for IT
This activity can be carried out by groups of children working with a word processor. The teacher should prepare the original text and make deletions appropriate to the children who are to undertake the activity. The use of the word processor by the teacher to prepare texts for this activity means that it is easy to modify the same original text for several groups of children and tailor the resource for their ability.

Children can then work together to restore the poem. This will involve them in the use of the cursor keys or mouse to manipulate the text. The final version can be printed out, compared with the original and used for display purposes.

Display ideas
Alternative restorations can be displayed alongside the original poem, together with appropriate illustrations.

Other aspects of the English PoS covered
Speaking and listening – 1a, b, c; 2a, b; 3b.
Writing – 1a, b.

A PERSONAL ANTHOLOGY

To motivate children to seek out poetry which they enjoy, and to share this with other readers.
†† *Whole class.*
🕐 *This is an open-ended project, which will have been preceded by activities aimed at enhancing children's enjoyment of poetry.*

Key background information
In this activity children will begin to compile an illustrated anthology of favourite poems, using a book that they have made themselves. This is best carried out as part of a longer-term project involving both bookmaking and the appreciation of poetry. It would fit well into activities taking place during a bookweek.

Preparation
Make an anthology of your own favourite poems, illustrated with a range of graphic material, including drawings, photographs, found pictures and collage.

Prepare a selection of blank books with the children, using a range of formats. *A Book of One's Own* by Paul Johnson (Hodder & Stoughton, 1990) provides a variety of suitable formats.

Resources needed
Blank books, drawing and writing materials, an array of visual materials for collage, a wide selection of anthologies and other poetry resources, including guides like the *Books for Keeps Guide to Poetry 0–16*.

What to do
Show the children your own anthology and explain how and why you have compiled it. Tell them that the blank books that they have made are to be used in the same way. Recap any work that the class has done on poetry, and initiate a discussion on favourite poems.

The compilation of the anthology can be integrated into continuing work on poetry as it unfolds in English, art, music and drama sessions.

Suggestion(s) for extension
This work can be extended by encouraging the children to make a database of favourite poems and anthologies, and by making tape-book sets, big books and dual-language editions of their anthologies.

Suggestion(s) for support
Children can be helped to compile an anthology during one-to-one reading and writing conferences with the teacher.

Assessment opportunities
The anthology can contribute to summative assessment by providing evidence of the child's interest in poetry and the range of her reading experience in this area over a set period of time.

Other aspects of the English PoS covered
Speaking and listening – 1a, b, c.
Writing – 1a; 2a, b.

Instructional texts

Instructional text has been given its own short chapter because it is such a widespread and potentially valuable source of reading development.

Most instructional texts are not found in books, though every classroom should feature such rich and fascinating items as cookery books, instruction manuals for machines and games, and texts which show children how to carry out scientific experiments or construct the paraphernalia of various hobbies. Every classroom should also feature examples of instructional texts culled from other sources: food wrappers and cereal cartons, game boards, computer screens, furniture assembly kits, toy boxes, and so on.

These texts are particularly valuable because they are highly structured, are very closely tied to immediate referents such as objects, actions and visible processes, and carry with them their own pay-off. A child struggling to read a novel or an information book does so in the fragile faith that the indeterminate end product will be enjoyable or at least useful. In the right circumstances, a child working with instructional texts knows that the objective is the game she wants to play, or the dish whose picture accompanies the recipe, or the toy whose pieces lie beside the set of instructions.

The set of procedures outlined in this chapter can all be applied to any instructional text. Clearly, the benefit to the young reader of following these procedures will only be gained if they are conducted alongside an authentic performance of the relevant physical task.

CLASSROOM MANUALS

To raise children's awareness of procedural genres by collecting and using a range of different examples of this genre.

†† *Whole class initially, then small groups working on a sorting activity.*

🕐 *Open-ended.*

Key background information

This is a collecting and sorting activity aimed at making children more aware of the diversity of procedural texts and more competent in their use. The rest of the activities in this chapter can all be based on the materials that the children collect and produce during this initial activity.

Preparation

Make a collection of procedural texts that you think will be of interest to the children, from as wide a variety of sources as you can. Your collection might include:

▲ recipes from books, magazines and packaging of foods;

▲ board game instructions;

▲ extracts from computer program manuals;

▲ instructions on how to make clothes, toys and construction kits;

▲ advice on how to look after pets.

Make a display of these texts, in no particular order, and invite the children to contribute to it.

Resources needed

Procedural texts, blank books, poster-making materials.

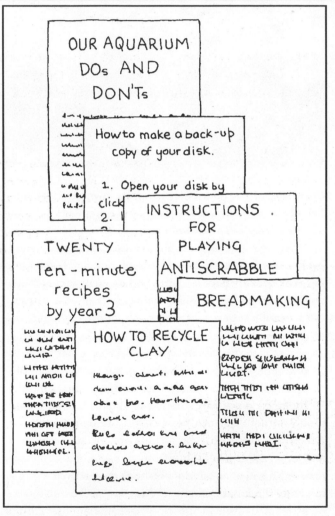

What to do

Discuss the range of texts with the whole class, and in particular talk about what they have in common. Ask the children for ideas on how to sort the texts into different categories. Can they identify which texts it might be useful to have on display in the classroom? Explain that you would like the texts to be sorted to make up a set of class manuals, and perhaps some charts could also be made that it would be useful to have on permanent display.

When the categories have been agreed, select small groups to work on each, and distribute the blank books and chart-making materials. At this stage, it is advisable to encourage the children to make sketch plans of the layout of the books and charts. In designing the books they might decide that certain texts should be rejected and that some need to be enlarged in scale, some to be rewritten and some to be illustrated with diagrams. Any previous work that children have done on editing, redrafting and publication should be referred to here, including such features of the book as the jacket design, contents list, index and glossary. In the case of items like recipe books, blank pages should be left for future contributions.

When the books and charts have been completed, the whole class can decide on suitable locations to display them. Books should be labelled according to the library's classification system.

Suggestion(s) for extension

Some children who have strong interests in particular activities, such as cooking, computer games and model making, can be encouraged to publish their own specialist journals (at regular intervals) in which procedures that they have learned about, or ones that they have devised themselves, can be shared with the class.

Suggestion(s) for support

As a preliminary to this type of activity, children can be encouraged to produce personal 'how to' books in which a variety of procedures that they find interesting can be written up through shared writing.

Assessment opportunities

Note the children's ability to make editorial decisions based on their reading and evaluation of the texts that have been collected.

Opportunities for IT

Children could use word processors or desktop publishing packages to write and format their instructional texts. If desktop publishing software is used the teacher, or children,

could set up a master page to ensure that there is a consistent format throughout the whole manual. Children could add pictures created using a drawing or art package or could scan in their own pencil drawings.

If the writing of these manuals is extended over a longer period of time, children will need to save and retrieve their work for each session at the computer. Children should also be introduced to appropriate formatting commands such as centring and justification to give their work an appropriate layout.

Display ideas
The deployment in the classroom of the resources that have been created can be decided by you and the children.

Other aspects of the English PoS covered
Speaking and listening – 1a, b, c; 2a, b; 3b.
Writing – 1a, b; 2a, b, c, d, e; 3a, b, c.

EVALUATING AND SIMPLIFYING

To raise children's awareness of readability factors and to enable them to produce clear written instructions.
†† *Pairs or small groups.*
🕐 *Three sessions of about 40 minutes each.*

Key background information
In this activity, children select texts that they think will be of interest to younger children, assess the accessibility of these texts to their intended audience, then rewrite and redesign these texts in order to improve them.

This activity involves paired reading in which older readers help partners from a younger age group, so it is best conducted by children accustomed to this practice. The ideal situation would be to incorporate this activity into a well-established paired reading programme, rather than to use it to establish such a programme.

Preparation
Ask the group you are working with to select a procedural text that they would like to use as the basis of a shared activity with a younger class. This should relate to a fairly short, simple and self-contained activity such as cooking a simple dish, playing a game or constructing a toy. The text should provide reasonably easy reading for the older group.

Arrange with another class for the paired reading of the procedural text to take place before going on to the shared activity. This will involve matching the children in the older group with the same number of children from a younger class, so the composition of each of these groups will need careful consideration.

Resources needed
One copy of the original text for each child in the older group, any material related to the selected activity, writing and drawing materials.

What to do
Session One
In the first session, supervise the children's paired reading of the text. The older children should practise a 'pause, prompt and praise' stratagem when listening to the younger children's reading. Any difficulties should be recorded carefully by underlining and annotating the text. If possible, the reading should be recorded on tape so that these points of difficulty can be examined in more detail in the next session. If the younger child becomes frustrated with the text, the older partner should simply read it to him. When the reading is over, the younger children can be asked to explain what the

text was about, and what will be needed in order to carry out the procedure it outlines. This 'retelling' will provide further evidence of the child's understanding of the text.

Session Two

Help the older children to compare their notes on the reading and locate the points at which the text presented difficulties. Discuss different ways in which the text might be amended to alleviate these difficulties, bearing in mind that simply shortening the sentences or using shorter words is by no means guaranteed to make the text easier to read. The children might consider providing a labelled diagram to use for cross-reference, adding illustrations, transforming the text into a cartoon strip, or using a more chatty style. Help them to redraft the text, allowing them the option of producing a range of rewrites.

Session Three

Supervise a paired reading session with the amended text. Afterwards, the children from both age groups should discuss the effectiveness of the rewritten text, before proceeding to carry out the actual task that the text describes.

Suggestion(s) for extension

The rewriting procedure can be applied to a range of procedural texts in the classroom. Translating instructions for using new computer programs into more comprehensible English is likely to be a strong candidate for further application of this practice.

Suggestion(s) for support

Text simplification is a sophisticated procedure best suited to experienced readers. Children's experiences in creating

their own procedural texts will raise their awareness of the issues involved. The 'Writing game instructions' activity on page 104 provides one way in which children might be helped to do this.

Assessment opportunities

Note the children's awareness of the factors involved in the readability of texts, and their ability to use this knowledge to adapt given texts.

Opportunities for IT

If the original text is typed into a word processor, much of the redrafting can be undertaken directly at the keyboard. Children could be shown how to use an electronic thesaurus to search for alternative words to make the text easier to understand. Copies of each of the re-drafts could be printed out and placed in a folder or displayed to show the different stages of the process.

Display ideas

Original and simplified texts can be displayed side by side, with appropriate annotations and photographs of the actual procedure being carried out.

Other aspects of the English PoS covered

Speaking and listening – 1a, b, c; 2a, b; 3b.
Writing – 1a, b, c; 2a, b, c, d, e; 3a, b, c.

FROM TEXT TO GRAPHICS

To explore different ways of presenting instructions by converting procedural texts into pictures.

†† *Small groups, children within each group working in pairs.*

⏱ *One hour.*

Key background information

In this activity children will explore alternative ways of presenting instructions, and attempt to formulate their own methods. The activity requires co-operation from another class, and would again fit well into a programme of paired reading.

Preparation

Collect a variety of wordless instruction formats from consumer items such as self-assembly furniture kits, seed packets and clothing care labels. Make a display using these items and invite the children to contribute to it.

Resources needed

Wordless procedural texts as described above, drawing materials, texts selected from the collection made in 'Classroom manuals' on page 98.

What to do

Introduction

Show the children examples of wordless procedural texts, pointing out the different ways in which the authors have used symbols or pictures to indicate actions, processes and sequences. Discuss why some procedural texts are wordless, and the advantages and disadvantages of such texts to particular audiences. The children might, for example, be able to contribute anecdotes about the frustrations experienced by members of their families while trying to construct furniture or other items from such texts. A more balanced view can be given by indicating, from your stock of texts, examples which could have been more comprehensible with supporting illustrations, or which are effective with no text at all.

Development

Ask the children to select one or two texts on a subject which they find interesting, and set them the challenge of turning these texts into wordless instructions which would be comprehensible to somebody who could not read any English. Refer back to symbols and formats used by published texts in order to help the children do this.

Conclusion

Allow children working on different texts to 'read' their completed wordless versions to each other and to comment on their effectiveness. Arrange for these versions to be presented to children in other classes so that their effectiveness can be evaluated.

Suggestion(s) for extension

This procedure can be applied to any situation in which children have to learn how to operate a particular process. Links can be made between this activity and the use of algebraic and scientific symbols to indicate relationships and processes.

Suggestion(s) for support

Help the children to incorporate drawings and diagrammatic representations of processes into their recording of work from all areas of the curriculum.

Assessment opportunities

Drawings made by the children will indicate their understanding of the original text and their ability to transform this into another representational medium.

Display ideas

Instructions expressed graphically can be incorporated into classroom displays wherever this is appropriate.

Other aspects of the English PoS covered

Speaking and listening – 1a, b, c; 2a, b; 3b.

Talk to the children about the content of the text that they will be working with, so that their background knowledge is activated.

Distribute the text cards and allow pairs of children to work out the best sequence for them. When this has been done, children should compare their versions of the reconstructed text.

Suggestion(s) for extension

As with the sequencing activities in preceding chapters, the difficulty of the task can be controlled through the selection of the original text and the number of segments into which it is divided.

Suggestion(s) for support

Conduct the sequencing activity as a shared reading session, drawing the children's attention to the cohesive features of text mentioned in the sequencing activities in earlier chapters.

Assessment opportunities

See the sequencing activities in previous chapters on pages 16, 24, 65 and 94.

Opportunities for IT

If the teacher produces the initial text using a word processor and then divides it into segments the children can use the 'cut' and 'paste', or drag and drop facilities to re-order the text into the correct sequence.

Other aspects of the English PoS covered

Speaking and listening – 1a, b, c; 2a, b; 3b.

SEQUENCING INSTRUCTIONS

To draw children's attention towards organisational features in procedural texts.

†† *Small or large groups, working in pairs.*

🕐 *20 to 30 minutes.*

Key background information

This activity is an extension of the sequencing activities outlined in previous chapters, and can be conducted using any of the texts collected in the 'Classroom manuals' activity on page 98.

Preparation

Select any procedural text related to current class interests, or provide a selection of such texts related to the interests of individuals within the group you wish to work with. Cut the text up into six to ten sections and delete all numerical clues to the original sequence. Paste each section on to card. Photocopiable page 154 can be used if this is appropriate. It is best if, as with photocopiable page 154, the text allows alternative possibilities to be discussed.

Resources needed

Texts prepared as above, or one copy of photocopiable page 154 for each pair of children.

What to do

Remind the children of any previous work that they have done on sequencing narrative or information text, and ask them to identify any features of the organisation of procedural text which will make the job of sequencing easier for them.

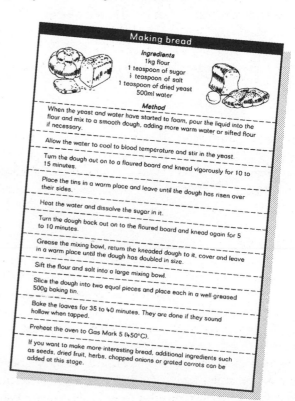

Making bread

Ingredients
1kg flour
1 teaspoon of sugar
½ teaspoon of salt
1 teaspoon of dried yeast
500ml water

Method

When the yeast and water have started to foam, pour the liquid into the flour and mix to a smooth dough, adding more warm water or sifted flour if necessary.

Allow the water to cool to blood temperature and stir in the yeast.

Turn the dough out on to a floured board and knead vigorously for 10 to 15 minutes.

Place the tins in a warm place and leave until the dough has risen over their sides.

Heat the water and dissolve the sugar in it.

Turn the dough back out on to the floured board and knead again for 5 to 10 minutes.

Grease the mixing bowl, return the kneaded dough to it, cover and leave in a warm place until the dough has doubled in size.

Sift the flour and salt into a large mixing bowl.

Slice the dough into two equal pieces and place each in a well-greased 500g baking tin.

Bake the loaves for 35 to 40 minutes. They are done if they sound hollow when tapped.

Preheat the oven to Gas Mark 5 (450°C).

If you want to make more interesting bread, additional ingredients such as seeds, dried fruit, herbs, chopped onions or grated carrots can be added at this stage.

Reference to photocopiable sheet

Photocopiable page 154 can also be used for 'Evaluating and simplifying' (page 99), 'From text to graphics' (page 100) and 'Reconstructing deletions from procedural text' (below).

RECONSTRUCTING PROCEDURAL TEXTS

To focus children's attention on procedural texts in the classroom, and to raise their awareness of the structure of such texts.

†† *Small groups, or the whole class.*

🕐 *10 to 15 minutes.*

Key background information

This is a short game that can be played as a regular routine with a small group of beginner readers, or with the whole class as an 'I spy' activity. The purpose is to draw the attention of beginner readers to the procedural texts displayed in your classroom, and to help them to read these texts by presenting them as a completion puzzle.

Preparation

The day before the activity, tell the children that when they have gone home you are going to alter one of the sets of instructions displayed in the classroom, and that when they return the following day, the designated group has to find the altered text and restore it.

Select a text that relates to an activity that the children are familiar with. Alter it by masking two or three of the instructions with card and Blu-Tack. This is best done with a large-scale text, using individual cards to cover separate words and phrases.

Resources needed

Any familiar procedural text which has been on display in your classroom. With children at the earliest stages of reading development, it is useful if the text is appropriately illustrated. Card and Blu-Tack will also be needed to mask portions of the text.

What to do

Ask the children to search the classroom and locate the altered text. Help them to read the portions of text that remain, using the location of the text (in the classroom) and any illustrations as clues. Encourage the children to reflect on what they have read and to predict the content of the first chunk of deleted text.

Provide feedback on their responses, directing them to the content of the preceding, and following, sentences if necessary. When this has been done, focus on the individual missing words. Ask the children to predict the first word; then disclose its first letter or letter blend and ask them to amend their predictions if necessary. Reveal the first word then proceed to the next one, repeating the process of predicting, amending and confirming, and referring back to the visible text and illustrations whenever this is necessary.

Continue until the entire text has been restored.

Suggestion(s) for extension

After the children have worked on activities which lend themselves to the creation of procedural texts (for example, technology projects, cookery, gardening), use shared writing to help them to produce these texts. The completed version can then be word-processed and certain portions deleted. Pairs of children can be given copies of these texts and asked to write in the missing words.

Suggestion(s) for support

This activity would be easier if the text used had just been written by the children themselves after they had engaged in the activity to which it refers.

A variant of the activity that some children might find more accessible is to cut up the set of instructions instead of masking them, and to present them in a shuffled form to the children for sequencing.

Assessment opportunities

Note the children's ability to use background knowledge of the task, to use illustrations and to use semantic, syntactic and graphophonic knowledge in predicting and identifying the deleted words.

Opportunities for IT

If children prepare their own original text on a word processor, and then delete items, other children can try to restore the text to its original form. The replaced words could be highlighted using bold, italic or even colour.

Other aspects of the English PoS covered

Speaking and listening – 1a, b, c; 2a, b; 3b.

WRITING GAME INSTRUCTIONS

To familiarise children with the process of creating procedural texts.

†† *Small groups.*

🕐 *Two sessions of at least one hour each.*

Key background information

In this activity, children will invent their own games and write instruction manuals for them. These manuals will then be evaluated by other groups, who will suggest revisions based on their ability to play the new games.

Preparation

Collect any paraphernalia that might lend itself to the invention of a new board or outdoor game: dice, counters, blank playing cards, 8 x 8 or 10 x 10 matrices, balls, skittles, hoops, chalk, nets, and so on.

Collect instructions from games like Scrabble and Monopoly and enlarge them so that they can be read easily by a small or large group.

Resources needed

Game-making resources, as described above. A copy of the writing frame on photocopiable page 155 for each child or pair of children.

What to do

Session One

Explain that the objective of the first part of the activity is to design a board or outdoor game, and that in the second part the children will be producing and refining a clear set of instructions for how to play the game. Some children might benefit from the added proviso that the game should be suitable for younger children to play, or that it should teach children something about language, maths or another area of learning.

Distribute the materials and allow the children plenty of time to design their games. As they work, encourage them to make notes which can be used later as the basis for instructions to go with the game.

Session Two

Present the children with the instructions for the printed games that you have collected. Read through them carefully with the children, and point out structural features and vocabulary choices designed to make the instructions clear to the reader. Ask the children to suggest improvements.

Distribute the writing frames, and make sure that the children understand the purposes of the different sections. They should then write a first draft of the instructions for their games. When all of the groups have produced first drafts, they can swap them and evaluate the clarity of each other's instructions by actually using them to play the games. As they do so, suggested revisions can be made in note form on the first drafts. When this has been done, the drafts can be returned and the suggestions for revision discussed.

Suggestion(s) for extension

If you have suggested that the games be designed for children in a younger class in your school, then feedback on the first draft should be obtained from that class. The game designers can visit the class, observe the games being played, help with the reading of the instructions, and make their own notes for the revision of these instructions. Again, this activity would work best if incorporated into an established cross-age paired reading project.

Suggestion(s) for support

Games can be designed by small groups under the supervision of the teacher, who can act as note-taker and scribe. Photocopiable page 155 can be reproduced as a chart for shared writing.

Assessment opportunities

Note can be made of the children's ability to use the procedural style competently, and of their critical skills in evaluating procedural writing produced by others.

Game instructions

Name _____ Date _____

▲ Invent your own game and fill in the details on how to play it below.

Game title _____

What you need

The purpose of this game is to _____

How to play

1

2

3

The game ends when _____

WORKING FROM FICTION

To link the reading and writing of procedural texts with children's wider literary experiences.

†† *A group of children who have read selected books, working with response partners.*

🕐 *40 minutes to 1 hour.*

Key background information

In this activity children will write procedural texts, such as recipes, instructions and directions, which are based on their reading of fiction. It would fit into a programme of activities linked to a book popular with individuals or groups within the class. It must be emphasised that this should be presented as a *voluntary* activity for children who may want to play around with the ideas represented in a favourite book. It would be worse than a waste of time to impose it on children who are not particularly interested in the books in question.

Preparation

Select works of fiction that you have read yourself which lend themselves to the generation of procedural text, and attempt to write examples of such texts yourself. Some suggestions include:

▲ *Macbeth:* a recipe for the witches' brew.

▲ *Treasure Island:* directions from the North Inlet to the treasure.

▲ *Moby Dick:* how to flay and butcher a whale.

Seek out texts with a similar potential that might appeal to children of the age that you teach, and ensure that the children have read or listened to them before introducing the activity.

Resources needed

Books, as described above, and examples of procedural texts, both your own and those published for authentic purposes.

What to do

Read selected passages from the books you have read yourself aloud to the children, and show them the texts that you have prepared. Explain that the purpose of the activity is simply to 'play about' with the text and to transpose some of its ideas into a procedural style.

Ask the children to locate passages from books they have read that are suitable for this type of activity, or indicate these passages yourself if you are working with familiar texts.

Remind the children of the structural features of procedural texts, and help them to write their own texts according to the conventions of this genre.

Suggestion(s) for extension

This activity can be linked to other response activities such as those outlined in the Fiction chapter, particularly 'Story

Opportunities for IT

The writing frame could be prepared by the teacher using a word processor or desktop publishing package. Children could then write their instructions at the computer, printing and saving the final draft. After they have played the game, and discussed changes to the rules, they could retrieve their original work and re-edit or sequence their instructions. The final version of the rules could be presented in an appropriate font and format and then printed out.

Display ideas

Games can be displayed alongside first and final drafts of their instructions, and visual material such as photographs of the games being played.

Other aspects of the English PoS covered

Speaking and listening – 1a, b, c; 2a, b; 3c.
Writing – 1a, b, c; 2a, b, c, d, e; 3a, b, c.

Reference to photocopiable sheet

Photocopiable page 155 provides a writing framework for the procedural style of text, which children can amend as necessary.

map' (page 32), and 'Introducing a reader's notebook' (page 15).

Suggestion(s) for support
The activity can be conducted as part of a programme of shared reading and shared writing.

Assessment opportunities
The process of transforming information from one style into another should provide the opportunity to make assessments of both reading and writing skills.

Opportunities for IT
Children could undertake the writing and drafting of their procedural texts using a word processor. They might start by typing in the original text to use as a basis and then delete sections of the original as they re-write it into the new style. This would help them ensure that they did not miss any sections. Alternatively, children could start by using the return key to separate each of the sections of the original text so that they start on a new line, and then re-write each separated section into appropriate language.

Display ideas
The completed pieces of writing can contribute to a display based on responses to a particular book or set of related books.

Other aspects of the English PoS covered
Speaking and listening – 1a, b, c; 2a, b; 3b.
Writing – 1a, b, c; 2a, b, c, d, e; 3a, b.

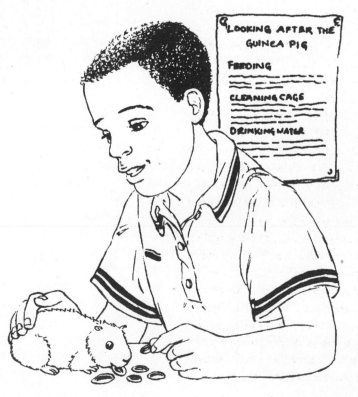

SELECTING AND USING AN INSTRUCTIONAL TEXT

To assess individual children's ability to use an instructional text.
†† *Children working individually, or in small groups.*
🕐 *Open-ended.*

Key background information
This is a simple, flexible assessment procedure which can take place towards the end of the school year. It should be based on the first activity in this section ('Classroom manuals' on page 98). If your classroom work ordinarily involves the use of a variety of instructional texts, this assessment will form part of the everyday activities of the class.

Preparation
See 'Classroom manuals' on page 98.

Resources needed
An instructional text selected by the child, and any material needed for the instructions to be carried out.

What to do
Inform the children that over a period of a couple of weeks or so, you would like each of them to select an instructional text from the collection that they have made and to carry out the activity it outlines. This might involve children working individually, or recruiting one or more helpers. The individual making the choice should be responsible for organising the resources required for the task, and should agree with you on a convenient time for carrying out the task.

Suggestion(s) for extension
Children who manage to carry out the activity without any difficulty could be asked to design their own extension to the activity, and to create an appropriate instructional text.

Suggestion(s) for support
The purpose of this activity is to assess how well the child can use the instructional text independently; but such texts vary widely in their readability, so the teacher should not be reluctant to give help with the reading of unfamiliar words or confusing phrases.

Assessment opportunities
Observe how successfully the child uses the text, and make a note of any help that you have to provide. Discuss any difficulties with the child afterwards, and try to judge these in the context of the level of difficulty of the selected text.

Other aspects of the English PoS covered
Speaking and listening – 1a, b, c; 2a, b; 3b.

Media

This final chapter presents a brief selection of activities related to the plethora of diverse texts that surround children in their everyday lives. Because such texts form a kind of linguistic wallpaper, vivid in some parts, patched and peeling in others, the inexperienced reader tends not to pay much attention to a lot of the print events surrounding him. In order for critical awareness to develop, the child needs to be made aware that every text has an author, and that every author has a set of motivations which might well impinge on the child's interpretation.

The first few activities are all concerned with newspapers, though they could be applied to any other form of journalism. The basic emphasis is on developing a knowledge of conventions, including the genre rules which underlie the way in which the writer addresses and influences the reader. Children are encouraged to make these rules explicit, and to play with them by writing imitations and parodies. Later activities are directed towards a small selection of environmental print items, such as junk mail and cartoons. Again, the teacher will be able to identify a great variety of other items which might usefully be explored through similar procedures.

The final part of this chapter outlines two or three games through which children's awareness of word structure might be sharpened. They provide a reminder of the prevalence of word games in the print environment, and of the need to ground literacy in activities which appeal both to curiosity and to the human need for play.

THE ANATOMY OF NEWSPAPERS

To familiarise children with the different ways in which newspapers are structured, and to raise critical awareness of the ways in which information is presented in the media.

†† *The whole class, working in groups of four to six.*

⏱ *One hour for the initial session, then open-ended follow-up.*

Key background information

In this activity the children will make a comparative study of different newspapers. The issues raised will be followed up in subsequent activities.

Preparation

Buy a range of newspapers on the day you intend to start the activity. You should have one for each group. Tell the children a few days in advance what they are going to do, and decide who will be in which group.

Resources needed

A range of broadsheet and tabloid newspapers, scissors, chart paper, felt-tipped pens.

What to do

Introduction

Explain to the children that the objective is to find out how many different types of information and other material are presented in newspapers, and how newspapers differ in the emphasis they give to these features. Ask the children to suggest categories into which these features might be divided, and list these on the board or on a chart. If any important categories are omitted, contribute these yourself.

Development

Hand out the newspapers and ask the children in the groups to separate the page sections and browse through them, locating examples of articles, photographs and other features that fall into the identified categories. When they have had enough time to do this, distribute chart paper, scissors, paste and pens, and ask the children to select representative items from each category and to incorporate these into a chart that shows the range of material presented by their newspaper. On the chart, the children should highlight the lead story and photograph selected by the newspaper that day. They should also make a note of the function of each print item displayed, and to whom they think the item is directed (male or female readers, older or younger readers, people with particular interests like gardening, cookery, money, and so on).

Conclusion

Each group should present their charts to the class and talk through their analysis of the newspaper. The following issues might be discussed:
▲ the differing amounts of gossip and trivia in the papers;
▲ the use of violent or sexist imagery;
▲ how vocabulary varies between and within newspapers;
▲ the role of print size, photographs, language play and layout;

READING

▲ the differing amounts of attention given to national and international news;

▲ the newspaper's political stance and attitude towards people in power.

Suggestion(s) for extension

The activity can be extended into a monitoring project in which the children keep a record of what is on the front pages of different newspapers over a week (or a longer period).

Older children can be helped to conduct a more detailed content analysis, in which the proportion of each newspaper devoted to the different categories is calculated and graphically displayed (see below).

All of the procedures outlined above can also be applied to magazines and comics.

This activity would be a useful preparation for the launching of a class newspaper.

Suggestion(s) for support

Prepare a chart yourself by cutting up a newspaper from an earlier date, then mounting and annotating the different categories of print item. Talk through what you have done with the group, then present an intact copy of a newspaper bought on the same day to the group and ask them to make a similar chart using the same categories.

Assessment opportunities

Note the children's awareness of the different functions served by the categories that they have identified, and how much critical awareness they show in their discussion of these functions.

Opportunities for IT

Children could record the observations of different newspaper front pages over a period of time using a database. The fieldnames could include areas such as title, cost, date, and categories for the type of story, use of photographs, and so on. If a range of newspapers is included, children can look for differences in the type of headline articles or the content of the front page.

More detailed analysis of the amount of space devoted to different types of news, photographs, advertisements, sport, and so on, could also be recorded using a database or spreadsheet. Groups of children could analyse this information for a particular newspaper over a period of time, or all the data for a range of newspapers can be stored on one spreadsheet.

The chart below shows one possible model:

The spreadsheet can be set up to calculate the percentage figures working from the number of pages in the newspaper and an estimate of the number of pages or part pages devoted to each category. It is also possible to set up formulae to calculate the average space devoted to each category for each type of paper. Results can also be printed out graphically. Children might make a more detailed analysis of a single paper on a page-by-page basis to look at how the structure of the paper is planned.

Display ideas

Completed charts can be displayed alongside each other, so that similarities and differences between newspapers are highlighted.

Paper	News	Gossip	Sport	Finance	Editorial	Adverts	Photos	Other
The Times	30%	2%	15%	10%	10%	20%	8%	5%
The Guardian								
The Sun								
Daily Mirror								

Other aspects of the English PoS covered
Speaking and listening – 1a, b, c; 2a, b; 3b.

MATCHING HEADLINES

To develop children's awareness of different styles of writing.

†† *Whole class or groups, with children working in pairs.*

🕐 *20–30 minutes.*

Key background information
This activity is intended to raise children's interest in different types of journalistic writing and design. The children should be encouraged to contribute the raw materials themselves.

Preparation
Ask the children to bring in newspaper stories that they find interesting. When you have a sufficiently large and varied bank of material, photocopy a selection of the stories, representing a range of newspapers, content areas (news, sport, reviews, gossip), forms of typography and styles of language. Make sure that you include articles on the same event or topic from different newspapers. Separate the headlines from the text of the photocopied articles, and mount the sets of headlines and articles on to card.

Resources needed
See above.

What to do
Introduction
Recap any work you have done on the analysis of newspapers, and explain to the children that the purpose of this activity is to match headlines with their texts by paying attention to such clues as keywords, typography and writing styles.

Development
Hand out the sets of cards and leave the children to get on with the sorting and matching, intervening only if frustration is apparent. (The number of articles given to each pair should depend on their level of stamina, ability and interest.)

Conclusion
When the task has been completed, ask each pair of children to talk through their decisions.

Suggestion(s) for extension
The activity can be made more difficult if typographical clues are eliminated. You can do this by retyping the headlines, the body of the text, or both. You could also provide more (or fewer) headlines than articles and ask children to correct the mismatch by writing the missing items.

Children can be asked to write a story for a given headline, or a headline for a given story, imitating the style of the newspaper from which the given part of the text is taken.

Suggestion(s) for support
Conduct the activity as a shared reading, using two or three enlarged texts. Help the children to identify key features of the texts by underlining important words and phrases as you read together.

Assessment opportunities
Note the children's ability to comprehend the texts and to use a range of text features in identifying the links between texts and headlines.

Opportunities for IT
Children could use a word processor to write stories for headlines. If the headline is set up on a desktop publishing package, different children can write stories for the same headline. The 'frame size' setting could limit children to a set space so that they would need to edit and draft their story to fit the given space. The results could be printed for a class display or for children's folders.

Other aspects of the English PoS covered
Speaking and listening – 1a, b, c; 2a, b; 3b.

GENERATING HEADLINES

To raise awareness of the distinctive vocabulary and syntax of different styles of journalism.

†† *Whole class for introductory activity, then pairs or small groups.*

⏱ *20 minutes.*

Key background information

This activity explores the use of high-impact and high-frequency vocabulary in the language of headlines, seeking to develop children's critical awareness of this aspect of journalistic language by engaging them in a writing task which parodies the usages in question.

Preparation

Ask the children to contribute to a collection of headlines from as many different newspapers as possible. When the collection has grown to include 100 or so headlines, help the children to produce a tally chart of recurrent items of vocabulary present in the samples. This information can be displayed on charts in the form of a wall dictionary of newspaper vocabulary.

Resources needed

The vocabulary chart, writing materials, one copy of photocopiable page 156 for each pair of children, an OHP transparency of this page.

What to do

Introduction

Project the transparency of photocopiable page 156, masking all but the first word of Part One. Ask the children to visualise this as a newspaper headline and to consider what sort of story it would signal. When the children have exchanged ideas, reveal the following lines one at a time, at each stage asking them to contribute suggestions for storylines. Do this for both Part One and Part Two, drawing the children's attention to the flexibility afforded by the introduction of function words in the latter.

Development

Distribute photocopiable page 156 and discuss the difference between function words and content words. Focus the children's attention on the content word list, and ask them to reflect on why these words should be so common in newspapers. Any earlier work that the children have done on onomatopoeia, alliteration and other aspects of phonology should be recapped here.

Ask the children to compose headlines by combining words from the function word list with words from the content word list. Any words from the list that the children have compiled themselves can also be included. Suggest a length restriction of two to seven words per headline, and ask the children to share ideas for the stories that might be attached to the headlines they are producing.

When a pair of children have produced three or four headlines, ask them to swap these with another pair. Each pair can then write stories to go with the headlines they have been given.

Conclusion

At the end of the session, the children should read out the headlines that they have produced and the stories that have been created to go with them.

Suggestion(s) for extension

The vocabulary tally chart can be extended, and a profile of the words used most often by different newspapers can be compiled. Children can be asked to extend the word lists on photocopiable page 156, adding words from their own reading and their own imaginations.

Examples of newspaper articles from the past (from history-book illustrations and personal archives) can be analysed to show how journalistic language has changed. The issue of whether or not this language has deteriorated can be discussed.

As with the previous activities, the work that the children do in this session can be used as a preparation for – or can contribute towards – the publication of a class newspaper.

Suggestion(s) for support

Present a selection of particularly vivid words from the content word list on photocopiable page 156, and ask the children to brainstorm associated words, phrases and stories in which these stimulus words might occur. Show them examples of authentic headlines in which these words occur. Conduct the article-producing phase of the activity as a shared writing session.

Assessment opportunities

Note the children's critical appreciation of the connotations of high-frequency words, and their ability to use these in original compositions.

Words for headlines

Name _____ Date _____

These words are commonly found in headlines in newspapers.

Part one

DOOM
DOOM PLEA
DOOM THREAT PLEA
DOOM THREAT PLEA CLUE
DOOM THREAT PLEA CLUE CHASE

Function words

AFTER
AGAIN AT
BY DOWN
FOR IN
OF
OVER ON
OUT
THROUGH
TO
UNDER
UP

Part two

SCIENTIST IN DOOM THREAT
DOOM SCIENTIST IN CLUE THREAT
PLEA FOR SCIENTIST OVER DOOM CHASE
SCIENTIST'S CHASE FOR DOOM CLUES
DOOM THREAT SCIENTIST IN PLEA FOR CLUES

Content words

AGONY ALARM ANGUISH ARREST ATROCITY AXE
BAN BEAUTY BID BLAST BLUNDER BOOT
CASH CHANCE COST CRASH CUT DASH DEAL DEATH DEFEAT DISMAL DRAMA
ENJOY ENTER EVIL EXIT
FACE FALL FATE FIGHT FLEE FOUND FREAK FRIGHT FREE FUN FURY
GAMBLE GET GLOOM GO GRAB GREED GUILT
HATE HAUNT HELD HIGH HIT HOME HOPE HORROR
INQUIRY

KILL KNIFE KNOCK
LIFE LOOM LOSE LOST LOVE LOW LUST
MAGIC MASS MERCY MUST MYSTERY
NASTY NEED NEW
OFFER ORDEAL OUTRAGE
POWER PRICE PROBE PROTEST PUZZLE
QUESTION QUIZ QUOTE
REJECT RIGHT RISE ROB ROW RUN
SCANDAL SEEK SEX SHAME SICK SINK SLAM SLEAZE SLUR STRIKE STRUGGLE STUN SWOOP
TAKE TEST TOP TRAGEDY
VICTIM VICTORY VIOLENT
WARN WHY WICKED WIN WOUND WRONG

Opportunities for IT

Children could use word processors to write stories for the headlines created by one of the children. They might also use the vocabulary chart to create a graphical representation of word frequency using a graphing software. A spreadsheet could be set up to show word counts from different newspapers.

Display ideas

Stories and headlines produced by the children can be displayed alongside examples from actual newspapers.

Other aspects of the English PoS covered

Speaking and listening – 1a, b, c; 2a, b; 3b.
Writing – 1a, b; 2a, b, c, d, e; 3a, b, c.

Reference to photocopiable sheet

Photocopiable page 156 provides an example of how high-impact words might be combined. You can extend the list with words from your own and the children's reading.

EXPLORING NEWSPAPER ARTICLES

To help children to develop reading skills and interest in journalistic texts.

†† *The whole class, working in pairs.*
🕐 *20–30 minutes for each activity.*

Key background information

The sequence of procedures outlined below can be applied to any newspaper article that is relevant to current issues or to the topic being pursued by the class. All of the procedures have been outlined in other chapters in relation to other kinds of text; suggestions for extension, support and assessment can be found under the appropriate headings in these activities.

Preparation

Select a relevant newspaper article and enlarge it if necessary. Remove the headline and cut the article into several segments, following the paragraph structure of the text.

Resources needed

One copy of the segmented article for each pair of children.

What to do

Each pair of children should be given a set of shuffled paragraphs. They should scan these before reading them carefully, looking for any clues to the correct order of the paragraphs, and making suggestions about the content of the intact article. The children should then be helped to conduct whichever of the following procedures you consider appropriate for their level of ability and interest:

▲ Reconstruct a coherent sequence for the segments.
▲ Write a headline for the article.
▲ Write a sub-heading for each segment.
▲ Underline key words and phrases in the article.
▲ Create a graphic or tabular representation of the information in the article.
▲ Write a letter to the editor in response to the article.
▲ Write an article arguing from a different position on the same issue.
▲ Rewrite the article in the style of another newspaper.
▲ Select or create a captioned illustration to accompany the article.

Opportunities for IT

The original story could be typed on to the word processor, or even taken from a newspaper CD-ROM, and then split into sections with the order altered. Children can then use the 'cut' and 'paste', or drag and drop commands to re-order the article. Any of the writing tasks in this activity could be undertaken using a word processor. Depending on the type of writing undertaken this would provide opportunities for children to develop their editing, presentation, formatting and organisational skills.

Other aspects of the English PoS covered

Speaking and listening – 3b.
Writing – 1a, b; 2a, b, c, d, e; 3b.

GENDER LANGUAGE IN NEWSPAPERS

To raise awareness of the different conventions that newspapers use in their descriptions of people, and how these might reflect stereotyped attitudes towards both the subjects of description and the readership.

†† *Small groups, reporting back to the whole class.*
🕐 *30–40 minutes.*

Key background information

This activity could take place within a project on media studies, or as a preparation for producing a school or class newspaper.

Preparation

Buy a range of tabloid and broadsheet newspapers for a particular day or week, or ask the children to compile such a collection themselves.

Resources needed

Newspapers, scissors, chart-making materials.

What to do

Explain the objective of the activity to the children. Give each group examples of broadsheet and tabloid newspapers, and ask them to scan them for words and phrases used to describe men and women. These should be cut out or copied and enlarged, then placed on a matrix which cross-references the title of the newspaper with the language it uses about men and women. (See Figure 1.) For each newspaper title and for each

gender, ask the children to compare the number of descriptions that make reference to:
▲ career and public position;
▲ relationship to a member of the opposite sex;
▲ physical appearance;
▲ age.

Ask the children to discuss the underlying attitudes that might be giving rise to these different types of language. If you find that the differences are more apparent in the tabloids than the broadsheets, discuss what this implies about the newspaper producers' attitudes towards their readership. If you have a school newspaper, a similar survey could be conducted.

Suggestion(s) for extension

This survey could be extended to include other types of journalism, such as comics, magazines and television reports, as well as to sources such as children's fiction from different historical periods.

The children can be encouraged to write to newspaper editors, asking them why they favour a particular type of description.

Suggestion(s) for support

Read aloud the opening words of descriptions to the children, without giving away the gender of the person being described. For example:
Heroic fire-fighter …
Thirty-year-old blonde …
Prominent politician …
Glamorous soap star …

	Men	Women

Daily Mirror	Di's brother
	Pop heart-throb
	  Terence Trent D'Arby
	Silver-haired academic
	  Dr. Stan Smith
		Supermodel Cindy Crawford
		TV's Linda
		Actress and Labour MP
		  Glenda Jackson

The Sun	Brainy Bamber Gascoigne Diana's dashing Major Lawyer Colin Scott Pasta-loving opera star Luciano Pavarotti	Sexy Angela Lea Angry bride Maria Kelly Glamorous Lisa Gough

Daily Telegraph	Defence Secretary
	  Lord Younger
	Journalist Keith
	  Waterhouse
		Lady Chalker, Minister for
		  Overseas Development
		Common-law wife of solicitor
		  Colin Harris

Figure 1

113

Ask the children to guess the gender of the subject, and use their responses to launch a discussion about the issues outlined above.

Assessment opportunities
Note the children's ability to scan the text and their awareness of the equal opportunities issues implicit in this task.

Display ideas
The charts made by the children can be displayed, together with photographs and stories linked to similar issues.

Other aspects of the English PoS covered
Speaking and listening – 1a, b, c; 2a, b; 3b.

IT'S A WELL-KNOWN FACT

Carrots help you see in the dark.
Wo___ ___ bad drivers.
___lligent than boys.

IT'S A WELL-KNOWN FACT

To highlight the fact that certain forms of language can be used to conceal the language user's motives.

†† *The whole class, working in pairs.*

🕐 *45 minutes.*

Key background information
In this activity children will discuss newspaper reports, identifying biased language and discussing the potential sources of bias.

Preparation
One copy of photocopiable page 157 is needed for each pair of children. Do the suggested activity yourself, and collect examples of real press reports which reflect the issues to be explored.

Resources needed
See above.

What to do
Introduction
Write the words 'It's a well-known fact' on the board and ask the children to complete the phrase, orally, in as many ways as they can. Discuss which of the children's suggestions are, in reality well-known facts. Pose the questions, 'How well known?' and 'Well known by whom?'

Development
Give each pair of children a copy of

It's a well-known fact

THE NEWS THAT COMPULSORY CORPORAL PUNISHMENT is to be introduced into all schools has been greeted with jubilation by a huge majority of the country's parents, teachers and children. With immediate effect, any breach of school rules, however trivial, is to be rewarded with the kind of sound thrashing that taught children the difference between right and wrong in happier, less crime-plagued times. So seriously does the Government take this initiative that it has ordered that any teacher refusing to carry out this policy will be liable to instant dismissal followed by imprisonment and a regime of physical chastisement.

'It's a well-known fact that children respect figures of authority,' said Jill Farr-Wright, the new Education Minister. 'I was a third-generation teacher before entering politics, and both my father and grandfather were broken-hearted at the breakdown in discipline due to the decline of corporal punishment. My grandfather flogged several boys to within an inch of their lives when he was a teacher, and with the exception of one child who succumbed to his injuries, they all sent him Christmas cards every year. If that doesn't prove something, I don't know what does.'

Psychiatrists working alongside toy trade entrepreneurs have disclosed that the recent dramatic rise in the price of toys has had a profoundly positive effect on the self-esteem of deprived children.

'It's a well-known fact that the more expensive a toy is, the more satisfaction a child derives from it,' said Dr G. Reed of the Children As Consumers Juvenile Protection Unit. 'By owning an expensive toy, children who find it hard to achieve in other areas derive an enormous sense of satisfaction. An expensive toy says "Your parents love you", especially if the child comes from an impoverished family. These toys convince individual children of their own worth, and stimulate healthy competition.'

The enhanced levels of theft, vandalism and friction between children often associated with the ownership of expensive toys also has positive consequences, the Department of Trade and Industry has revealed.

'Fighting to maintain ownership of valuables constitutes personal growth for the budding consumer,' Junior Minister V. Nallity commented last night. 'It creates a keen sense of ownership and prepares children for the home security responsibilities they will assume in later life.'

photocopiable sheet 157, and ask them to read through the passages before:
▲ underlining those parts of the text with which they agree;
▲ underlining in a different colour those parts of the text with which they disagree;
▲ noting whose interests are being served by the statements;
▲ noting whose interests and opinions are not represented in the reports;
▲ noting any real-life press reports which they come across which raise any related issues.

Conclusion
Pairs of children can share their responses to this activity with each other before the responses of the whole class are compared.

Urge the children to look out for authentic texts in future projects which relate to this theme.

Suggestion(s) for extension
Children can collect examples of newspaper reports and subject them to the same analysis.

Suggestion(s) for support
The entire activity can be done orally, if appropriate.

Assessment opportunities

Note the children's ability to scan the texts for evidence of bias and distortion.

Display ideas

Authentic examples of biased newspaper reporting can be displayed, with the children's annotations and underlinings marked on them.

Other aspects of the English PoS covered

Speaking and listening – 1a, b, c; 2a, b.

Reference to photocopiable sheet

Photocopiable page 157 provides a parody of biased reporting.

ENVIRONMENTAL PRINT

To heighten children's awareness of the range of types of writing that surround them, and to help them to become aware of the origins and purposes of these texts.

†† *The whole class, working in small groups.*

🕐 *30-minutes for the introductory session, then open-ended follow-up.*

Key background information

This activity would fit well into a project on the local environment.

Preparation

Take a series of photographs of environmental print in the vicinity of the school. These should range from single words, such as those found on traffic signs, to complex clusters of text, such as a well-loaded newspaper stand. Try to include as many different examples as you can: labels, warnings, persuasive advertisements, reminders, acknowledgements (bus tickets and other types of receipts, for example) and so on. Make a display of your work, draw the children's attention to it, and ask them to look out for examples of environmental print that you have overlooked.

Resources needed

Photographs, photocopies of the photographs for distribution, drawing and writing materials.

What to do

Introduction

Present each group with a selection of items copied from your display. Ask them to discuss the origin and purpose of each one. In most cases the purpose will be fairly obvious, though young children might be a bit unsure about who actually issues advertisements, traffic signs and warnings about litter.

Development

Ask each group to visualise a particular environment, such as a railway carriage, a bus, a launderette, a supermarket or a cinema. Ask them to make a display of all the different types of print that they would find in this environment, and to annotate each type of writing with its function and possible author. Unofficial writing, such as graffiti, fly-posting and political slogans, should also be included.

One group could be given the task of envisioning the street outside the school as it might be in ten or a hundred years' time, and drawing some of the types of environmental print (both official and unofficial) that might be current at that time.

Conclusion

Children should compare their work and discuss the following points:
▲ the scope of the intended audience for each type of print (some will be directed to everyone in general, others will be specifically targeted);
▲ which types of message are best conveyed by single words and which need more extended writing;
▲ which types can stand alone and which need illustration;
▲ the variety of types of message found in each environment (commands, labels, warnings, slogans and so on);
▲ which items are necessary and which are dispensable, making it clear to whom particular items are necessary.

Suggestion(s) for extension

A group of children can be given the job of redesigning the environmental print for a particular location; making messages clearer, adding necessary messages which are missing, and editing out messages which are not necessary.

More detailed ideas for extending this type of work to more specific items of environmental print are outlined in subsequent activities.

Media

JUNK MAIL

To raise critical awareness of the types of persuasion through text that adult readers are subjected to.

👫 *Whole class, working in small groups.*
🕐 *30–40 minutes.*

Key background information
This activity would be a useful element of a topic on the environment or on aspects of media studies.

Preparation
Enlist the co-operation of parents and guardians in amassing as wide a range of junk mail as you possibly can. To give the children some idea of the scale of the junk mail phenomenon, the collection should cover a set period of time such as a week or a month, and should be displayed in such a way that the volume and variety of the material are presented vividly.

Resources needed
Junk mail, charts for recording the children's findings.

What to do
Introduction
Give each group a representative selection of material and allow them to sort it into whatever categories they find most useful.

Development
Ask the children to work in pairs or individually, and to make notes on the following points for each item of junk mail:
▲ features which suggest the intended audience;
▲ the use of vivid words and phrases to attract interest;
▲ the use of language and images appealing to vanity, greed, fear or compassion;
▲ the use of rhetorical devices such as questions, startling statements and commands;
▲ the contrast between the types of information given in large print and those given in small print.

The junk mail and the children's notes on it should be incorporated into a chart which can be presented to the whole class.

Conclusion
When the children have compared their findings, ask them to discuss the advantages and disadvantages of this phenomenon, reminding them (if you are old enough) what it was like to receive post before junk mail became so prevalent.

Suggestion(s) for extension
If the children are sufficiently interested, you could ask them to compose a piece of junk mail arguing for or against a ban on junk mail.

Suggestion(s) for support
The best support for this activity is to take a group of children on a print walk, either inside the school or in its immediate vicinity. As each item of print is encountered, the teacher can guide discussion using the points outlined above. It is useful to take along a tape recorder as a 'talking notebook', so that each child's observations can be recorded and later discussed and written up.

Assessment opportunities
This activity will enable you to assess the children's awareness of environmental print, their ability to comprehend it, and the level of their critical awareness of its influence and origins.

Opportunities for IT
Children could use a word processor, desktop publishing or drawing package to design the new messages. This would encourage them to consider the use of different font styles to highlight the formality of the message. If a graphics package is used, children can design different-sized labels, use different colours and include borders to make their notices stand out. The resulting messages could be displayed or used within the school.

Display ideas
Your photograph display can be extended to include contributions from real and imaginary environments researched by the children.

Other aspects of the English PoS covered
Speaking and listening – 1a, b, c; 2a, b; 3a, b, c.
Writing – 1a, b, c; 2a, b, c, d, e; 3a, b, c.

The children could also be asked to write back to the publishers of the material, enclosing a summary of their critical comments.

Suggestion(s) for support
Items of junk mail text can be enlarged, and their salient features underlined and annotated with questions which direct the children's attention towards the persuasive and potentially deceptive nature of this material.

Assessment opportunities
Note the children's ability to appreciate rhetorical language and other textual features aimed at the manipulation of the reader.

Opportunities for IT
Some more advanced word processors have the facility for 'mail merge', where a standard letter is written with spaces left for personal information such as the name and address of the person to whom it is being sent. A database of names and addresses is then merged with the letter so that each letter appears to be written personally. Older or more able pupils might like to experiment with this facility. They could try to mail merge a personal letter about a school trip or event to each child in the class. Children would need support to set up the database and put the relevant field codes into the letter.

Even if children do not have an opportunity to see the mail merge at work, teachers should use the facility to highlight the use of IT in the wider world and the way that personalised mail can be used to influence people. Children might also discuss how companies obtain the names and addresses of people for mailing lists and the morality and environmental issues connected with junk mail.

Display ideas
See above.

Other aspects of the English PoS covered
Speaking and listening – 1a, b, c; 2a, b; 3b.

COMICS
To develop children's general reading skills through working with words and phrases in a context that they will find entertaining. To develop awareness of the specific language conventions found in comics and cartoons.

†† *The whole class, working in small groups.*

🕐 *20–40 minutes for each activity.*

Key background information
This is an open-ended set of procedures that can be used with comics and cartoon strips. The activities can be carried out in any order.

Preparation
Enlist the children's help in compiling as large and varied a collection of comics and cartoon strips as you can. You may need to photocopy and enlarge some of these for certain activities.

Resources needed
A collection of comics; drawing and writing materials.

What to do
▲ Cut a cartoon or comic strip into its separate frames, shuffle the frames and ask the children to reconstruct the story.

▲ Delete the print from speech balloons and captions. This can be done either with selected balloons and captions or with the whole text. Ask the children to use the graphics and any remaining text as clues in restoring coherent dialogue and captions.

▲ Cut out the speech balloons, enlarge them, photocopy them and shuffle them. Arrange the children into pairs, give each pair a set of balloons and ask them to fit these into a sequence and explain their sequence if necessary. This can then be used as a starter for a written story. When the activity has been completed, the story can be compared with the one from which the speech balloons came. This might help children to understand the incoherence which sometimes occurs in their own stories when they concentrate on writing dialogue and sound effects to the exclusion of all else.

▲ Focus on the onomatopoeic words in the text. Delete these and ask the children to experiment with substitutes. For example, what would be the effect of replacing human sounds with animal ones, or substituting gentle sounds for strident ones?

▲ Ask each group to sort their selection of comics into those aimed at boys and those aimed at girls. They can then carry out a content analysis of the comics, recording their findings about the content of stories, features and adverts and about differences in vocabulary, typography and illustration on charts to be presented to the rest of the class. The class as a whole can then discuss the assumptions about boys' and girls' interests which underlie the design of these texts. Follow-up work might involve writing to authors, illustrators and editors.

▲ Select from each comic any items of language that seem to you to be characteristic of the producer's perceptions of the attitudes and interests of the intended audience. These could be snippets of dialogue from speech balloons, captions for illustrations, editorial comment, readers' letters, or alluring words and phrases from the front cover. Type these out in a uniform style and mount them on to cards, then ask the children to match them to an array of comics. When this has been done, ask them to justify the 'matches' they have made. Draw their attention to such issues as the presumed gender appeal of certain types of language, the use of informal words and idioms, and the sense of exclusiveness implicit in the use of technical terminology.

Suggestion(s) for extension

Fluent readers can make a collection of historical stories which have been told in comic-strip form ('The Odyssey', the *Ramayana* and 'picture biographies' of the Buddha, Christ, Guru Gobind Singh and Mohammed are all readily available in comic book form). These can be compared critically with prose versions.

Children can enlist the aid of adults in making a historical collection of comics. The changing depiction of individual characters can then be traced, as well as more general changes in the content, presentation and language of the comics. This type of investigation would be a very valuable component of any topic on social change.

Suggestion(s) for support

For each activity, work with an enlarged text and demonstrate the first steps of the procedure. To begin with, use texts which the children have contributed to the collection themselves, and with which they are familiar. The compositional aspects of tasks which require writing can be performed orally, and the scribing done by the teacher or another helper.

Assessment opportunities

Note the range of reading skills which the children bring to each activity, their aesthetic appreciation of the special language of comic books, and their critical awareness of gender and producer/consumer issues.

Opportunities for IT

Children could create a simple database about the different types of stories found in different comics. This would require some discussion about the categories that stories might fall into. Children could then interrogate the database to find the most common types of story, numbers of stories, the relationship between the intended audience for the comic and the stories included. Examplar fieldnames and data might include:

Title	The Beano
Cost	20p
Audience	B/G
No. of stories	13
Sport	0
Space	2
Animals	1
Hobbies	0
Crime	0
Ghosts	2
Fantasy	3
Cartoon	3
Others	2

Looking at the cost and number of pages might also provide some interesting statistics on value for money!

Display ideas

See 'What to do'.

Other aspects of the English PoS covered

Speaking and listening – 1a, b, c; 2a, b; 3a, b, c.
Writing – 1a, b, c; 2a, b, c, d, e; 3a, b, c.

PLAY SCRIPTS

To develop a range of reading skills and to familiarise children with the conventions of drama texts.

†† *Small groups.*

🕐 *20–40 minutes for each activity.*

Key background information

As with the previous activity, the procedures outlined below are open-ended and can be carried out in any order.

Preparation

Collect a set of drama texts appropriate for the age range and interests of the children you teach. Most of the more recent reading schemes incorporate such texts, and *Drama and Short Plays* compiled by Alan Brown (*Collections* series, Scholastic 1993) is a versatile collection which incorporates many photocopiable pages.

Resources needed

A drama text collection, writing materials.

What to do

The first priority is for the children to perform and appreciate the texts. They should have copious experience of this before being presented with any of the more analytical activities outlined below.

▲ Take a self-contained stretch of dialogue and cut it up into segments corresponding to individual turns in the dialogue. Ask the children to reassemble it.

▲ Delete one character's part from a dialogue and ask the children to use the remaining text in order to write in the missing part.

▲ Present the children with an intact stretch of conversation, but delete the character part indicators. Ask the children to read the dialogue and to mark in the character names.

▲ Present the children with an unfinished scene and ask them to improvise their own completion to it, taking one part each. This can be done either spontaneously or after discussion and the writing of a script. The children can then compare their completion with that given by the original text.

▲ Give the children one short scene from the middle of an unfamiliar play. Ask them to read and act it out, and then to speculate on the personalities and motivations of the characters, the events that have preceded the portion they have read, and the events which are to follow.

Suggestion(s) for extension

All of the above activities can be extended steadily to more challenging and less familiar texts, and can be used as a preparation for the children's writing of their own plays.

Suggestion(s) for support

Work with texts which the children have already acted out, and use drama rather than 'cold' reading as the basis for any of the above activities. Texts which have been transcribed from taped dialogues and dramas created by the children themselves make very good starting-points.

Assessment opportunities

This set of activities should enable you to observe a range of reading skills, including the children's ability to use oral intonation in bringing the texts to life.

Opportunities for IT

If the original text is prepared using a word processor, children can re-assemble the text into the correct sequence or can mark the character names into a text where the names have been deleted from the play script.

Other aspects of the English PoS covered

Speaking and listening – 1a, b, c, d; 2a, b; 3a, b, c.
Writing – 1a, b, c; 2a, b, c, d, e; 3a, b, c.

CROSSWORDS

To familiarise children with spelling patterns and the conventions of using a dictionary.

†† *Children working individually, in pairs or in small groups.*

🕐 *20 minutes.*

Key background information

This is a very flexible strategy that can be adapted to the vocabulary of any subject area.

Preparation

Select the vocabulary that you want to cover with the children; ideally, this will be a set of terms related to the topic that the children are about to study. Devise a crossword matrix for these words, then write in the words, and write a set of clues of appropriate difficulty. These clues should reflect the definition of each of the terms you have selected, but should not simply be copied from the dictionary that the children will be using. There should be scope for the children to compare clues and definitions, and to decide whether or not they match.

Write the clues out in random order, with no indication of which word on the crossword grid they relate to.

Resources needed

Crosswords, clues, dictionaries at an appropriate level of sophistication.

What to do

Hand out the crosswords, the clues and the dictionaries. Explain to the children that the purpose of the game is to search for the definitions of the words on the crossword matrix, and to use the information they find in the dictionary to match the scrambled clues to the words on the grid, writing in the correct number and direction (across or down) for each clue.

Suggestion(s) for extension

Children who are interested in word games can try to create similar puzzles for each other.

Suggestion(s) for support

Conduct the activity as a shared reading session, using a simple dictionary and providing a closer match between the clues given and the dictionary definitions.

Assessment opportunities

Note the children's ability to locate words and definitions in the dictionary by using all the structural guides supplied.

Opportunities for IT

Children could be introduced to electronic dictionaries and thesauruses such as those on handheld spelling devices, or could use the dictionaries of word processors or desktop publishing software. Some of the newer palmtop computers also have inbuilt dictionaries and even anagram facilities which could be used by children to solve the more difficult clues to the crosswords.

Display ideas

A selection of blank crosswords can be enlarged and displayed for individuals and groups to work on during spare moments. They can be accompanied by other crosswords (with clues) cut from newspapers and magazines.

Other aspects of the English PoS covered

Speaking and listening – 1a, b, c; 2a, b; 3b.

120

MORPHEMIC WORD WEBS

To compose assemblies of words based on similar roots, then discuss their relationships and the ways in which such relationships are depicted in dictionaries.

†† *The whole class – children working in groups, with partners or individually.*

🕐 *10 to 15 minutes.*

Key background information
This activity is aimed at raising children's awareness of word structure, spelling patterns and relationships between words. Like the 'Alliterative word web' activity on page 82, it is a valuable routine to practise on a daily basis.

Preparation
Take a selection of words which are related to a current class topic or story. Look at each word individually and brainstorm as many other words as you can which are related by morphology, arranging the new words in a web around the original (see Figure 1). Display your word webs and explain to the children what you have been doing. Show them an enlarged photocopy from a page of a dictionary, displaying the conventions for representing cognate forms of a word.

Resources needed
Notebooks and writing materials.

Figure 1

night *noun* 1. The time between sunset and sunrise, the hours of darkness. T' time between bedtime and morning. 2. N *noun, plural* nights.

nightfall *noun* pproach of darkn dusk.

garment worn wh women.

What to do
Write a familiar word on the board or on a chart, and around it write two or three other words which are morphologically related to it. Ask the children to copy this into their notebooks, and to add as many other related words as they can think of. Allow five minutes or so for this, then ask them to read out the words that they have produced. Write these out on the board or chart. Discuss the meanings of these words and the different ways in which they relate to the original word.

Suggestion(s) for extension
A dictionary of words related to a particular topic area can be written by the children, incorporating morphologically-related forms.

Suggestion(s) for support
Conduct the activity orally with children who have trouble writing independently. Write their responses on a chart and draw their attention to structural relationships between the words.

Assessment opportunities
Note the children's ability to perceive visual and semantic relationships between words.

Opportunities for IT
When children have completed the original word web they could be allowed access to handheld electronic dictionaries, or the dictionaries or thesauruses that accompany word processors or palmtop computers, to extend the range of words in the web.

Display ideas
Word webs can be displayed on charts. This will be particularly appropriate if the words are related to a topic being explored by the children.

Other aspects of the English PoS covered
Speaking and listening – 1a, c; 2b.
Writing – 1a, b, c; 2a, b, d.

FREE-ASSOCIATION WORD WEBS

To generate as many words as possible related to a given word, and to discuss how the relationships between these words and the given word might best be displayed.

†† *The whole class, working individually, in pairs or in groups.*

⏱ *10 to 15 minutes.*

Key background information
Like the other word web activities, this should be conducted on a daily basis and not allowed to drag on for too long. The idea here is to explore more open-ended relationships between words, and to encourage the children to design and use their own thesauri.

Preparation
Take a selection of words related to a story or topic that you have been exploring with the class. Write each word down in the middle of a piece of paper, and around it write down all the words associated with it that you can think of – indicating, if you can, the relationship between each of the new words and the original word. Put your work on display and talk to the children about it.

Resources needed
Notebooks and writing materials, thesauri using different principles of organisation.

What to do
Write the stimulus word on the board or on a chart. Write any words sparked off by this stimulus around it, and talk to the children about why these words occurred to you. Ask

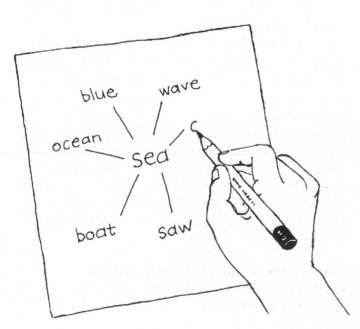

the children to copy this web and extend it as far as possible. Allow about five minutes for this, then ask them to read out the words that they have produced. Add these to the chart and discuss how they are related to the stimulus word. Synonyms and antonyms will be particularly useful for achieving the objective of the lesson, but the idiosyncratic responses you will probably receive might be more interesting.

If the children are not already familiar with thesauri, show them one or two examples and explain how such books are organised and how a writer might use them. Many word-processing programs provide computerised thesauri, and children should be familiarised with these.

Suggestion(s) for extension
Children can be encouraged to develop their word webs into personal thesauri, using principles of organisation from published sources or developing their own.

Word webs can also be used as a starter for poetic or descriptive writing. The words generated from the stimulus word can be incorporated into phrases, and the order and wording of the phrases can be manipulated until a satisfying composition has been produced.

Suggestion(s) for support
This type of writing can be supported by oral word-association games, for example: 'tennis - elbow - foot'. The children sit in a circle and the first player calls out the first word that comes into her head; the next player responds with a word that is associated with it in some way; the next player responds to the previous player's word; and so on, going round the circle.

Children who have difficulty with the kind of rapid writing required for this activity can work orally with a scribe.

Assessment opportunities
Children's vocabulary and their sensitivity to relationships between words can be assessed through this activity.

Display ideas
Word webs can be displayed as vocabulary resources. They can be organised on thesaurus principles, with separate displays for synonyms and antonyms; or they can be left as open-ended and idiosyncratic free-association webs. In either case, children should be free to add to them over time.

Opportunities for IT
Children could be introduced to the thesauri which are incorporated into many word processing or desktop publishing programs or which are an integral part of laptop or palmtop computers.

Other aspects of the English PoS covered
Speaking and listening – 1a, b, c; 2a, b; 3a, b.
Writing – 1a, b, c; 2d, e; 3c.

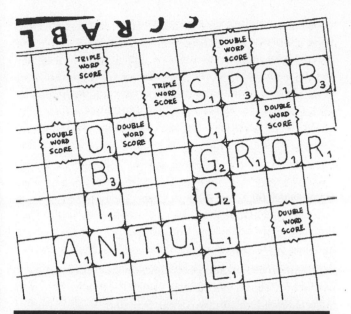

ANTISCRABBLE

To familiarise children with more complex sound-spelling associations, to extend their interest in imaginative wordplay, and to provide experience in the use of dictionary conventions.

†† *Small groups.*

🕐 *20–40 minutes.*

Key background information
This is a word game based on the familiar game of Scrabble. It can be played to sharpen children's spelling awareness, their dictionary skills or their knowledge of word structure; or it can be used purely as an imaginative recreation.

Preparation
Photocopy selected pages from a dictionary, highlighting in different colours such features as the pronunciation guide, word class indication and definition for various entries. Using a Scrabble or Boggle set, make up some non-existent words, concoct definitions for them, and write formal dictionary entries for them.

Resources needed
A Scrabble game, photocopies of dictionary pages, writing materials.

What to do
Read your own imaginary words to the children and ask them to guess what these might mean. Encourage them to base their guesses on such features as onomatopoeia and morphemic structure. Read your definitions to the children and show them the dictionary conventions that you have followed in writing them.

Explain to the children that they are going to be playing a game which explores spelling patterns, sounds, meanings and definitions.

Show the children how to play Antiscrabble. This is played in exactly the same way as conventional Scrabble, except for the following rules:

▲ Any word that can be found in a published dictionary is disallowed.

▲ Only words that can be *pronounced* are allowed; the spellings of the words must therefore follow the same rules as 'real' English words. This condition can stimulate some useful discussion on which letter strings are permissible in English spelling.

▲ The player must offer a coherent definition for each word played.

Record the game on tape, and when it is over, select a few particularly interesting words to form the subject of the children's written definitions. This phase of the session should only be introduced after the children have played the game a few times.

Suggestion(s) for extension
This activity can be related to any of the other activities on the phonology and morphology of language. Many dictionaries provide families of related verbs, adjectives, complex nouns and compound nouns for the entry that they define; it would be useful for interested children to do the same thing for a selection of the words that they have created in the game.

The words that are generated can be used to write nonsense poetry; or you can challenge the children to create their own thematic ABC of imaginary animals, materials or machines.

Suggestion(s) for support
Join the game as one of the players, clarifying the rules as you go along and prompting the children by encouraging them to think of the sound of a particular word, or a possible association with a known word.

Assessment opportunities
Note the children's ability to identify permissible spelling patterns, their familiarity with dictionary conventions, and their awareness of word morphology and onomatopoeia.

Opportunities for IT
Children could use a word processor or desktop publishing package to present their final list of defined words. They could be introduced to the kind of formatting commands which enable them to present their work in a standard dictionary format, using indents to split definitions from the words and italics to highlight the pronunciation from the definition itself.

Other aspects of the English PoS covered
Speaking and listening – 1a, b, c; 2a, b.
Writing – 2a, b, c, d; 3b, c.

NOT THE NINE O'CLOCK NEWS

To create an audiotape from readings of a spoof news-script based on the children's own oral compositions.
†† *The whole class for preliminary oral work, then sessions with individual children.*
🕐 *30 minutes for group work, then about 10 minutes each for sessions with individual children.*

Key background information

In this activity, the children will be required to read unfamiliar material; but they will be supported by the fact that the material, prepared by the teacher, is based closely on their own oral compositions.

Preparation

Tape some examples of television and radio news readings. If possible, you should also tape examples of humorous parodies of these readings. If you cannot do this, try writing your own humorous parody of a news broadcast.

Resources needed

Tapes of news broadcasts, tape recorder, microphone, word processor.

What to do
Introduction

Encourage the children to discuss any current news story which has attracted their attention. Play the news tapes. Read out your own transcript and draw the children's attention to the distinctive features of broadcast text. Ask them to try to present some news stories that they are interested in (orally) as a news bulletin.

Development one

Play the children the parody tapes, or read out a humorous parody of a news broadcast that you have written yourself. Explain that the purpose of the activity is for each person to contribute one news story to a class 'Not the Nine o' Clock News' broadcast about impossible events.

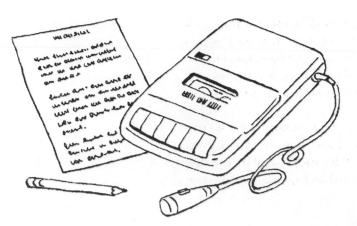

Ask the children to sit in a circle around the tape recorder. The microphone can be passed round until one person feels that they are ready to contribute. This activity will probably generate a lot of laughter: you will need to keep the tape switched on and the microphone circulating, capturing any false starts and collapses into laughter that occur.

When the children have all contributed, allow them to listen to the whole tape and to suggest ways in which this 'rough draft' of the broadcast might be made more coherent.

Development (2)

Make a transcript of the children's stories, sticking to their storyline and vocabulary, but 'tidying up' the text where necessary. The length of each story will be based on your own assessment of the children's reading stamina.

Hold individual sessions with each child for the tape-making activity. Allow each child to read through their own story as many times as is necessary to produce a confident reading for the tape. Provide help with difficult words where necessary, and model the type of intonation and the reading pace that are typical of news broadcasting.

Conclusion

After each child has contributed, the tape can be played to the whole class.

Suggestion(s) for extension

The group can follow a similar procedure to create parodies of weather forecasts, interviews, sports commentaries and other broadcast texts.

Suggestion(s) for support

Children who are not yet capable of reading independently can be supported by the following basic procedure:
1. Read the text to the child without requiring her to contribute to the reading aloud. Use appropriately stressed intonation when doing this.
2. Read the text again, inviting the child to join in whenever she feels confident enough.
3. Invite the child to start off the reading. Join in the reading whenever the child falters.

Assessment opportunities

Note the degree of confidence with which the child reads, the 'naturalness' of the intonation patterns, and the cues that the child uses when dealing with less familiar words.

Display ideas

The tape can be included in the class listening collection, with an appropriately-designed cassette cover and a set of word-processed and illustrated transcripts.

Other aspects of the English PoS covered

Speaking and listening – 1a, b, c, d; 2a, b; 3a, b.

Photocopiables

The pages in this section can be photocopied for use in the classroom or school which has purchased this book, and do not need to be declared in any return in respect of any photocopying licence.

They comprise a varied selection of both pupil and teacher resources, including pupil worksheets, resource material and record sheets to be completed by the teacher or children. Most of the photocopiable pages are related to individual activities in the book; the name of the activity is indicated at the top of the sheet, together with a page reference indicating where the lesson plan for that activity can be found.

Individual pages are discussed in detail within each lesson plan, accompanied by ideas for adaptation where appropriate – of course, each sheet can be adapted to suit your own needs and those of your class. Sheets can also be coloured, laminated, mounted on to card, enlarged and so on where appropriate.

Pupil worksheets and record sheets have spaces provided for children's names and for noting the date on which each sheet was used. This means that, if so required, they can be included easily within any pupil assessment portfolio.

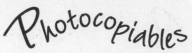
Document restoration (1), see page 21

The *Marie Celeste*

Name _____   Date _____

▲ This message was found inside a bottle washed up on the beach.
Read it through and imagine what the rest of the message might have said.
Finish off the message in the space below.

The Marie Celeste

17th November 1902

To the finder of this bottle,

*If our ship is ever found, it will be empty. I am writing this
letter to explain what happened to us. When I finish it, I
will put it into a bottle and fling it into the sea.*

*Last night, everybody was woken up by a great light in the
sky and the sound of beautiful voices singing. We came out
on deck, and saw a wonderful sky ship anchored in the
clouds. The sailors of this sky ship were winged creatures
who fluttered about our masts and rigging. They sang to us
in a language we could not understand. Then the leader of
these wonderful creatures spoke to us in English, and told
us that*

What happens next? see page 23

Prediction (1)

There was once a head teacher who ran an enormously posh school, so exclusive and expensive that only her own three daughters could afford to go there. Two of them were sensible girls, but the youngest was very mischievous.

One day, the head teacher announced that she had to go on a long journey to visit another school. She told her daughters that she was leaving them in charge of her own school.

'You may play in the grounds and stroll in the orchard,' she told them, 'and you may enter any room in the school, except for the tiny room at the very top of the bell tower. That room is extremely dangerous.'

When the daughters found themselves alone, they soon became bored with the grounds and the orchard, and they took to exploring the school. Within a week they had searched every room, but none of them dared to approach the tiny room at the very top of the bell tower. Then one day when her sisters were picking apples in the orchard, the youngest daughter decided to climb the staircase to the top of the bell tower. At first she had no intention of going into the forbidden room. She just wanted to enjoy the view from the staircase windows – but when she reached the door of the tiny room at the very top, something made her open it and step inside.

There was nothing in the room except an old school desk, and a curious old exercise book which lay on the desk. She was about to open the book when she saw the writing on its cover. It said *'On no account should this book be opened.'*

The youngest daughter was frightened and wanted to leave the room, but something made her stretch out her hand to the book and open it. What she read inside froze her blood.

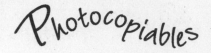
Sequencing unfamiliar text, see page 24

Death conquers all

'What are you running away from, old fellow?' said one of the youths.

'From Death,' said the old man. 'I have seen Death hiding in a cave and I must escape from him.'

'We're not frightened of Death,' said another one of the young men. 'Show us where he is hiding, and we'll show Death who is master around here.'

While he was in town, the younger man began to think about how rich he would be if he had all of the money himself. He bought plenty of food and wine, but he also bought poison and poured it into the wine bottle.

They began to count the gold in order to divide it up fairly between them. After a while, they became tired and hungry. They decided to have dinner, so the youngest man was sent to the nearest town to buy food and wine.

The man dropped his sticks and fled from the cave. Further down the beach he ran into three youths who were lounging on the sand.

The old man pointed along the beach and then hurried away. The three young men walked down the beach and soon found the cave. When they saw the chest full of gold inside it, they forgot all about Death and began to rejoice at their good luck.

When the young man returned to the cave, his two companions stabbed him to death. Then they sat down to eat the food he had brought and to drink the poisoned wine. Within minutes, they too were dead. Death had conquered after all.

There was once an old man who found a cave by the sea while he was gathering driftwood after a storm. Looking into the mouth of the cave, he saw a large sea-chest standing open, and in the chest was more gold than any person could count in a day.

While he was away, the older men began to talk about how much more money they would have if there were only two of them to share it. They decided to kill the younger man when he returned.

 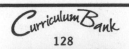

Sequencing unfamiliar text, see page 24

Winter is coming

Later still, a fox padded by and saw the young frog sitting there.

'Go to sleep, young frog,' he said. 'Winter is coming and you will surely freeze.'

But the young frog stayed awake.

- -

The next thing he knew, the warm spring sun was shining down through the water of the pond. All of his brothers and sisters were awake already, and they were making fun of him for having tried to see what Winter was like.

'Never mind,' he said. 'I did see a little of the Winter, *and* I had a better sleep than any other frog in the pond as well.'

- -

Winter came. The young frog shivered and yawned. How nice it would be to settle into the mud for just a few minutes, he thought.

- -

The young frog ignored them. He decided that he would become the first frog to stay awake for the whole of the Winter. So when all the other frogs had gone to sleep in the mud at the bottom of the pond, the young frog sat alone on the river bank and tried to stay awake.

- -

Later, a hedgehog on his way to his long Winter sleep shuffled past the bank and saw the young frog sitting there.

'Go to sleep, young frog,' he said. 'Winter is coming and you will surely freeze.'

But the young frog stayed awake.

- -

Once upon a time there was a young frog who wanted to know what Winter was like. All of the other frogs thought that he was silly. They told him that frogs had to go to sleep for the Winter, and that any frog who tried to stay awake would come to no good.

- -

The young frog jumped into the pond just before it froze over. He settled into the mud and fell fast asleep.

- -

As he sat there, the geese who were flying south for Winter looked down and saw him.

'Go to sleep, young frog,' they said. 'Winter is coming and you will surely freeze.'

But the young frog stayed awake.

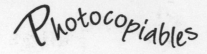
The missing piece, see page 26

Nasr-ed-Din

Name _____   Date _____

▲ Fill in the missing words from this story.

One day, the richest man in town came riding past Nasr-ed-Din's house as he was ladling a delicious stew from the pot into a bowl.

'Good day, Nasr-ed-Din,' he said. 'That's a wonderfully big pot of food you have there. Why not give half of it to a hungry traveller? I've been riding for hours and would dearly love to share your dinner.'

'You are welcome to a small bowl of my stew,' Nasr-ed-Din replied, 'but I can't give you half of it. What's left has to last me through the week.'

'Through the week?' asked the rich man, who had decided to try to trick Nasr-ed-Din. 'There's no need to worry about that. Haven't you heard that

_____ ?'

Nasr-ed-Din looked at the rich man, then he smiled.

'If _____ ,'

he said, 'then you might as well take half of my stew.'

The rich man dismounted from his magnificent horse and sat down to dinner with Nasr-ed-Din. The stew tasted every bit as delicious as it smelt, and the rich man ate so much of it that he fell fast asleep as soon as his bowl was empty.

While he was asleep, a beggar walked by and asked Nasr-ed-Din for money.

'Why not take that horse and sell it in the next town?' Nasr-ed-Din said, nodding to the rich man's horse tethered to his fence.

'Take that horse?' the beggar said. 'But it's worth more than your house!'

'My friend asked me to give it away to the first person who walked past my house, and you are the lucky one.'

The beggar decided to take advantage of this opportunity before Nasr-ed-Din changed his mind. He untethered the horse, mounted it and rode it away. Later that day he sold it for a fortune, and lived the rest of his life in comfort.

Meanwhile, back at Nasr-ed-Din's house, the rich man was waking up.

'Thank you for a magnificent dinner, Nasr-ed-Din,' he said. 'But now I must be on my way. Where has my horse got to?'

'I gave it away to a beggar,' Nasr-ed-Din said.

'You did what!' the rich man roared, 'What gave you the right to give away my horse, the most magnificent steed in the kingdom?'

'I thought that you wouldn't need it any more,' Nasr-ed-Din said. 'After all,

_____ .'

Rotary story, see page 27

Story starters (1)

Nico lived with his dad in a flat down the road from the school. Every morning he walked to school with Clyde. One day Clyde came along carrying a brand new rucksack, and he told Nico that there was something inside it that nobody in the world had ever seen before.

Three friends were sitting on the river bank in the sunshine.

'I'm bored,' said the otter.

'I'm fed up,' said the badger.

'I want something exciting to happen,' said the hare.

'No wonder you're bored, sitting there doing nothing,' said the voice of the fox from the wood behind them. 'Come with me, and I'll show you something that will give you a big surprise.'

Zinnia lived with her grandparents on a farm in the mountains. She was far away from shops and schools and other children, but she was never lonely. This was because she had learned how to talk to the animals, and every day she chatted to the cows and hens and goats as she went about her work. One morning, she was woken up by the sound of two animals she had never heard before, whispering in the yard below her window.

Rotary story, see page 27

Story starters (2)

For three months in the spring of 1880, the man they called Buck Moose roamed the trackless badlands between Squantum Gulch and Fever Canyon. For three months he heard nothing but the creak of his saddle leather and the whisper of wind in the prairie grass, saw no living creatures but his horse and the wheeling vultures, felt no fear in spite of the unbroken solitude of those days and nights. Then one May morning, he rode into the ghost town of Silver Gallows; and there, outside the ramshackle saloon, he came upon a scene that was to end his drifting days for ever.

When the first of their space ships landed, we expected the aliens to be friendly. They were small and soft, and they sang to each other in quiet bleats and mews. They reminded us more of cuddly toys than of the monstrous beasts that we had been dreading. We expected them to be friendly, and at first they were. They gave us cures for diseases that had never been cured before. They grew forests for us on deserts that our industries had poisoned. They taught us how to ride the solar wind from planet to planet. It was my job to look after the aliens during their visit, and it was my fault that things started to go wrong.

It was Gruddy's idea to play the April Fool's Day joke on Mr Benson. Gruddy did most of the planning, and when it ended up with Old Benzy being rushed to hospital with a broken leg, only Gruddy laughed. But out of the four of us who took part in the adventure, guess which one wasn't standing outside the Dragon's Den the next morning, waiting to see whether we'd be suspended or not? It looked like Gruddy had got away with it again.

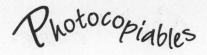

Who's to blame?, see page 30

Blue Riding Hood (1)

Once upon a time there was a clever young woman called Blue Riding Hood who enjoyed playing tricks on people.

Every Sunday, Blue Riding Hood walked through the forest to her grandmother's house, where the old lady gave her dinner in exchange for a basket of cakes.

One Sunday morning, Blue Riding Hood strayed from the path to pick some foxgloves to sell at the market. When she had finished, she realised that she was lost. She wandered about for an hour before sitting down on a tree stump, sobbing in frustration.

'Don't cry,' said a gentle voice. 'Are you lost?'

'What does it look like?' Blue Riding Hood snapped, looking up into the beautiful brown eyes of the great big wolf who had stepped out of the trees.

'There's no need to worry,' the wolf said. 'I know the way to your grandmother's house and I will guide you there.'

The wolf took Blue Riding Hood's basket full of cakes between his teeth and led her out of the forest. By the time they arrived at Grandmother's house, it was getting dark.

'Here we are,' the wolf said. 'Now that I have helped you, will you pay me?'

'What do you want?' Blue Riding Hood said suspiciously, taking up the basket that the wolf had set down.

'Nothing much,' the wolf replied. 'Just those lovely cakes in your basket; half for me and half for my poor starving cubs.'

'You can't have any of them; those cakes have got to pay for my dinner.'

'If you won't give me the cakes, I will have to take them. I hope it won't be necessary for me to bite you in order to do so.'

'I was only joking,' Blue Riding Hood said, thinking quickly. 'Take the cakes, but let me spice them up a bit for you first.'

Blue Riding Hood stripped the petals off the foxgloves and sprinkled them over the cakes.

'Eat them up quickly while they're still fresh,' she said, 'and take the rest home to your poor hungry children.'

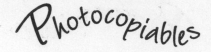

Who's to blame, see page 30

Blue Riding Hood (2)

The wolf tucked into the cakes, not realising that foxgloves are poisonous. He was on his third cake when he gave a great groan of agony and dropped dead. Blue Riding Hood dusted the petals off the rest of the cakes and went into Grandma's cottage.

'What time do you call this?' the old woman snapped, 'and where are the rest of my cakes?'

'I got lost in the forest and a wolf tried to steal them. Please Granny, can I have my dinner?'

'You can dine on darkness tonight,' Grandma said, snatching the basket from her granddaughter. 'Get out of my house!'

'But it's dark, Granny. I can't go out now!'

Granny was deaf to Blue Riding Hood's pleas, and chased her out into the night. A woodcutter returning from work found her wandering in the forest, alone and afraid. When he heard of her Grandma's hard-heartedness, he became very angry.

'I'd like to teach that Grandma of yours a lesson she won't forget,' he said.

'Come with me and I'll show you how to do it,' Blue Riding Hood said.

She led him to where the wolf's body lay and ordered him to flay it; then she dressed up in its skin. They crept up to Grandma's doorstep, the woodcutter smashed the door down with his axe, and Blue Riding Hood rushed in on her Granny snarling and howling. Granny flung herself out of the window, fled into the forest, and was gobbled up by the bears that very night.

Blue Riding Hood and the woodcutter got married and settled down in Granny's house, where they lived very happily on the life savings they found tucked away under the bed. They kept the skin of the wolf as a hearth rug, so that on long winter evenings, as they sat side by side before the fire, they could remind themselves of the great joke that they had played on Granny the night they had first met.

▲ Nobody in this story behaved very well, but perhaps some people behaved better than others. Discuss the story with the others in your group and try to put the four characters in order of blame.

Tales with a moral, see page 31

Tales with a moral (1)

A thrush caught a big fat snail one day and flew away with it towards her nest. On the way, she rested on a twig over a pond. When she saw her reflection in the pond, she thought that it was another thrush with another big fat snail.

If I'm quick, she thought, I could swoop down and snatch that snail off her. Then I would have two snails.

The thrush swooped down to the water, but as soon as she opened her beak the snail fell out and sank to the bottom of the pond.

One day Peacock and Sparrow met in the woods.

'You poor, dull, grey, little thing,' said Peacock. 'Don't you wish you were as rich and exciting and colourful and big as I am?'

'No,' Sparrow replied, 'I'm quite happy as I am.'

Then Eagle flew overhead, looking for his dinner. Sparrow flew up into a tree, where Eagle could not see him because he was so little and dull. Peacock tried to hide as well, but he was too heavy to fly, and Eagle easily spotted his colourful plumage. Eagle flew down and gobbled him up.

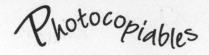
Tales with a moral, see page 31

Tales with a moral (2)

Once upon a time, a hungry fox was prowling through a wood when he saw a family enjoying a picnic. He decided to creep up on them and snatch some of their food. Just as he was about to leap forward and snatch a pie, he heard voices behind him. He crept towards them and saw another family having a picnic at the edge of the wood. Their food looked tastier than the first family's food, so he decided that he would steal from them instead. Then he noticed that although their food looked tastier, there was not so much of it, so he turned around and crept back to the first family. Then he thought again about the second family's food. It really was too good to miss! He turned around and returned to them, but found that they had eaten all the food. 'Never mind,' thought the fox, 'I'll go back to the first family.' By the time he arrived, the first family had also finished all their food. Still hungry, the fox prowled away.

Long ago, when pigs had noses as long and graceful as elephants' trunks, Pig and Eagle were friends.

'How I wish I could have a nose as long and beautiful as yours,' said Eagle, 'instead of this short and ugly beak.'

'What does having a beautiful nose matter?' said Pig. 'How I wish I could fly!'

Eagle decided to give his friend a treat, so he picked him up in his claws and flew a little way with him.

'This is wonderful!' Pig shouted. 'Take me higher!'

Eagle flew higher, but Pig asked to go higher still.

So Eagle flew higher again, but Pig demanded to be taken yet higher.

At last Eagle was exhausted, and Pig suddenly slipped out of his claws. Down and down and down he plunged, and landed flat on his beautiful nose. To this day, all pigs have squashed little snouts where once their beautiful trunks grew, and none of them have ever learned to fly.

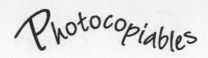

Visualising characters, see page 33

Character profile

Name_____ Date _____

A profile of _____

from _____

by _____

Appearance _____

_____

_____

_____

_____

_____

_____

_____

Biography _____

_____

_____

_____

Habits _____

_____

_____

_____

My opinion of this person _____

_____

_____

_____

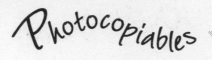

Visualising characters, see page 33

My favourite character

Name _____   Date _____

My favourite character is _____

This is what s/he looks like:

I like this person because _____

_____

_____

_____

even though _____

_____

_____

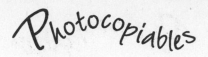

The Structure of the Egg

Name _____   Date _____

▲ Read this passage. Which parts do you think give useful information about what an egg is made of? Which parts are not so useful?

At the centre of an egg is the yolk. This word is pronounced 'yoke', and comes from *geolca*, an Old English word for yellowness. The central part of the yolk develops into the chick, and the surrounding area provides food supply for it while it develops. If you imagine yourself scrunched up inside a bagful of nutritious custard, you might have some idea of what the chick experiences before hatching.

Surrounding the yolk is the albumen or egg white, which contains water reserves for the chick. The word *albumen* is derived from the Latin word for white and is related to other words you might know, like albino and albugo. Egg white is wonderful stuff, and is used in the making of meringues and other treats.

The yolk is held at the centre of the egg by two braided strands of protein known as the *chalazae*. This lovely word is pronounced 'ka-la-zeye' and is from the Greek word for hailstone. During incubation the hen rolls the egg to keep it evenly warm, and the *chalazae* gently twist themselves to keep the developing chick in position. It is a wonder that the poor chick does not have nightmares, though perhaps it does.

Just inside the shell there is a layer consisting of two membranes, which help with insulation. This is like wearing two shirts under your sweater to keep yourself warm. Towards the end of incubation, an air space develops between these two layers at the blunt end of the egg. You have probably noticed this when you have opened a hard-boiled egg for breakfast, especially if you open your eggs at the more sensible end. The fully developed chick breathes through this airspace by pushing into it with its beak.

Relevant or not?, see page 54

Kitchen herbs: basil

Name _____   Date _____

▲ Read this passage. Which parts do you think give useful information about herbs? Which parts are not so useful?

Basil is one of the most useful herbs to keep in your kitchen. Herbert Smith, known to his friends as Herb the Horrible, should definitely not be kept anywhere near your kitchen. Basil is a pale green, leafy herb with a lovely smell. It can be eaten raw in salads, or added to tomato sauce. Basil Fawlty, the hotel owner from *Fawlty Towers*, is another famous basil, but should not be added to either salads or tomato sauce. Fresh basil can also be ground up with olive oil, garlic, Parmesan cheese and pine nuts to make a delicious sauce known as pesto. This sauce has nothing to do with pests like headlice, blowflies and rats. Pesto sauce can be put on spaghetti or spread on bread. You cannot do this with lice, flies and rats. You can also add pesto to soups. To grow basil, you need good soil and a warm, sunny position. You cannot grow it inside a dark fridge or a hot oven. A kitchen window-sill would be an ideal position for a pot of basil. If you grow basil in your garden, it will help to keep pests away from your tomato plants.

Diagram labelling, see page 60

The parachute

Name _____ Date _____

If you jump out of a plane your body will fall towards the Earth. Within 12 seconds, it will be falling at a speed of 54 metres per second. A person hitting the ground at this speed would be killed instantly. The job of a parachute is to slow the body down so that it reaches the ground at a safer speed of about 7 metres per second.

The parachute does this job by providing the parachutist with an enormous extra skin in the form of a canopy. This canopy effectively expands the surface area of the parachutist so that air resistance to his or her fall is hugely increased, and the speed of the fall is therefore reduced.

The canopy of the parachute is the umbrella-shaped expanse of nylon fabric that floats above the parachutist, attached to his or her body with rigging lines. When not in use, the canopy and rigging lines are folded away inside a pack which is fastened to the parachutist's body by a harness. The pack is held shut with securing pins to which the ripcord is attached.

When the parachutist pulls the ripcord, the pack opens up and releases a small pilot chute. When this opens, it pulls out the main canopy and rigging lines. As the canopy fills with air, the parachutist's rate of descent decelerates rapidly. The harness protects the body from shocks while this happens. When the parachute is fully open, the parachutist can direct it to the ground by operating guide ropes which control steerage slots in the canopy.

READING

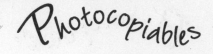

Constructing a timeline, see page 61

The Forests of the Moon

The emergence of a rain forest amongst the craters and dust seas of the moon was first noticed in 1999 by Cynthia Rainstone, an amateur astronomer working from her garden shed. Ms Rainstone's discovery was reported two years after the passage through the Earth's exosphere of Comet Malachite, and astrobiologists have speculated that the forests grew from spores deposited by the comet.

Computer-enhanced images of the new forest revealed that within a year of the emergence of the first trees, the canopy had reached a height of 50 metres, and that the foliage was densely populated by a wealth of species whose behaviour and physical characteristics appeared to be completely different from those typical of terrestrial fauna.

Scientific interest in this new ecosystem was, of course, intense; and seven years after Ms Rainstone's discovery, the first international expedition landed on the moon to carry out explorations of the forest. The scientists were not, however, the first people to arrive. Two years earlier, a fleet of space freighters had been sent out secretly from Earth by Hackco, the multinational logging company; and by the time the scientists arrived, they had already cleared an extensive area of the forest, shipping the high quality timber back to Earth.

An emergency delegation of scientists appealed to the United Nations to suspend the logging operation until a full scientific survey had been made of the forest. At its first meeting, the scientists revealed that fruits discovered in the forest contained the full spectrum of human nutrients, as well as compounds with versatile healing properties and the power to raise levels of intelligence and good-naturedness among subjects who had volunteered to eat them. The forest creatures which had been examined all appeared to be non-aggressive and intelligent. Moreover, the capability of the trees to grow rapidly in a very thin atmosphere and with almost no water merited intensive and prolonged research.

The argument over who, if anyone, had the rights to the forest raged for ten years, and during this time the last of Earth's tropical rain forests vanished. It was this event which eventually swayed the opinions of the decision makers. The moon was declared open for commercial exploitation, and the scientists were granted a square mile 'protected research zone'. Within a year of the decision being made, seven of Hackco's rivals had sent their own freighters to the moon. In 2019, the last of the trees in the lunar forest was felled. Two years earlier, the research zone had been abandoned, its trees and the creatures who dwelt within them having succumbed to the pollution caused by the lumberjacks.

Comet Malachite is expected to return in approximately ten thousand years.

Introducing writing frameworks, see page 64

Onchlids: an endangered species

▲ Read this passage then complete the activity on photocopiable page 144.

Onchlids inhabit the rain forests of Borneo and are among the region's most spectacular mammals. Onchlids resemble other great apes in several ways: they are humanoid in appearance, occasionally travel bipedally, and engage their young in an extended period of learning.

Several other features are unique to this animal. Female onchlids may grow to be twice the size of males. The majestic female who leads the onchlid pack usually has a vivid green tinge to her fur and is known as the emerald mama. The female skull differs from the male in having pronounced, horn-like protuberances in the region of the temples. At the start of the rainy season, these develop into magnificent green antlers from which sprout leaves and flowers. By the end of the season, they are laden with a variety of fruits, each of which is unique to the onchlid. The weight of the ripening fruit contributes to the shedding of the antlers, which are then used as walking sticks by older members of the pack. The fruit is dried to supplement foraged food during the dry season.

The female onchlid also has more formidable canine teeth than the male, and a wider range of facial expressions.

Like chimpanzees, onchlids show signs of having mastered the use of tools. Doctor D. Seever, who has conducted most of the research in the onchlid enclaves of the rain forest, reports that musical instruments, cooking utensils and bicycles left in the vicinity of the onchlids' dwellings have all been used with a great deal of creative ingenuity.

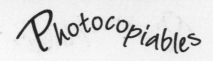

Introducing writing frameworks, see page 64

Comparison/contrast frame

Name _____   Date _____

▲ Read through 'Onchlids: an endangered species' on page 143, then complete the sentences below.

Onchlids and chimpanzees are alike in several ways. They both

_____

_____

_____

However, there are also differences. Chimpanzees

_____

_____

_____

_____

while onchlids

_____

_____

_____

_____

Another difference is that

_____

_____

_____

_____

The most interesting thing that I have learned about onchlids is that

_____

_____

_____

_____

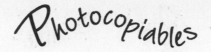

Sequencing, see page 65

The recovery of the River Thames

By 1960, one of the most important rivers in Britain was on the brink of death. The River Thames, which flows through London, was so polluted that few organisms could survive in it. Factories along its banks poured waste into its waters, adding to the pollution caused by raw sewage. The river was a health risk to people who lived near it.

- -

Another danger associated with the Thames was that of flooding. The water level rises rapidly whenever there is a high tide. If strong winds occur at the same time, there is a real danger of the river bursting its banks. The communities living alongside the Thames had long been threatened by the devastation that a serious flood can cause.

- -

Recently, there have been changes for the better. The water is getting cleaner as the old docks and factories close down. The surviving factories now have to obey stricter anti-pollution laws.

- -

New sewage works have also opened, so there is less dumping of poisonous filth into the river. The water is much cleaner now, and supports a wider variety of water birds, fish, plants and other wildlife.

- -

The general public have become more aware of environmental issues. Groups of walkers and wildlife enthusiasts have successfully campaigned for better footpaths along the river, so that everybody can enjoy its improved scenery.

- -

The danger of flooding has also receded in recent years. A magnificent tidal barrier has been built across the river at Woolwich. It consists of movable sections which are usually lowered to let water traffic pass. But whenever there is a flood risk from tidal surges, the sections are raised from the river bed to form a protective wall.

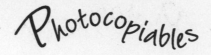

Sequencing, see page 65

The recovery of the Thames: expository frame

Name _____   Date _____

▲ Read through 'The recovery of the River Thames' on page 145 and fill in this sheet.

Preliminary notes

Dangers	Improvements

Before my reading, I knew that _____

_____

_____

I have now learned several things more about the Thames.

Firstly, _____

_____

_____

Another thing I learned is that _____

_____

_____

The most interesting thing I learned is that _____

_____

_____

I would still like to find out _____

_____

_____

Role-play, see page 68

Acid rain

▲Read this passage and the passage on photocopiable page 148, then complete the activity on photocopiable page 149.

By the end of the 1980s, it was becoming clear that acid rain was causing serious damage to woodlands, rivers, crops and historical buildings in Britain. In 1989, an all-party committee of MPs published details of ancient forests and historical monuments that had already been affected, and recommended that urgent action be taken to control emissions of sulphur dioxide from power stations (thought to be the main cause of acid rain).

The Department of the Environment rejected the report, arguing that the damage to national forests was entirely due to the droughts of the mid-1980s, even though the latter part of that decade had been exceptionally wet. It also asserted that there was no connection between industrial pollution and declining stocks of fish in rivers and the North Sea.

The CEGB, which then ran the power stations, argued that existing controls on sulphur dioxide emissions were adequate, and that any additional measures were bound to put up the price of electricity. Managers in other industries also warned that anti-pollution measures would cost jobs.

No serious measures were taken until 1997, when up to 90 per cent of British woodland was already dying, and the Houses of Parliament at Westminster had started to dissolve.

READING

Role play, see page 68

Acid rain destroying Britain's heritage

An all-party group of MPs warned yesterday that Britain will lose 50 per cent of its forests by the end of the 1990s unless steps are taken to curb emissions of sulphur dioxide from power stations.

The report from the Commons Environment Committee also warned that historic buildings are being eroded, crops damaged and fish stocks poisoned by this chemical, which falls to the earth as acid rain.

The committee chairman's call for immediate action sparked off a storm last night among power bosses and the Department of the Environment. Electricity supremo Sir Sterling Watt claimed that his industry's anti-pollution standards are the highest in Europe, and that further improvements would lead to steep rises in the price of electricity. Top industrialist Ted Brimstone also warned that the measures advised by the committee would cost jobs. 'This country's got to choose between having people in work at the cost of a few dead trees, or having thousands more on the dole spending their enforced leisure time in flourishing woodlands,' he said. 'We can't have both.'

Meanwhile at the Department of the Environment, Forestry Minister Tim Burr claimed that the visible damage to Britain's woods has nothing to do with acid rain. 'We've had a few very dry summers in recent years,' he said, 'and the damage done then is still working its way through. Very soon, things are going to start getting better again.'

Leading architects greeted the report as a confirmation of their warnings about the state of many of the country's best-known buildings. 'Liverpool Cathedral is being eaten away like a wedding cake,' Luke Bungalow claimed today, 'and Big Ben looks like it's been steeped in vinegar.'

Environmental activist Theresa Green called for an immediate shutdown of all power stations and industries. 'What this country needs is a return to pre-industrial society. It's perfectly possible for us to generate all the power we need from windmills, solar energy and the composting of sewage.'

Role-play, see page 68

Acid rain: discussion framework

Name _____   Date _____

Issue: *Should anti-pollution measures be taken to control acid rain?*

▲ Read through the texts on acid rain then complete this sheet.

Arguments in favour	Arguments against

Some people think that urgent measures should be taken against industrial pollution because _____

_____

_____

_____

_____

Others argue against this because _____

_____

_____

_____

My opinion is that _____

_____

_____

_____

Playground poetry, see page 77

Playground poetry

Dip dip dip
My blue ship
Sailing on the water
Like a cup and saucer
Dip dip dip.

Eeny meany macka racka
Rara rye ya dominacka
Chicka pocka lollipopa
Om pom push aye.

Sarah fifarah
Chickle-arah bomb-arah
Bomb-arah fifarah
That's how you spell Sarah.

Michelle, fifichelle
Chickle-ichelle bomb-ichelle
Bomb-ichelle fifichelle
That's how you spell Michelle.

One fine day in the middle of the night
Two dead men got up to fight
Back to back they faced each other
Drew their swords and shot each other.

Nursery rhymes, see page 78

Nursery rhymes

Ride a cock horse to Banbury Cross
To see a fine lady upon a white horse
With rings on her fingers and bells on her toes
And she shall have music wherever she goes.

There was an old woman tossed up in a basket
Seventeen times as high as the moon
Where she was going I couldn't but ask it
For in her hand she carried a broom.
Where are you going to up so high?
May I go with you?
Aye, by and by.

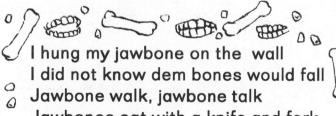

I hung my jawbone on the wall
I did not know dem bones would fall
Jawbone walk, jawbone talk
Jawbones eat with a knife and fork.

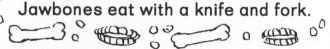

When I was a little boy
I washed my mummy's dishes
I stuck my finger in my eye
And pulled out little fishes.

My mother called me a good boy
And bid me do it again
I put my finger in my eye
And got three score and ten.

There was a crooked man and he walked a crooked mile
He found a crooked sixpence behind a crooked stile
He bought a crooked cat, which caught a crooked mouse
And they all lived together in a little crooked house.

Riddles, see page 80

Riddles

A My first is in with, in ship and in shop
My second in clip, but not in clop
My third is in buzz, in busy and bee
My fourth is in his, but not in she
My fifth is in hiss, in serpent and snake
My sixth is in rack, but not in rake
My seventh's in mug, in supper and grub
My eighth is in Puss, but not in pub.
What am I?

B My first in rat, and also in cap
My second in goat, but not in boat
My third is in log, in sob and in dog
My fourth is in pump, in gut and in lump
My fifth is in tie, and also in sty
My last is in lip, in milk and in sip
If you try to catch me I'll give you a nip.
Who am I?

C
Two legs sat upon three legs
With one leg in his lap;
In comes four legs,
Runs away with one leg.
Up jumps two legs,
Picks up three legs,
Throws it after four legs
And makes him bring back one leg.

D Thirty white horses on a red hill
Now they stamp
Now they champ
Now they stand still.

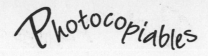

Nonsense rhymes, see page 87

Nonsense

Name _____   Date _____

▲ Read the verse below. How do you imagine the scene looks? Draw a picture of it in the box.

[ ]

'Twas brillig, and the slithy toves
Did gyre and gimble in the wabe;
All mimsy were the borogoves,
And the mome raths outgrabe.

[ ]

▲ Invent your own words to complete the verse, and draw a picture of the scene described in the box.

'Twas _____ and the _____

Did _____ and _____ in the _____

All _____ were the _____

And the _____

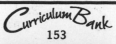

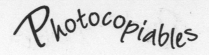

Sequencing instructions, see page 102

Making bread

Ingredients
1kg flour
1 teaspoon of sugar
½ teaspoon of salt
1 teaspoon of dried yeast
500ml water

Method

When the yeast and water have started to foam, pour the liquid into the flour and mix to a smooth dough, adding more warm water or sifted flour if necessary.

Allow the water to cool to blood temperature and stir in the yeast.

Turn the dough out on to a floured board and knead vigorously for 10 to 15 minutes.

Place the tins in a warm place and leave until the dough has risen over their sides.

Heat the water and dissolve the sugar in it.

Turn the dough back out on to the floured board and knead again for 5 to 10 minutes.

Grease the mixing bowl, return the kneaded dough to it, cover and leave in a warm place until the dough has doubled in size.

Sift the flour and salt into a large mixing bowl.

Slice the dough into two equal pieces and place each in a well-greased 500g baking tin.

Bake the loaves for 35 to 40 minutes. They are done if they sound hollow when tapped.

Preheat the oven to Gas Mark 5 (450°C).

If you want to make more interesting bread, additional ingredients such as seeds, dried fruit, herbs, chopped onions or grated carrots can be added at this stage.

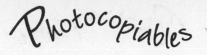

Game instructions

Name _____ Date _____

▲ Invent your own game and fill in the details on how to play it below.

Game title _____

What you need

The purpose of this game is to _____

_____

_____

_____

How to play

1

2

3

The game ends when _____

_____

_____

_____

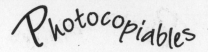

Words for headlines

Name _____ Date _____

These words are commonly found in headlines in newspapers.

Part one

DOOM
DOOM PLEA
DOOM THREAT PLEA
DOOM THREAT PLEA CLUE
DOOM THREAT PLEA CLUE CHASE

Function words

AFTER

AGAIN AT

BY DOWN

FOR IN

OF

OVER ON

OUT

THROUGH

TO

UNDER

UP

Part two

SCIENTIST IN DOOM THREAT
DOOM SCIENTIST IN CLUE THREAT
PLEA FOR SCIENTIST OVER DOOM CHASE
SCIENTIST'S CHASE FOR DOOM CLUES
DOOM THREAT SCIENTIST IN PLEA FOR CLUES

Content words

AGONY ALARM ANGUISH ARREST
ATROCITY AXE
BAN BEAUTY BID BLAST BLUNDER
BOOT
CASH CHANCE COST CRASH CUT
DASH DEAL DEATH DEFEAT DISMAL
DRAMA
ENJOY ENTER EVIL EXIT
FACE FALL FATE FIGHT FLEE FOUND
FREAK FRIGHT FREE FUN FURY
GAMBLE GET GLOOM GO GRAB
GREED GUILT
HATE HAUNT HELD HIGH HIT HOME
HOPE HORROR
INQUIRY

KILL KNIFE KNOCK
LIFE LOOM LOSE LOST LOVE LOW LUST
MAGIC MASS MERCY MUST MYSTERY
NASTY NEED NEW
OFFER ORDEAL OUTRAGE
POWER PRICE PROBE PROTEST PUZZLE
QUESTION QUIZ QUOTE
REJECT RIGHT RISE ROB ROW RUN
SCANDAL SEEK SEX SHAME SICK SINK
SLAM SLEAZE SLUR STRIKE STRUGGLE
STUN SWOOP
TAKE TEST TOP TRAGEDY
VICTIM VICTORY VIOLENT
WARN WHY WICKED WIN WOUND
WRONG

It's a well-known fact, see page 114

It's a well-known fact

THE NEWS THAT COMPULSORY CORPORAL PUNISHMENT is to be introduced into all schools has been greeted with jubilation by a huge majority of the country's parents, teachers and children. With immediate effect, any breach of school rules, however trivial, is to be rewarded with the kind of sound thrashing that taught children the difference between right and wrong in happier, less crime-plagued times. So seriously does the Government take this initiative that it has ordered that any teacher refusing to carry out this policy will be liable to instant dismissal followed by imprisonment and a regime of physical chastisement.

'It's a well-known fact that children respect figures of authority,' said Jill Farr-Wright, the new Education Minister. 'I was a third-generation teacher before entering politics, and both my father and grandfather were broken-hearted at the breakdown in discipline due to the decline of corporal punishment. My grandfather flogged several boys to within an inch of their lives when he was a teacher, and with the exception of one child who succumbed to his injuries, they all sent him Christmas cards every year. If that doesn't prove something, I don't know what does.'

Psychiatrists working alongside toy trade entrepreneurs have disclosed that the recent dramatic rise in the price of toys has had a profoundly positive effect on the self-esteem of deprived children.

'It's a well-known fact that the more expensive a toy is, the more satisfaction a child derives from it,' said Dr G. Reed of the Children As Consumers Juvenile Protection Unit. 'By owning an expensive toy, children who find it hard to achieve in other areas derive an enormous sense of satisfaction. An expensive toy says "Your parents love you", especially if the child comes from an impoverished family. These toys convince individual children of their own worth, and stimulate healthy competition.'

The enhanced levels of theft, vandalism and friction between children often associated with the ownership of expensive toys also has positive consequences, the Department of Trade and Industry has revealed.

'Fighting to maintain ownership of valuables constitutes personal growth for the budding consumer,' Junior Minister V. Nallity commented last night. It creates a keen sense of ownership and prepares children for the home security responsibilities they will assume in later life.'

INFORMATION TECHNOLOGY WITHIN READING

This brief outline looks at the key features of the main types of software used in this book, and gives some information for teachers about appropriate ways of using them with children.

Word processing

The activities in this book can be used to introduce and develop a range of skills which give children a wider experience of the ability to edit, organise and develop their text, as well as to present it for a range of audiences. Children should be encouraged to originate work on the computer. This means that the writing tasks need to be of a suitable length for the children's keyboard skills. Group writing tasks are also useful in giving more children access to writing on the computer. Writing can also be read and edited away from the computer – in which case, children will have to save and retrieve their work in order to edit it.

Once the children have written their text, they need to consider how it should be presented to the readers. They will need to be taught how to change the fonts and font sizes. They should also be introduced to some of the concepts of good design (limiting the number of fonts used on a page, restricting line lengths to make text easier to read and using bold or italic fonts to highlight important areas of text). It is important that the children are taught how to position text on the page without using the space bar. This means that they need to know how to use some basic formatting commands, such as centring, justification, tabs and rulers.

Where activities such as sequencing involve moving text around the page, the 'cut and paste' facility is helpful. Word processors differ in the way that they achieve this. Some of the older or simpler word processors do not have this facility, and children will be forced to delete and then retype their work. In more recent word processors which have a mouse, children can highlight the text to be moved by dragging the mouse across it. It can then be 'cut' out of the text and placed on a clipboard hidden in the computer's memory. The mouse is then moved to the new position, and the text is 'pasted' there. On some word processors, this can be achieved by simply dragging the highlighted text to the new position. This is called 'drag and drop'.

Desktop publishing

Many word processors have some desktop publishing facilities, for example the ability to add, move and resize pictures. However, most DTP packages are 'object orientated', which means that pictures or blocks of text are placed inside frames that can be resized or moved around the screen. The frames can be given different borders and backgrounds, and can overlap each other on the page. Text can also be made to 'flow around a frame'.

Most DTP packages also have master pages, allowing the teacher to set up a specific page format which automatically appears as each new page is stated. When children are writing a book or creating a newspaper, this helps them to maintain a consistent format for each page. DTP packages also have the facility to set up text styles, so that all headlines or picture titles appear in the same size and type of font. If a change is made to that style, then all the occurrences of that style throughout the document are also changed. This also helps to ensure consistency across the whole document.

Multimedia authoring software

This software is a relatively recent addition for most schools, but is proving to be a very versatile and powerful medium. It combines many of the features of a word processor or desktop publishing package, but its main new feature is that the different pages of a child's work can be linked together. Depending on the way that the links are created, children can move to different parts of the presentation by simply clicking with a mouse on a symbol, word or picture. Such presentations usually begin with a title page which allows the user to move to different chapters of a story or sections of a text.

Another important feature of this software is its ability to handle a range of different types of media. These can include text; pictures from art and drawing packages; digitised pictures from scanned images, icon cameras and video cameras; sounds from audio CD-ROMs or sound samplers; and even moving pictures taken from a CD-ROM or captured using a video camera. Some of the latter areas require specialised equipment; but the mixing of text, pictures and simple recorded sound can be undertaken with a minimal amount of equipment. The data files created by such work can be very large, and a computer with a hard disk and a large memory is needed. If the final presentation is to be moved to other computers via a floppy disk, this will also limit the number of pages and the amount of pictures and sound bites that can be included.

Work with authoring packages is best undertaken as part of a longer project, with children working in groups. A class presentation can be split between several groups, with each one preparing the text and pictures for its section and deciding how the pages are to be laid out and linked. Children will need support when they first start to put their ideas into the computer. They will need to know how to create frames, alter text styles, add colours, import graphics and sound files from other disks and make the links between pages. A class structure can be set up in advance by the teacher to provide a starting-point for group work. It is a good idea for the teacher to spend some time with the software before embarking on a project with the children.

IT links

The grids on this page relate the activities in this book to specific areas of IT and to relevant software resources. Activities are referenced by page number rather than by name. (Bold page numbers indicate activities which have expanded IT content.) The software listed is a selection of programs generally available to primary schools, and is not intended as a recommended list. The software featured should be available from most good educational software retailers.

AREA OF IT	TYPE OF SOFTWARE	ACTIVITIES (page nos.)				
		CHAPTER 1	CHAPTER 2	CHAPTER 3	CHAPTER 4	CHAPTER 5
Communicating Information	Word Processor	16, 19, 21, 23, 24, 26, **28**, 30, 31, 32, **36**, 38, **39**, 45	54, 57, 61, 63, 64, 65, 68, 70	76, 77, 78, **80**, 82, 84, **85**, 87, 88, 90, 94, 96	98, 99, 100, 102, 103, 104	110, 111, 112, 115, 116, 117, 120, 121, 123
Communicating Information	DTP	**28**, 30, 32, **36**, 38, **39**	61, 71	77, 78, **80**, 82, 87	98, 103	115, 117, 123
Communicating Information	Art/graphics	32, 46	60, 61	88, 90		115
Communicating Information	Multi-media authoring	**36**	**72**	76, 78, **80**, **85**		
Communicating Information	Electronic mail			77		
Information Handling	Database	**39**, 43	51			108, 117
Information Handling	Spreadsheet					108, 110
Information Handling	Branching database	35				

SOFTWARE TYPE	BBC/MASTER	RISCOS	NIMBUS/186	WINDOWS	MACINTOSH
Word Processor	Pendown Folio	Pendown 2 Folio Impression Style	Write On Caxton	Claris Works Creative Writer Word	Claris Works Word Word Writer's Toolkit
DTP	Typesetter	Desktop Folio Impression Style Ovation First Page	Newspaper Caxton Press	Microsoft Publisher	
Art Package	Image	1st Paint ProArtisan Revelation	Paintspa Plus	Colour Magic Kid Pix	Kid Pix Fine Artist
Multi-media Authoring		Magpie Genesis Key Author		MMBBox2 Genesis	Hyperstudio
Database	Grass	Junior Pinpoint Keynote Find IT Bodymapper	Grass Sparks	Claris Works Junior Pinpoint Information Workshop Bodymapper	Claris Works Bodymapper
Branching Database	Branch	Retreeval	Branch		
Electronic Mail	CAMPUS/ Internet	CAMPUS/ Internet	CAMPUS/ Internet	CAMPUS/ Internet	CAMPUS/ Internet

	MATHS	SCIENCE	HISTORY	GEOGRAPHY	D&T	IT	ART	MUSIC	RE
FICTION	Reading resources survey (statistics).		Use of historical fiction. Restoring old documents.	Stories from around the world. Making a story map.	Making props for dramatic interpretations of stories. Bookmaking.	Use of word processor for text manipulation. Text disclosure programme. Making a bibliographical database.	Responding to stories by drawing. Visualising characters.	Musical interpretations of stories.	Stories with a moral.
INFORMATION BOOKS	Use of tables, sets etc to display information.	Reading aloud and discussing science texts.	Making timelines. Reading and discussing historical texts.	Reading aloud and discussing geographical texts.	Designing and making an information book.	As above.	Making graphic interpretations of texts.		
POETRY			Riddles, nursery rhymes and playground poetry from the past. Poetry past and present.	Riddles, nursery rhymes and playground poetry from around the world. Poems in various languages.	Designing and making a personal anthology.	As above.	Drawing etc in response to poetry. Illustrating an anthology.	Musical interpretations of poetry. Setting speech to music.	
INSTRUCTIONAL TEXTS	Procedural texts involving weighing and measuring.	Procedural texts. involving		Exploring environmental print in the local area.	Designing and making a game.	As above.	Illustrating a set of instructions.		
MEDIA			How newspapers and other media have changed over time.		Designing and making a newspaper.	As above.	Making comic strips and cartoons. Illustrating newspapers.		